REDEFINING MULTICULTURAL EDUCATION

REDEFINING MULTICULTURAL EDUCATION

Inclusion and the Right to Be Different

Third Edition

Ratna Ghosh
Mariusz Galczynski

Canadian Scholars' Press, Inc.
Toronto

Redefining Multicultural Education: Inclusion and the Right to Be Different, Third Edition
Ratna Ghosh and Mariusz Galczynski

First published in 2014 by
Canadian Scholars' Press Inc.
425 Adelaide Street West, Suite 200
Toronto, Ontario
M5V 3C1
www.cspi.org

Canadian Scholars' Press Inc. gratefully acknowledges financial support for our publishing activities from the Government of Canada through the Canada Book Fund (CBF).

Library and Archives Canada Cataloguing in Publication
Ghosh, Ratna, author   Redefining multicultural education : inclusion and the right to be different / Ratna Ghosh, Mariusz Galczynski. -- Third edition.

Includes bibliographical references and index. Issued in print and electronic formats.
ISBN 978-1-55130-628-5 (pbk.).--ISBN 978-1-55130-629-2 (pdf).-- ISBN 978-1-55130-630-8 (epub)

1. Multicultural education--Canada. 2. Multicultural education. 3. Educational change--Canada. I. Galczynski, Mariusz, 1983-, author II. Title.

LC1099.G56 2014   370.1170971   C2014-903109-2
C2014-903110 -6

Text design by Aldo Fierro
Cover design by Gordon Robertson

Printed and bound in Canada by Webcom.

Canada

MIX
Paper from
responsible sources
FSC
www.fsc.org   FSC® C004071

To the many students who prompted us to reflect on the issues in this book.

TABLE OF CONTENTS

PREFACE

Since the second edition of this book was published, societies around the world have become much more diverse. The need to reckon with this fact is urgent, owing to intensified globalization, worldwide migration, growing identity politics among religious/cultural/ethnic groups, and increasing self-awareness of previously marginalized groups, who are different due to gender, religion, ethnicity and culture, sexual orientation, and/or (dis)ability. Yet the social landscape is still constituted by groups that have power and define the rules, while others struggle to achieve a degree of presence and empowerment in our rapidly changing world. This maintains the power asymmetry between haves and have-nots. In fact, the traditional democratic view of superficial equality between these groups (e.g., one person, one vote) leads to an unequal and unjust contest because the playing field is not level: it is like a boxing match between a featherweight challenger and his heavyweight opponent, duking it out under the same rules of the game. With the spread of democracy, the demand for recognition and rights by all groups is rising, and with that comes the demand for education. People realize that knowledge is power and the path to reaping the benefits of economic mobility.

Diversity is not only a characteristic of modern societies, but also an asset in the competitive global market. We recognize that diversity of perspectives and ideas is essential to innovation. Diversity implies a kaleidoscope of ideas, structures (including values and beliefs), and people: the potential of a spectrum of perspectives derived from multi-dimensional differences. This is why our schools need to foster inclusion of different groups and recognize diversity as a defining feature of excellence. And it is not only essential to acknowledge the crucial role of education in promoting the acceptance of differences—critical multicultural education must also create a safe space for all students, helping to reduce feelings of alienation among students from certain groups, mitigate violence and bullying, and counter the radicalization of youth. Every student must feel an equal participant and stakeholder in the enterprise of education. No one should feel abandoned, stranded, alienated, or excluded.

Unfortunately, educators sometimes lack the skills and knowledge necessary to deal with controversial and contentious issues in the classroom and school environment, from bullying to radicalization, even to terrorism. Despite commonplace media reports of violence in American as well as Canadian schools, research indicates that teachers avoid such topics in class because they are uncomfortable and unsure how to establish ground rules for discussion, not to mention how to overcome their own unresolved conflicts on the complex issues surrounding diversity. Given the pre-eminent role of schools and education in the development of a peaceful and inclusive society, this book attempts to provide teachers with some critical education tools that can be used to engage students in dialogue and exploration so as to work towards a just society.

In this third edition, we have taken into account not only the changing social landscape of education but also recent research developments in the areas of multicultural education, culturally responsive pedagogy, and the realities of new rapid means of electronic communication. In addition, we have been stimulated by the fact that, in the last decade or so, students have become much more aware, informed, and critical—undoubtedly due to the prevalence of electronic and social media. As such, this book encourages more vigorous student participation both in the classroom and beyond it, moving away from the "transmitter-receptor" educational model towards a more Socratic style, where teacher and pupils discuss and learn together the foundations and limitations of knowledge. This is indeed an exciting new era in education, as well as in teacher-student relationships.

This new edition of *Redefining Multicultural Education* builds on the earlier editions in many ways. Since the publication of the first edition in 1996, the first chapter has been expanded to provide a broader conceptualization of multicultural education, with further discussion of issues related to gender identity, religious expression, (dis)ability, and privilege. Similarly, Chapter 2, on the history of multicultural education in Canada, has been updated, and the sections on Quebec and on First Nations education, in particular, have been significantly expanded. Additional sections throughout the book have been brought up to date, including those on second-language education, anti-racist education, technology and classroom use, and multicultural evaluation. This edition also includes new sections that critically examine an array of issues that are increasingly prominent in educational debates: bullying and cyberbullying, environmental awareness, extremism, and competing human rights. In addition, the appendix of useful resources for multicultural education has been comprehensively updated. It includes links to primary source policy documents, educational organizations and advocacy groups, multicultural resources and lesson plans for teachers, open-access publications aimed at educators, and university-based research centres in Canada and the United States.

Drawing on our own experiences teaching multicultural education at the post-secondary level to pre-service teachers, we have also supplemented each of the chapters in this book with original and innovative activities that ask students to interactively engage with key issues and concepts. These extension activities strive to help multicultural educators bridge the divide between theory and practice. Each activity incorporates central tenets of critical multicultural education and is described in a step-by-step plan for implementation.

While the activities are intended for use with university students enrolled in education courses, we have designed them so that they can be easily modified for pedagogical use with students in a primary or secondary classroom. We also kept in mind that educators sometimes feel reluctant to incorporate multicultural principles into their teaching and lesson planning because they feel that they must prioritize the curricular content over anything "extra." In response, we have included a Curricular Connections section after each activity that models how teachers can infuse the curriculum with multiculturalism—in the social sciences, natural sciences, performing arts, and physical education alike. Our hope is that all educators feel empowered to address multicultural topics in their classrooms, no matter what their subject areas or grade levels of specialization.

PREFACE TO THE FIRST AND SECOND EDITIONS, 1996 AND 2002

The traditional view of education is that it seeks to impart objective knowledge of our universe, and of our social and political institutions. A more penetrating analysis of this subject, however, would show that in practice the knowledge being disseminated is skewed toward perpetuating the worldview and interests of the dominant group in power. That is, our institutions and educational system tend to propagate a worldview that is predominantly Eurocentric, Judeo-Christian, middle class, white, and male. Of course, the powerful social undercurrents, traditions, and institutions that promote this worldview are well supported by academic theories and statistics that appear to be objective. In democratic societies, all citizens seek equality, which they can aspire to if not achieve. The equality rhetoric persists despite inequalities in society and education.

Multicultural education programs have aimed at dealing with equality for racially and ethnoculturally diverse students, but judging by the persistence of inequality of particular groups in society, they have generally been ineffective. More radical programs, such as anti-racist education and feminist pedagogy, focus on particular groups and emphasize equity issues, racism, and sexism in school content and structure. However, they remain within the traditional framework that directs attention to diversity rather than involving a new vision in which the norm is redefined to include all groups of students. They do not go to the root of the problem: how society and education create difference as a disadvantage rather than utilize it as an enriching dimension.

The main thesis of this book is that multicultural education must be inclusive and attempt to develop a society in which "difference" is not a negative concept. Inclusivity means encompassing students from diverse groups (based on gender, race/ethnicity, social background, and so on) as much as students from the white dominant culture (English or French). Multicultural education must deal with cultural difference (which is created in relation to a cultural norm) rather than mere ethnocultural diversity.

The focus in this book is on the politics of difference in education rather than on diverse ethnic cultures, because schooling involves the relationship between cultural visions and differential power. The politics of difference stresses the power inequality that results when students of difference are calibrated against norms and traditions established by the dominant group. In this context, a focus on cultural diversity (instead of "difference") is inadequate because the concept is neutral and, in particular, fails to pinpoint the power inequalities embedded in our social and cultural institutions.

This book seeks to relate to multicultural education the recent revolutionary theoretical developments in the social sciences that challenge traditional knowledge and meaning. It is a response to the need for a text that deals with the significance and implications of the revolution in the understanding of knowledge for teaching and learning, and in multicultural pedagogy. In laying the groundwork for such a project, the book suggests a restructured vision of multicultural education based on new conceptions of "difference" and "knowledge." Both theory and practice concern us here. However, while a brief discussion of theoretical concepts is given, the focus is on practice. Theory explains the relationships between concepts—the connection of knowledge and power—and between the educational performance of students, their life chances, and cultural differences. These differences are socially created on the basis of race/ethnicity, gender, and class. Practice shows how the process of schooling signifies and represents these relationships.

It is neither desirable nor possible for multicultural education to be "difference-blind." Human beings are different from each other in various ways, and this does not translate into deficiency or deviance when they differ from a traditional norm; it simply means that they are different, but also that they have the right to be different. Indeed, multicultural education should focus on the validation of their cultural, social, and gender differences, and the development of their individual identities. The aim of multicultural education, thus, is to empower all students with an ethical and democratic vision of society within which they can make a variety of contributions appropriate to their talents, needs, and aspirations.

Redefining Multicultural Education is directed at teachers, as well as students who are working to enter the teaching profession. If, as Marshall McLuhan has said, the medium is the message, then the focus of a redefined multicultural education is the teacher. The matrix of contemporary society points to an urgent need for the redesign of pedagogy. On the one hand, there is pressure in education for a dramatic shift from teaching to learning—that is, moving away from the idea of packaged knowledge given by teachers to the concept of discovery of knowledge by students. On the other hand are the demands of a postmodern, post-industrial society in which the revolution of rising expectations in terms of human rights and justice, along with the electronic and communication revolution, pose a tremendous challenge to education. The priority is to rejuvenate the methods of education and change its organizational structure and culture, rather than merely manage old-style institutions. Although schools are often considered among the most conservative institutions in society, the response of educational establishments to the information revolution gives much hope for radical innovations demanded by global challenges in an interdependent world.

This book was written to fill a perceived need for a suitable text for my classes at McGill University. The stimulus came from my discussions with my husband, Ashok Vijh, whose perceptions, as a physical scientist, on the construction of knowledge and the nature of difference were very challenging, to say the least. During the time I was writing the book I greatly appreciated his understanding of the disorder it caused in our lives, although it gave him the opportunity to perfect his culinary skills. My son Partho's pursuit of excellence and encouragement was a great motivation to me. I could not have worked on this book without the support and patience of my mother, Indira, when she visited us during this period. I owe the development of my social consciousness to my father, the late Dr. Gauri Sankar Guha, whose exemplary life has been a great inspiration to me. Thanks are also due to Ann Torchinsky for many useful discussions; I benefitted greatly from her long experience in teaching. For the initial manuscript, I want to thank Elaine Correa for her assistance and Samia Costandi for her help with the index. I greatly appreciate the invaluable help given to me by Ayaz Naseem in the preparation of the second edition. Many thanks to those who reviewed the various drafts of the manuscript: Kogila Adam Moodley, University of British Columbia; Robert Lawson, Ohio State University; Marie McAndrew, Université de Montréal; Keith McLeod, University of Toronto; Iain Munro, Queen's University; Douglas Ray, University of Western Ontario; and John Young, University of Alberta. Finally, I acknowledge all the students who have given me so much pleasure over the years and who helped me learn about the importance of "difference" in the construction of knowledge.

ACKNOWLEDGEMENTS

Ratna Ghosh has been privileged to be able to discuss and debate the conceptual basis of many of the issues related to the deconstruction of knowledge at home with her husband, Dr. Ashok Vijh, who though a physical scientist also has a deep interest in the epistemology of knowledge.

Mariusz Galczynski is grateful to Ratna Ghosh for her invitation to participate in the preparation of this book and for her invaluable academic, professional, and personal mentorship. He would also like to thank his mother, Elzbieta Galczynska-Jagen, for her continued support, as well as all of his past school-teachers for their extraordinary dedication to the teaching profession and their exemplary safeguarding of the classroom as a comfortable and stimulating space for all students.

ACKNOWLEDGMENTS

Chapter 1

MULTICULTURAL EDUCATION

Samantha was the most self-assured and outspoken student in Mr. Hopson's Grade 1 class. As part of a classroom activity just before Thanksgiving, Mr. Hopson asked each student to write a few sentences about a family tradition and to draw a picture of how his or her family celebrated that tradition. Samantha was particularly engaged in this assignment because her stepmother had just bought her a new set of markers, which she was eager to share with the classmates at her table. She drew stick figures to represent her entire family gathered around two turkeys, both with colourful feathers, to represent that she got to celebrate the same holiday twice—once with her mom's side and again with her dad's side. Later, when Mr. Hopson made his way around the room, he stopped at Samantha's table and noticed that the children seated there were quarreling over their drawings. In fact, Manuela was in tears and Ainsley had torn his paper in half. When Mr. Hopson asked what happened, Manuela and Ainsley blamed Samantha for ruining their pictures by scribbling all over them with a brown marker. When the teacher asked Samantha about her actions, she unwaveringly explained that she was helping her classmates finish because they forgot to colour in the people.

- On what basis did Samantha construct difference between herself and the other students?
- Do you think that Manuela and Ainsley recognized difference in the same way as Samantha? Why or why not?
- Should children be encouraged to recognize difference on their own? Is there a particular age or level of development when this is most appropriate?

INTRODUCTION

Multiculturalism is a hotly debated and controversial concept. It means different things to different people. To conservatives, "multi-cultures" (ethnic and racial) means anything that is not white. In this interpretation, European–North American values prevail, although equal opportunity appears to be a possibility. The liberal meaning of multiculturalism stresses the equality of all races (by ignoring difference) so that socio-cultural and economic differences (education, occupation, and income) are seen as the only barriers to equal opportunity. In education, these interpretations have resulted in the study of "exotic" cultures, "multicultural days," and compensatory programs such as language learning (English/French). A more radical version of multiculturalism stresses respect for cultural differences in values, behaviours, ways of learning, and socio-cultural practices. Consequently, the recent trend in multicultural education programs has been to focus on shared participation through prejudice-reduction strategies and equity programs. All of this has taken place within the dominant educational framework of a monocultural pedagogy in which other ethnocultural groups have been accommodated.

Lack of conceptual understanding of the term "multiculturalism" has led to its misinterpretation. The popular perception is that it is a policy that caters to "ethnic groups" and this enables the majority groups (anglophone or francophone) to watch from the sidelines so that white privilege is kept intact: it is never in question, never under attack (McIntosh, 1990). The anglophone and francophone groups who are white do not define themselves as "ethnic" and multiculturalism does not seem to affect them. Anglophones and francophones are perceived as not having any ethnicity. The federal government refers to people from Asia, Africa, and Latin America as "people of colour" or "visible minorities," while Quebec refers to them as "cultural communities." The majority groups do not assume a position in the framework of "multiculturalism." They not only distance themselves from identities of colour and culture, but they also privilege themselves (as the majority) and do not see the disadvantages of discrimination, so that they do not have to share the power that they now have (Ghosh, 2011).

This book attempts to redefine the concept of multicultural education in perspective and in methodology. First, it defines multicultural education as one that allows full development of the potential and critical abilities of all children regardless of their "differences." These differences have been based on racial, ethnic, gender, and class stratification in society (as well as on differences such as disabilities and sexual orientation). Social stratification is the hierarchical ranking of groups in society and should not be confused with individual inequalities (Ogbu, 1994). Stratification implies a differential relationship between dominant groups, who are at the top of the hierarchy, and subordinate groups, who are at the bottom. These stratifications are based on socially created categories built on physical (race/ethnicity), biological (sex), and economic (class) characteristics. The meanings attributed to these categories have changed over time and are not fixed. The significant point, however, is that there is as much variation within groups as between them. Addressing inequalities in education requires more than structural changes; education must focus on the forces of social stratification and on the power that is represented in the social and historical construction of difference and its maintenance. The emphasis of multicultural education must be the politics of difference, not ethnic cultures.

It is also important to understand that multicultural education is not only for minority groups. Minority status here is defined in the sociological sense, in terms of lack of power, not in terms of culture. "Minority groups" include racial/ethnic groups (usually non-white groups), women (who may actually be a numerical majority), and the working class because of their lack of access to power, privilege, and societal rewards. White students must develop a consciousness of ethnicity and the cultures of other students; although "whites often fear that they will have much to lose if racism ends … in fact they have much to gain. Racism exacts a cost from both those who are hurt and those who benefit from it; the ending of racism will be both humanizing and liberating to all" (Derman-Sparks & Ramsey, 2006, p. 2). Whiteness cannot remain invisible and outside the framework of multiculturalism, which recognizes the need for a profound shift in the ways that we view the world. A significant goal of multicultural education is to teach all children critical consciousness so that they can question the conditions in society that allow inequalities to exist within the democratic rhetoric of social justice. Dominant-group children must learn to challenge prejudice and discrimination simply because their privileged position makes it less likely that they will do so. Education must prepare white students for a multicultural society and non-white students for a society in which they are likely to encounter discrimination.

Second, multiculturalism is a right to difference. Studies (Bourdieu & Passeron, 1977; McLaren, 1994) have uncovered how the unequal power relations in school have a differential impact on the construction of students' identities. Focus on the politics of difference does not imply a blindness to difference. Humans are deeply diverse—in their inherent characteristics (gender, age, physical and mental health, physical attributes, aptitudes, and so forth) as well as in their external situations (place of birth, social background, and so on). The effect of ignoring these differences, in fact, may be unjust and inegalitarian (Sen, 1992). Modern democratic societies (influenced by ethical theories) demand that all citizens, as human beings, have certain rights and equal opportunities. Differences based on race, sex, and place of birth, for example, are individual characteristics that are irrelevant to people's intrinsic worth and do not determine their functioning and capabilities (as recognized in human rights legislation). Ethnic, gender, and class differences are constructions in which individuals are ranked according to their membership in a specific group rather than on their individual merits. In multicultural education, social, gender, and cultural differences (among others) must be validated because they are an important part of one's identity.

Third, multicultural education must be seen to be radically different from a framework in which students of difference equate the school curriculum and culture with the dominant-culture privilege. The ambivalence resulting from being ignored and denigrated, or merely accommodated, within a largely Euro-centric, Judeo-Christian, male, middle-class culture places minority students in a disadvantaged position. Change in curriculum is essential not only because a more comprehensive picture of culture and the world would enrich the education of students, but also because the principle that all human beings have equal value demands that some students not be given a demeaning picture of themselves in school through the curriculum and school environment. As Taylor (1992) points out, "Nonrecognition or misrecognition can inflict harm, can be a form of oppression, imprisoning someone in a false, distorted, and reduced mode of being" (p. 25). This implies that the curriculum, methods of teaching and evalua-tion, and norms and standards of excellence must incorporate the worldviews, histories, and experiences of all children—dominant and minority—rather than only those in the dominant group.

Fourth, multicultural education must deal with the total culture of the school. It must be aware of the differential treatment of students who have very dissimilar experiences because of certain differences based on race, gender, culture, or class. Both students and teachers should be "transformed by the study of the other, so that we are not simply judging by our original familiar standards" (Taylor, 1992, p. 70). One aim of multicultural education is to provide a learning environment free of painful experiences of discrimination and inequality. As a philosophy, multicul-turalism must permeate the school culture so that all students can be empowered to cope with existing realities and have a democratic vision for the future.

Fifth, multicultural pedagogy must create new spaces in what Gadamer has called the "fusion of horizons" (quoted in Taylor, 1992, p. 67). This implies that the school should not create the "other" by making borders around group differ-ences. The school must not create a centre (an ethnocentric norm) that inevitably creates a periphery (the "other"). Rather, the centre and periphery must come together in one space.

Multiculturalism involves understanding multiple realities, creating a new level of consciousness that includes, but advances beyond, a monocultural frame of reference through interaction with other cultures. Multicultural education must empower students to negotiate with the margins of their identities.

Finally, multicultural education must aim to transform, not merely reform, the relations and meanings in education. For educators, this redefinition involves an understanding of how differences and inequalities are constructed—by people—

around ideas of race, ethnicity, gender, and class. The operative concepts here are identity and empowerment.

Multicultural education requires a knowledge of and sensitivity to the social consequences of expressing difference through prejudice and discrimination in the form of racism, sexism, and classism. While difference is a social concept, it is something we learn—not something we are born knowing. The pedagogical importance of difference lies in the persistence of inequalities in educational performance as well as in the development of identity and empowerment, which affect how students are taught and how they think of themselves.

It is of critical importance in multicultural education to focus on identity development—gender and ethnic at the individual level, and social and political at the community and national levels. The strategy is to separate the two aspects of ethnicity: identity and culture (Buchignani, 1980). The focus must not be on "immigrant" cultures as such, but on ethnic identity and how that merges with an overall Canadian identity. The teacher's role is to help students interpret their social relations so they integrate ethnic identity at the individual level into a national Canadian identification.

MULTICULTURALISM, INCLUSION, AND THE RIGHT TO BE DIFFERENT

In 1971, Prime Minister Pierre Trudeau announced a "policy of bilingualism within a multicultural framework." Bilingualism was based on the concept of two "founding nations," the English and the French. The policy ignored Canada's Native population. Multicultural policy had four objectives: (1) to assist all cultural groups to develop the capacity to grow and contribute to Canada; (2) to assist minority groups in overcoming cultural barriers to full participation in Canadian society; (3) to promote inter-group relations; and (4) to provide facilities to minority groups for language learning. The 1988 Multiculturalism Act focused on the weakest part of the policy, the third objective, by building on the equality provisions in the Charter of Rights and Freedoms through its Race Relations Directorate. The focus, however, is on exposing mainstream Canadians to different cultures so that they will be accepted. The dominant groups (English and French) remain outside the framework of multicultural policy. Canadian multiculturalism stands apart from that of other immigrant countries (i.e., the United States, the United Kingdom, Australia, New Zealand) not just because of how it has responded to the needs of minority, immigrant, or indigenous groups, but also because of the specific demographics of the Canadian population and the breadth of these people's needs, the constitutionalization of Canada's practices of accommodation, and the appropriation of diversity into Canadians' sense of national identity (Kymlicka, 2003).

Multicultural means many cultures. Multiculturalism is an ideology, a system of beliefs determined by the existence of many cultures. Therefore, to understand multiculturalism it is important to know that culture refers to the way in which a group of people responds to the environment. Culture is a way of seeing the world in terms of cognition, emotion, and behaviour. It is a concept that is constantly changing.

Cultural characteristics based on biological differences of gender, race, and ethnicity are the first things most people see. For instance, women think in ways that correspond to their difference in status from men and their lack of power in society. Economic status places people in different classes, which have their own cultures.

All of Western knowledge is influenced by gender, class, and European culture. The concept of multiculturalism has implied ethnic cultures. This book suggests that the notion of multiculturalism must include the dominant group that defines the norm, as well as the groups considered different from that norm because of social concepts of race, ethnicity, gender, class, religion, and lifestyle. It is these differences that are the basis of problems for students and others. These differences are socially created and serve to separate groups of people and form boundaries. They are inherently political because they veil domination and exclusion, and are symbolic of some form of underlying power struggle (Goldberg, 1992).

The demands of multiculturalism extend from the principles of equal dignity and equal respect, which must simultaneously allow for the right to be treated the same as everyone else, with identical rights and immunities, as well the right to difference, with recognition as having a unique identity (Taylor, 1994). Thus, inclusion is predicated on the right to difference and encompasses the full spectrum of difference in all its forms. This makes diversity embedded in and synonymous with multiculturalism.

But difference is a comparative term. *The Oxford Dictionary* defines it as "that which distinguishes one thing from another." Several questions arise from this definition: Different from whom? Different in what way? Different for whom?

Different from Whom?

To answer this question, we must identify those at the centre of power—the dominant group. The dominant group is not a homogeneous whole. In Western multicultural societies, members may represent some or all of the following characteristics: white, male, middle class, Christian, and heterosexual. In North America, the dominant group exhibits these characteristics, and those who are not in that image are created to be the "other." The dominant group is defined by its position of power in society and the way it relates with members of less powerful subordinate groups. The characteristics represented by the dominant group become the standard of and model for rationality and morality (Rothenburg, 1990).

Those who are not members of the dominant group are different, and this difference may be the basis for discrimination. Non-whites are subjected to racism, the working class is exposed to classism, and females experience sexism. However, these categories represent status and position in society rather than difference. Racism, classism, and sexism imply power and domination of white over black, middle class over working class, male over female. The common element is power. The task of multicultural education is to reveal the structures of power relations and inequalities.

Different in What Way?

Those who are different—"they," the "other"—are defined by the dominant group—"we," the "norm." Both "we" and "they" are socially constructed generalizations used by the dominant group to negatively single out individuals belonging to groups whom they consider to be subordinate. The terms "we" and "they" enhance and perpetuate the physical and economic differences that are used to categorize people, and maintain inequalities between "us" and "them." Difference is created when individual students are identified and differentiated according to their group affiliations in terms of race, ethnicity, gender, and class.

Different for Whom?

Although the concept of multiculturalism has changed over time, Canada's official multicultural policy addresses minority cultures, the "others," rather than both the dominant (English and French) and minority (other ethnocultural) groups. The ideology of multiculturalism does not include the dominant groups because they are not part of subordinate ethnic or cultural minorities. Multiculturalism has come to connote a policy for non-white groups because whiteness has become invisible. This ensures that the dominant-group members maintain their positions of power (Carby, 1992), while ethnocultural groups are assigned to the lower status of the "other" or "they." Multicultural educators should ask how the social constructions of whiteness and difference are learned and perpetuated, how they are created and have changed over time, and what opportunities students are given to challenge and change these ideas. The pedagogical aim is to focus on how students "learn to identify, challenge, and rewrite such representations" (Giroux, 1993, p. 21).

As a social concept, difference has traditionally been discussed by comparing opposites: difference/similarity, we/they, white/black, male/female, middle class/working class, good/bad, superior/inferior, strong/weak. Schools socialize students to respond to human differences with dislike and apprehension by ignoring, destroying, or incorporating differences. The simple focus on binary opposition may consciously or unconsciously mask the more complex underlying power hierarchies in gender, race, and class relations—for example, white is superior to black, male is more powerful than female.

These issues indicate not only that there are several definitions of difference but also that they are not fixed in any one time and place (that is, historically and across cultures). Multicultural education means recognizing that differences are constructed on the basis of the lack of power and the subordinate identity of people and groups. The implication of this for teaching strategies is that educators need to understand the social and historical construction of difference (for example, that the concept of race took on a new meaning with colonialism). Educators must know the effects of practices that label, devalue, and exclude the knowledge of the "other," the minority ethnocultural groups and females. They must also evaluate how schools deal with differences in social and pedagogical interactions that influence the way teachers and students define themselves and each other.

THE CONSTRUCTION OF DIFFERENCE

Concepts of race, ethnicity, gender, and class are social constructions. They serve to separate certain groups from others, whose identities are defined by the groups in power, in order to safeguard their position of privilege. As sociological ideas, these concepts have changed over time and are not fixed. Although in contemporary Canada racism is seen as discrimination directed mainly at non-white people, this was not always the case. For example, Eastern Europeans were subjected to racism in Canada at the turn of the 20th century because they were seen as being of a different race and ethnicity. Viewing whites as one racial group is a relatively recent phenomenon, and Banks (1995) points out that in the nineteenth and early twentieth centuries some white races were considered superior to others. The classifications of race, ethnicity, gender, and class have no relevance either as a basis for assignment of rights or as grounds for prejudice and discrimination. They indicate changing power and social relations (for example, women did not always have the right to vote). Inherently political because they veil domination and exclusion, these classifications are symbolic of some form of underlying power struggle (Goldberg, 1992). They are also ideological because they reflect people's beliefs. As Buchignani (1980) explains, difference as a concept "operates on those who hold it, as a way of seeing part of the world around them; once formulated, it provides the basis for action consistent with it" (p. 80). Thus, we must understand the politics of difference to make sense of, for example, the reality that until fairly recently blacks were not allowed by law to live in white neighbourhoods in South Africa.

The injuries caused by racial, ethnic, gender, and class discrimination are often hidden, but they are nonetheless painful. For students at risk—those who are largely poor, female, or from minority ethnocultural groups—multicultural education should ensure that school is not a place of hurtful experiences based on difference.

Identity

A significant aim of multicultural education is the development of a positive self-concept and identity in students. Educators need to understand the dynamics involved in the construction of identity. Recent theoretical developments in the social sciences have focused on the social process involved in identity development.

Identity is based on several elements such as race, gender, nationality, and sexual preference. It emerges at the individual level, but each person also has several social identities (for example, gender, ethnic, and class affiliations) that have implications at the political (such as being seen as a minority) and social/cultural levels. Social distance, or the perceived feelings of separation between groups, is based on experiences of tolerance and prejudice as well as socio-economic and educational status. For some students, the combined effects of racism, sexism, and class disadvantages are profound indeed.

Identities are always in the making and are the result of an individual's history and culture, class, and ethnicity/race as well as his or her experiences as male or female. These factors assume meaning in social relations. Ethnic identity formation is related to dominant-group perceptions of a particular ethnocultural group as well as their own perceptions and responses (for example, to their treatment in school). Because individuals have several identities, the teacher's role is to help students interpret their social relations. The success of multicultural education will depend on its ability to create unity within the diversity—to integrate a positive ethnic and gender identity at the individual level with a national Canadian identity.

The challenge for Canadian society and educators is to examine the complex process of identity construction and develop a harmonized Canadian identity that includes the individuality of various cultural, ethnic, and social identities.

Privilege

In conceptualizing multiculturalism as inclusive of multi-layered cultures of difference, we must reflect on how the phenomenon of privilege confers subtle and not-so-subtle advantages on groups that represent the dominant majority in society. Peggy McIntosh (1990) explains that although we can agree that minority groups in our society are disadvantaged in certain ways, it is much more problematic for us to admit to the inverse of this idea: that representatives of majority groups must therefore be over-privileged. But such logic does ring true if we realize that identifying with and being identified as a member of the societal norm allows a person to live his or her life without being forced to defend or justify an unalterable part of his or her identity:

> For instance, when candidates who represent visible minorities run for high political office, are they not pressed about how their race affects their views as leaders? When a woman with children is the CEO of a successful company, is she not asked about how she manages to balance both her personal and professional lives? If a gay teacher gets engaged to be married, is he or she permitted to openly express elation in front of students and coworkers? Conversely, in examining these situations through the lens of privilege, we would need to acknowledge, respectively, that white politicians are very seldom asked about how their whiteness influences their views, that high-powered businessmen are rarely saddled with expectations about raising their children, and that heterosexuals are free to make references to their partners in public settings without much threat of repercussions. These examples—and we could cite similar ones to uncover privilege in terms of class, (dis)ability, religion, age, etcetera— illuminate unfair societal advantages, which are reinforced through the education system. (Galczynski, Tsagkaraki, & Ghosh, 2012, p. 149)

In a truly multicultural education, then, students must be guided by teachers to become cognizant of the interlocking hierarchies in our society (McIntosh, 1990) if they are to develop empathy and respect for one another—and affect change. Most importantly, they must recognize the privileges they enjoy because they have been normalized. Otherwise, the politics of difference, which signify the uneven power relations between dominant and subordinate groups, will remain unchallenged (Ghosh & Abdi, 2004).

Knowledge

Our place in society and what we know affect how we understand the world. Traditionally, the school system has taught the male, Western, middle-class knowledge that was thought to provide "the truth" because it was the accepted way of knowing. Knowledge was thought to be "value-free"—that is, it was considered a "given" and therefore objective, rather than socially created and subjective. It has recently been argued that knowledge in the physical and social sciences is defined by the people who create it (the context) as well as by socio-cultural and historical forces. For example, the word "race" originally referred to a group of people. It has evolved to acquire a very different connotation in con-temporary society for both dominant and minority groups. Therefore, knowledge is not only socially constructed, but also reflects both the objective reality and the subjectivity of the knower (Banks, 1995; Code, 1991). The position or location of the knowledge creator, then, becomes crucial because the knowledge produced is influenced by the person's particular situation or place in the social (gender, race, ethnicity) and economic (class) structure. The realization that knowledge is constructed has challenged the idea of universal, value-free, and "objective" knowledge, which has tended to exclude the experiences of women, and peoples of other races, ethnicities, and classes.

Multicultural education's challenge to traditional views of knowledge chan-ges how we approach the teaching profession and pedagogy. By questioning how curriculum is designed, multicultural education offers alternative ways of teach-ing that represent different worldviews. How are students who are different in terms of race, ethnicity, gender, and class socially and culturally affected by the curriculum? Does the curriculum serve students differently depending on these differences? In other words, are male, white, middle-class students better off in the school system? Do teachers assume that their pedagogical practices are equally good for all students even though their students learn in different ways? Can teachers assume that teaching techniques are suitable for all students? How can students' historical, social, and cultural experiences become primary sources of knowledge so that they can be active participants in the learning process?

These questions transform the process of teaching by focusing on the relationship between teaching and learning rather than on the content or subject matter only. They also change the student-teacher equation, in which, as Freire (1970) has pointed out, knowledge is not just an object to be transmitted from the teacher who has the knowledge to the students who do not. As Lusted (1986) states, "Knowledge is not the matter that is offered so much as the matter that is understood" (p. 4).

Empowerment

Simon (1987) defines empowerment as the process by which students critically adopt knowledge outside of their experiences so as to have a vision of a world that is "'not yet'—in order to be able to alter the grounds upon which life is lived" (p. 375). Therefore, empowerment means creating conditions that bring someone into a state of ability or capability to act (Ashcroft, 1987). In school, empowerment means that a student can "develop the ability, confidence, and motivation to succeed academically" (Cummings, 1986, p. 23). Conversely, students are disabled by school experiences that do not develop academic and emotional foundations. Student empowerment should be both a tool for enhancing academic performance and an educational end in itself; the ultimate aim is that students will become responsible and effective citizens.

Educational institutions and teachers do not empower students, since empowerment is acquired, not given. In empowering education, conditions are created that allow the transformation of students' potential power into actual power or empowerment. Education that empowers emphasizes a process of inquiry and discovery in which knowledge can be personally acquired, not given in packaged form as a fixed entity. It focuses on development as personal growth, schools that operate as communities, and curriculum that gives full expression to multiple voices. Multiple voices are the worldviews and experiences of a variety of people. Each student has multiple voices because each cultural dimension of identity creates a different voice (dominant/minority, male/female, heterosexual/homosexual, etc.). An empowered student is one who can state, defend, and demonstrate values. The teacher plays a crucial role in facilitating and creating a symbiotic relationship: students need conditions that encourage inquiry, while the teacher uses the multiple worldviews to create an environment of full expression.

THE BASIS AND CONSEQUENCES OF DIFFERENCE

Differences elicit a variety of responses including stereotypes, prejudice, and discrimination. Stereotypes are social constructs in which groups of people are identified in terms of fixed images associated with specific attributes, particularly those of colour or culture. Prejudice is an attitude (usually negative) developed toward members of a group; it is an opinion made in advance and not based on evidence. Discrimination is the behaviour resulting from prejudice. It grants or denies individuals or groups opportunities and rewards based on group characteristics, such as ethnicity, sex, class, religion, and language. In schools, especially, discrimination may take on forms of bullying and cyberbullying.

Racial Stratification and Racism

According to contemporary biologists, there are no races, only racists. Scientifically, we all belong to one human race, but the concept of race exists very much in our social consciousness as a means of classifying people. The concept of hierarchy among races is closely related to the colonialism and slavery that occurred during the expansion of European nations to the other continents.

Initially, populations were categorized by physical (e.g., skull measurement) and behavioural characteristics, and the conquering nations were placed at the top of the hierarchy. Racial superiority justified the Europeans' mission of civilizing and saving the souls of the conquered indigenous peoples. Racism developed as an ideology of power to rationalize the subordination and oppression of local populations. This ideology randomly classified people on the basis of biological criteria such as actual (skin colour) or assumed (e.g., non-whites are less intelligent) physiological and genetic differences. These earlier theories of innate differences among races have been scientifically refuted in the twentieth century. Race now exists as a socially defined category.

Race is a separate construct from ethnicity, although they are closely connected in people's minds. Whereas both concepts are socially defined, ethnicity is based on cultural criteria (such as religion, language, customs, institutions, and history), while race is constructed on the basis of physical criteria (Van den Berghe, 1967). Discrimination based on ethnicity, however, is also racism because it is grounded on physical and cultural characteristics (such as mode of dress or eating habits).

The complexion of Canada is changing rather fast. Whereas in 1971 about 62 percent of immigrants came from Europe, in 2006 as much as 58 percent of immigrants came from Asia (including the Middle East) (Statistics Canada, 2008). So, the word "multiculturalism" has come to be associated with the word "immigrant," and the very word "immigrant" has a connotation of non-white groups: "visible minorities," which is the term used by the Canadian federal government to describe minorities who are non-white and non-Aboriginal. Surveys of attitudes toward immigration have indicated that many Canadians feel that too many immigrants are visible minorities. Their fear is not only that "Canadian culture" will be reshaped, but that visible minority immigrants will put a strain on the country's welfare programs. This attitude prevails, despite statistics showing that immigrants increase the average total income in Canada (Beaujot & Rappak, 1988). As of the 2006 Census, five million Canadians—or over 16 percent of the country's population—self-identified as representing a visible minority. Moreover, visible minorities actually comprise the majority of the population in certain Canadian cities, including Toronto and Vancouver (Statistics Canada, 2008). It is important to note, however, that although labelling "visible minorities" ostensibly highlights their recognition, individuals who are non-white tend to be "invisible" in positions of power.

Religion and Intolerance

Whereas the Canadian Constitution establishes the right for all Canadians to freely practice their religious beliefs, debate over religious expression in Canadian schools has a long history. As Christian churches were closely linked to the establishment of early education systems in both English and French Canada, the growing dimensions of diversity among the Canadian population have led to conflict over issues of religious accommodation. Egbo (2009) explains that religious minorities have challenged the privileging of Christianity in education by asking for federal support of their own alternatives to publicly funded Christian schools. According to Seljak, "Those who clamor for more accommodation of the rights of religious minority groups are, in a way, trying to broaden the definition of who and what is identified as legitimately Canadian.... These debates are important because they define boundaries of Canadian identity and the limits of Canadian tolerance" (2007, p. 36). Yet it is also important for Canadians to question whether religion, particularly in its more fundamentalist forms, is actually on the rise—or whether it is just the presence and participation of non-Christians in Canadian society that is increasing (Jedwab, 2007).

Prevalent forms of religious intolerance worldwide include anti-Semitism and Islamophobia. Trends of hostility towards Jewish and Muslim populations have well-documented historical roots as reactions to difference, particularly in the contexts of establishing or preserving perceptions of national identity. This explains why periods of increased immigration, such as the opening of borders through the constitutionalization of the European Union in the early 2000s, tend to witness a resurgence of religious intolerance (Bunzi, 2008). Both anti-Semitism and Islamophobia may be interpreted as forms of racism, as they are predicated upon prejudiced attitudes and hostilities in relation to racial/ethnic otherness as much, if not more so, than religious otherness: "Antisemitism and Islamophobia have to be considered as the same family of racial prejudices. Obviously different in some aspects, they however share a long sequence of similarities regarding the folkways evoked and the discourses subtly diffused" (Alietti & Padovan, 2013, p. 599).

Secularity, agnosticism, and atheism are also expressions of religious identity, even if they represent separation from or negation of principles and beliefs expressed by followers of traditional faith-based religions. In an inclusive multicultural classroom, it is necessary to create space for non-religious students in addition to their religious peers in order to avoid seeing religious identity through a deficit-model lens.

Gender Stratification and Sexism

Feminist theorists distinguish between sex, which is biological, and gender, which is a social construct (Ambert, 1976). Gender stratification is a social ranking that gives females a subordinate status. Much of the bias in schools is expressed through sexist language and stereotyping of sex roles and is, therefore, referred to as sexism.

From the time they are identified as female, girls are attributed certain "feminine" characteristics that position them to feel inferior and to grow up to expect and do less, all of which reinforces the hierarchical gender order that confers greater power and resources on men (Berkowitz, Manohar, & Tinkler, 2010). Because of this, sex-role stereotyping can be discriminatory against girls/women as well as boys/men, as it pressures them to live up to norms perceived, respectively, as "feminine" or "masculine." In classrooms and schools, deviation from these gendered roles is often linked to bullying, sexual harassment, and gender-based violence (Janigan & Masemann, 2008).

Sexism in education has been amply substantiated over the last three decades in terms of its impact on the lives of female students. While the late 1990s and early 2000s have witnessed an alleged "boy crisis" in education, scholars point out that such perceptions perpetuate a false gender myth that fails to acknowledge the interplay between race and class differences (Barnett & Rivers, 2004). If policy-makers are to successfully address gender imbalances in education, they must not insist on "gender neutral" policies, which fail to acknowledge that Canadian society, for all practical purposes, remains patriarchal. Accordingly, "while both female and male needs should receive equal consideration in our school systems, the outcomes of such scrutiny should lead to different treatment for women, as they comprise a marginalized group" (Egbo, 2009, p. 290).

Sexual Orientation and Homophobia

According to conservative estimates, a typical Canadian high school classroom of twenty-five students will include two or three students who are gay, lesbian, or transgender (Crook & Truscott, 2007). This is important for multicultural educators to consider because students who identify as lesbian, gay, bisexual, transgender, or questioning (LGBTQ) are much more likely than their heterosexual peers to hear homophobic remarks, have low self-esteem, be physically assaulted, drop out of school, or commit suicide. In general, "as a society we remain perplexed about how to deal with homophobia, even though we know that the gay, lesbian, transgender, and bisexual population make up a significant portion of our society" (Grant and Sleeter, 2009, p. 260). Thus, LGBTQ students face the tremendous obstacle of a society that privileges individuals who belong to the dominant heterosexual norm and often antagonizes those who do not. In response to this reality, Canadian courts have increasingly ruled that public schools have "a positive duty to provide a safe and supportive learning environment for all students," even occasionally finding them liable for not having taken adequate steps to provide such an environment (Crook & Truscott, 2007, p. 151).

Teacher education programs typically do not train teacher candidates to deal with issues that arise from differences in sexual orientation. Redman and

Redman (2011) point out that, as in many areas related to multiculturalism and diversity, terminology is important and can be quite sensitive in relation to sexual orientation. In fact, "microcultures in one geographical area may use certain terms to define their sexual orientation and related situations, whereas in other areas, those same terms may be viewed as irrelevant or even offensive" (p. 122). Teachers need to be aware of these terminological differences—for example, the appropriateness of using the term "queer," which is commonly used in academic fields but sometimes considered pejorative or even hate speech when invoked in interpersonal communication—when issues related to sexuality are discussed in the classroom. Some scholars prefer to use the term "affective orientation" in place of "sexual orientation" in order to emphasize aspects of identity and self over biological differences or sexual practices.

Mental and Physical (Dis)ability

As is the case with underprivileged groups in terms of race, gender, and sexual orientation, the recognition of those with physical or mental disabilities as different propagates stereotyping and discrimination. In labelling students with mental or physical disabilities as "exceptional" or "special needs," school policies emphasize their difference. Because such individuals' differences are measured against a vaguely defined norm, one that is "able," the term disability labels them as deficient (Galczynski et al., 2012). Some scholars posit that the "importance of physical [and mental] difference lies solely in discriminatory social reaction to or ignorance of the effects of that difference" (Koch, 2001, p. 370), which reminds us that individuals with disabilities must deal not only with the limitations of their conditions, but also with the impositions of societal barriers. As a result, "building an identity influenced by both exceptionality and diversity [can] create a feeling of double jeopardy" (Manning & Manning, 2009, p. 41).

Disability scholars and activists have gone beyond understanding disability as just a physical or mental condition to interpret the label as a signifier of shared socio-political issues; for example, "a person who is paralyzed from the waist down has a physical disability, but if the person has a wheelchair, and if the physical context is wheelchair accessible, the person may actually not be disabled most of the time" (Grant & Sleeter, 2011, p. 12). In this way, (dis)ability functions as culture, and individuals find membership in that culture because of their physical or mental differences.

Class Stratification and Classism

Class indicates economic status, which is related to education, occupation, and income. While race, ethnicity, and gender are inherited, class is often evaluated in terms of skilled versus unskilled, intellectual versus manual labour, and professional versus blue-collar workers. The distinction is based on occupational level as well as the quality of our possessions, such as the make of car we drive. Classism refers to discrimination against classes that differ from middle-class culture and values. Values are different for the working class, the unemployed, and those living below the poverty line—by far the largest population in Canada and about one-quarter of the school population. Although an individual's economic status can be changed (usually with higher levels of education), class status tends to persist. Education is thought to be a significant factor in maintaining class structure (Bowles & Gintis, 1976). Schools fail the children of the poor when their values and culture are left out of the school curriculum. This alienates poor children, whose experiences of poverty (e.g., undernourishment, substandard housing and unfavourable living conditions, absences from school due to sickness) extend the cycle of underachievement and cause high dropout rates. The most damaging implications, however, remain invisible: personal experiences of failure, hopelessness, alienation, and lack of opportunity.

In our society, "education is often heralded as the gateway towards socioeconomic mobility, but such a correlation is overly simplistic if it ignores the reality of inequity within the education system, both in terms of access and educational quality" (Galczynski et al., 2012, p. 159–160). For instance, a recent survey of American university admissions directors found that universities prioritize the recruitment of students who do not need financial aid and are willing to pay non-discounted tuition (e.g., international students) over the admission of those who are less financially secure. In addition, college aid packages increasingly rely on "gapping," or necessitating that students who do not meet full financial need take out additional private student loans (Jaschik, 2013). While we may assume that higher education facilitates social mobility, research confirms that similarly able students consistently enroll in different types of universities based on their socio-economic backgrounds. In a study of high school valedictorians and their pathways to university, Walton Radford (2013) found that high-achieving students from poorer backgrounds limit themselves to less selective (and typically less expensive) post-secondary institutions, and that such decisions continue to affect their access to occupational prestige and power throughout their lives.

MULTICULTURAL PEDAGOGY AND THE SCHOOL

While multicultural education focuses on student diversity, its aim should be to provide the best education for all: it should not only be concerned with minority groups, but also with dominant-group children. A redefined multicultural education is concerned with providing all students with the best possible education, and that implies a pedagogy that is inclusive of various ideas and possibilities.

Why should we be concerned with providing the best education for all children? Why should we try to have an education that includes various cultures and languages? The obvious answer is that the loss of diversity in culture and languages would mean a lack of intellectual diversity. A single cultural framework, as in an assimilationist model of education, would limit the human potential of minority cultures, further dispossessing the minority-group children who are different from the mainstream culture in terms of ethnocultural group, socio-economic context, gender, and lifestyle.

Why do particular groups of children fail? Conversely, why does the school fail certain groups? Who are these children? In order to answer these questions it is important to examine the explanations for low achievement among certain groups of students. It is equally important to examine existing programs that are based on those explanations. This leads to a redefinition of multicultural education. A redefined multicultural education must include goals that are "responsive to the imperatives of human dignity, justice and rights, social responsibility, interdependence and responsiveness and to the full development of the human personality" (Lynch, 1992, p. 36). This section makes some suggestions along these lines and ends with a brief discussion of the notion of change.

Multicultural Approaches in Education

The main focus of multicultural education has been the education of children who are racially and ethnically different from the dominant group. Because earlier interpretations excluded broader definitions of culture—those that encompass gender, sexual orientation, class, and (dis)ability—the term "inclusion" was relegated to discussions of whether or not to include special needs students in "mainstream" classrooms. However, just as the field of special education has come to recognize the many benefits of including all kinds of students in the same classroom and the perpetual costs of segregation, so must multicultural education incorporate the principle of inclusion to ensure equitable opportunities for all students in school and in their adult lives.

The liberal theories of multicultural education measure success from a Eurocentric, male, middle-class norm. Equality is taken to mean "same"—the nearer to the norm, the greater the possibility of being equal. This handicaps those, such as visible minorities, who cannot (even if they wanted to) become the "same" as the dominant group. The result is structural inequality, in which those who are not the same because of their ethnicity, gender, and/or class are subjected to unfair competition in order to fit the "norm" of the dominant culture.

Radical theories, on the other hand, focus on structural discrimination in the school, rather than on the student, as the problem. The structures in school are seen as being devised for a homogeneous population (anglophone and francophone), and as working, perhaps unintentionally, against minority groups. Students from other cultures are judged by standards that are not fair to them because these standards reflect the needs and aspirations of the dominant group. Thus, the system disables minority students. This systemic discrimination seeps through the policies of ministries of education and school boards. These barriers are built into the supposedly "neutral" institutional structures, policies, and practices that exclude people or deny them equitable treatment (Ontario, 1993) because they were devised for homogeneous populations, not for diverse student bodies. Because these structures and policies are not created with diversity in mind, "the capital and language codes of a dominant culture make academic success particularly difficult for those who do not belong" (Carnoy, 1989, p. 6). Thus, power inequality becomes central to the problem of discrimination, and children of minority groups are being socialized into failure.

Research shows that students who fail are the poor, ethnic minorities, and females (especially those whose lives are influenced by a combination of two or three of these factors). The difference of these students from the dominant group is constructed on the basis of three factors. The first factor is class. Class differences are constructed and reinforced through education (Bernstein, 1977; Bourdieu & Passeron, 1977; Bowles & Gintis, 1976). Studies demonstrate that there are variations in school success for ethnocultural minorities and females related to class differences—that is, when they belong to higher socio-economic groups they are likely to do better in school. The second factor that creates difference is low group status in society. Cummings (1986) uses international data to show how power and status relations between dominant and minority groups influence school performance. Third, difference is created especially for those groups who have internalized the inferior status attributed to them by the dominant group (women, non-whites, the working class).

Some ethnic minority groups in Canada and the United States are reported to achieve highly in academic and socio-economic terms. This fact may raise the question of why certain groups are upwardly mobile despite the common experiences of racism. Ogbu (1978) suggests that some "immigrant" minorities and "autonomous" groups succeed because they are not totally dominated. For example, some successful Asian immigrants have enough cultural resources to resist discrimination and the internalization of the dominant group's negative attributions. Autonomous groups like the Jews are, numerically, a cultural minority in North America, but they are not subordinated economically or politically. Feuerstein (1979) suggests that groups that get cut off from their culture suffer from intergenerational transmission disruption, which means that cultural transmission gets disrupted between generations. So, a cultural group that does well in school may not continue to do so if cultural values are not transmitted to the next generation. The overall evidence is that positive association with the dominant as well as with one's own culture is related to school success. Individuals and groups who do not perceive themselves as victims succeed, through a variety of strategies, in deflecting the discrimination of the dominant group. Takaki (1989) refers to the success of some Asian minorities in the US educational and economic system as the "model minority syndrome." The success of these minorities has created resentment in dominant as well as in other minority groups and has led to racial harassment. Another problem is stereotyping members of these groups, thereby masking the difficulties faced by minority ethnic students who achieve despite the odds. Moreover, it ignores their failures and may make their school experiences painful.

Research indicates that social status influences school performance. Cummings (1986) found that when the social status of a group changes, the educational performance also changes. For example, Finnish students are reported to fail academically in Sweden, where they are a low-status group, but to do well in Australia, where they are a high-status group (Troike, 1978). Similarly, the Burakumin, a historically outcast and geographically isolated group tracing back to the Japanese feudal era, perform poorly within Japan, but just as well as other Japanese students in the United States (Ogbu, 1978).

The structure and process of education classify children from some groups as low achievers (Coard, 1971), with the result that large numbers of them are either dumped into special education classes or drop out of school altogether. The solution to this dilemma can be found not in trying to fit these groups in, but in changing the rules and structure of the educational game. For example, if square pegs will not fit into a board that has only round holes, we cannot blame the pegs for this failure. Should we change their shape to fit them into the holes? Or should we make space for them in the board? So it is with children. Many do not fit into the school system. The history of First Nations people clearly demonstrates that changing a group of people to fit into society through assimilation does not work and destroys their distinctiveness. The solution lies in changing the structure of education in order to recognize diversity—of race, ethnicity, gender, and class—rather than in blaming the students. Such change would involve redefining what is valid knowledge, adopting a variety of teaching styles, reinterpreting the concept of achievement, and devising evaluations to deal with student diversity. An expanded notion of education that validates a diversity of skills, talents, values, goals, and aspirations is essential.

Through the influence of radical theories, the meaning of multicultural education has now broadened. The trend in existing multicultural education programs is to include human rights and prejudice reduction strategies, cross-cultural communication, and, more recently, a comprehensive approach for involving parents and community. The programs may vary considerably, but the general focus is on developing respect for other cultures. For example, global education and development education are aimed at internationalizing student perspectives through the study of the interdependence of nations and systems and worldwide issues relevant to the future of humanity. Environmental education deals with issues related to a sustainable life at the local and global levels. Human rights education is focused on developing student awareness of individual rights and responsibilities, sensitizing them to the rights of others and encouraging responsible action to protect the rights of all. It deals with the content as well as the process of education (Tarrow, 1990). Peace education expands the concept of peace beyond the absence of war and violence (physical and structural) to include human rights and justice (Tarrow, 1993). "Education about peace" deals with content; the broader term "education for peace" (or educating for positive peace) involves cognitive, attitudinal, and behavioural objectives.

More recently, critical pedagogy and critical feminist pedagogy have enlarged the scope of multicultural education in three significant ways: (1) by re-examining the notion that Western European values, philosophies, and narratives constitute "universal truths" and are the only valid knowledge; (2) by pointing out the inequalities and discrimination resulting from cultural differences; and (3) by focusing on identity development and empowerment in education.

Related to these perspectives are two programs that look at the broader structures in education. Anti-racist education started in Britain in the 1960s and has been implemented in two Canadian provinces, Ontario and British Columbia. It focuses on structural and individual discrimination (particularly racism and its intersection with class and gender) and on social reconstruction, which seeks a society based on equality and social justice. Feminist pedagogy is concerned with sexism (and the overlapping oppressive formations resulting from race and class). It challenges women's deprecation and devaluation in knowledge, and goes on to define the "other voice" (meaning women's experiences). While each of these programs is necessary, neither is sufficient on its own. The terms anti-racist and feminist are exclusive—the first focuses on race, while the second concentrates on gender—although each includes the other. It is necessary to not only incorporate all "others" but also to alter the rules of pedagogy, the definition of the norm.

Redefining Multicultural Education

Given that education programs based on the official definitions of multiculturalism and interculturalism have been inadequate in addressing the fundamental problems of difference and its social connotations, what can we propose to make education programs meet the needs of all children?

The term "multicultural education" is retained here but redefined to be an inclusive term relevant at the structural and individual levels in education. It has an integrated approach that incorporates human concerns at the local, national, and global levels into one framework. It includes cognitive (knowledge), affective (feelings), and ethical (moral) spheres relevant to education.

The goal of redefined multicultural education is to ensure that all students are empowered (through the development of knowledge, skills, attitudes, and values) to participate with confidence as informed citizens. It seeks to impart to students a social vision of a democratic society within an interdependent global context.

Redefined multicultural education is aimed at students from both dominant and minority groups (not only the latter). Its framework is inclusive, integrated, and student-centred, and is based on co-operative approaches to teaching and learning. It emphasizes a more inclusive classroom ethos and an ethical-affective approach in which learners are active participants.

Redefined multicultural education is based on the assumption that any system and practice that discriminates against specific groups on the basis of their difference from the dominant group is unacceptable and therefore requires radical change at all levels, including structural/institutional, individual, and philosophical.

The Structural and Institutional Levels

One of the aims of multicultural education is to identify and eliminate structures and hidden mechanisms that result in differential educational experiences for students of various races, ethnicities, classes, or other categories. The goal is an equal chance for all students to develop their full potential for economic survival and their concern for social justice. Equal chance does not mean the "same" but implies that different students have different needs; the structure of education should be inclusive enough to satisfy those needs equally without labelling some as deficient because they are different. The dominant-group norm is biased against minority students and must be changed to include other groups. All actors in the educational system are implicated in this process, and true multicultural education is good education for all. Unless multicultural education is seen as being good for all, the major beneficiaries of the school system will continue to be the dominant group.

The Individual Level

The role of education in producing responsible citizens is to help all students develop the skills necessary for the workforce and gain knowledge of democratic principles. In addition, an awareness and understanding of the principles of the Universal Declaration of Human Rights, the Canadian Charter of Rights and Freedoms, and provincial human rights codes are essential. All students must understand that rights and responsibilities go hand in hand. Dominant-group students must realize their special responsibility to unlearn stereotypes and work toward the elimination of unequal relations. Mainstream children are central to a redefined multicultural education because it is their relationship to other ethnocultural groups that is crucial in creating difference.

The Philosophical Level

A redefined multicultural education is not only concerned with the curriculum; it also involves a philosophy of knowledge and learning based on recent theoretical developments in the social sciences. The way we look at the world is influenced by our knowledge of it and how that knowledge is acquired. For example, feminist theory challenges the traditional elite male perspective in knowledge creation; the "new sociology" has influenced analysis of the socially constructed nature of knowledge; critical theory links knowledge to power; and postmodern, post-structural, and post-colonial theories challenge monocultural philosophies as representing "universal truths" and all of humanity, emphasize a cultural politics of difference, and focus on identity, culture, and power.

The mandate of a redefined multicultural education is the radical transformation of the structure and culture of the school so that the formal educational system represents the perspectives and knowledge of the diverse groups (including the dominant one) that make up society. The framework of this reconstruction upholds certain universal human values and rights. It focuses on the politics of difference and culture by instilling responsibility in and empowering all students to develop confidence through a strong cultural and political identity and to communicate across differences.

The intent of a redefined multicultural education is to move beyond "managing" difference to a point where difference becomes an intrinsic component of the "norm." This involves a transformation of the philosophy and ideology of the prevailing educational system—a change that impinges on every aspect of pedagogy.

The Change Process

A redefined multicultural education suggests potentially significant changes. Restructuring involves much more than changing policy; it means a break with the past and the status quo. The shift is radical—from an unquestioning acceptance of "facts" (thereby maintaining inequality) to a critical awareness of the politics of knowledge creation. It means recasting all aspects of education to reflect the experiences and intellectual viewpoints of those who have historically been left out. Such a process goes to the roots of the sociology of knowledge construction and validation.

What makes any educational change significant is that the student is at the centre, and his or her learning and motivation are at stake. Restructuring has a price tag, but so does the status quo, which is already unjust for so many. The changes caused by redefining multicultural education may involve simple and inexpensive procedures such as innovative teaching practices; these can range from utilizing different learning materials to altering teaching strategies and educational philosophies. The meaning of change is created by the educational actors involved, their perceptions, and their position in the system. Change means different things to different people: the teacher's perception is likely to be different from that of the student or the school principal.

The fact that change alters pre-existing values and conditions makes it important to involve all the actors in the change process, particularly teachers. Studies indicate that when people feel part of the policy and process of change, they are more likely to try harder to make it work. Change must deal with more than implementation; it should involve sustained and intensive effort to create "the conditions for people to change how they deal with change" (Fullan, 1992, p. 121). The process of change involves both interpersonal (between individuals) and intrapersonal (within individuals) dimensions.

Fullan (1992) points out that the most important aspect of change is the creation of the institutional capacity to restructure. It is related to the mobilization of all resources in the education system around the student. Change must also be institutionalized as the result of a collective effort. To have a lasting effect, it has to take root and must be internalized. Any change in education must be judged by its impact on students and be aimed at improving student learning and school experiences.

CONCLUSION

It is important to emphasize again that, theoretically, multicultural education seeks to elucidate the unequal power relations that have historically developed around differences. This constitutes a powerful undercurrent that propels all social interactions—in society and in schools. The aim of multicultural education is to explore the common space enriched by the variety of talents, cultures, histories, and experiences that difference represents. It is the garden in which the diversity of flowers defines its beauty. In education, diversity must be used as a creative force rather than as a force that cripples the development of society.

At present, not all students have the right to be different. The rationale for redefining multicultural education is to help these students develop positive identities and make them critical, democratic citizens. The purpose of multicultural education should be to challenge how we see the world, given the continued existence of racism, poverty, violence, and the abuse of human rights. Multicultural education holds value for all groups and individuals: "If we so marginalize or devastate people that, ultimately, they cannot become productive, contributing, or participating members of society, we are all diminished. If we can create inclusive, respectful conditions that support all people—both at home and abroad—in meeting their needs, in receiving an education, and in fulfilling their dreams, we will all benefit" (Shields, 2013, p. 100). The success of multicultural education programs will depend on their ability to create unity within the diversity of Canadian society.

While multicultural education has tended to focus on students from minority backgrounds, we need to look at education for all students. In particular, the relations in educational practice between the dominant and subordinate groups must be re-examined. Such a process is based on the assumption that schools need to reverse the powerlessness of some groups in society if these groups are to succeed. A redefined multicultural education aims to help all students develop the potential to gain knowledge and confidence in order to contribute to a democratic vision of society.

REVIEW QUESTIONS

1. How are the concepts of "identity" and "empowerment" central to multicultural education?
2. How are race/ethnicity, gender, sexual orientation, class, and (dis)ability related to equality of opportunity in education? Which of these factors do you think most affects educational opportunities in local, national, and global contexts?
3. How is discrimination harmful to the well-being of both minority and dominant groups?
4. How have historical trends influenced the assignment of "traditional" gender roles? Whose traditions are they? Are these gender roles consistent from one culture to another?
5. Are individuals from certain religious backgrounds more welcome to express their beliefs than others? What makes certain religious traditions seem more unusual than others?
6. What are the connotations of labelling someone as "handicapped" or "disabled"? How do you think these labels affect the perceptions that people with special needs have of themselves? How do they affect others' perceptions of them?
7. What kinds of students are "at risk" of failure? Is there anything inherent in these students that leads to school failure?

8. Who should be responsible for redefining multicultural education in a way that breaks with the status quo and empowers all students to succeed?

9. How can multicultural education help build a strong Canada?

REFERENCES

Alietti, A. & Padovan, D. (2013). Religious racism: Islamophobia and anti-Semitism in Italian society. *Religions, 4*, 584–602.

Ambert, A. (1976). *Sex structure.* Toronto: Longman Canada.

Ashcroft, L. (1987). Defusing "empowering": The what and the why. *Language Arts, 64*(2), 142–156.

Banks, J. (1995). The historical reconstruction of knowledge about race: Implications for transformative teaching. *Educational Researcher, 24*(2), 15–25.

Barnett, R.C., & Rivers, C. (2004). *Same difference: How gender myths are hurting our relationships, our children, and our jobs.* Cambridge, MA: Basic Books.

Beaujot, R., & Rappak, J.P. (1988). The role of immigration in changing socio-economic structures. *The Review of Demography and Its Implications for Economic and Social Policy.* Ottawa: The Royal Society of Canada.

Berkowitz, D., Manohar, N.N., & Tinkler, J.E. (2010). Walk like a man, talk like a woman: Teaching the social construction of gender. *Teaching Sociology, 38*(2), 132–143.

Bernstein, B. (1977). *Class, codes, and control.* London: Routledge/Kegan Paul.

Bourdieu, P., & Passeron, J.C. (1977). *Reproduction in education, society, and culture.* Beverly Hills, CA: Sage.

Bowles, S., & Gintis, H. (1976). *Schooling in capitalist America.* New York: Basic Books.

Buchignani, N. (1980). Culture or identity: Addressing ethnicity in Canadian education. *McGill Journal of Education, 15*(1), 79–93.

Bunzi, M. (2008). Between anti-Semitism and Islamophobia: Some thoughts on the new Europe. *American Ethnologist, 32*(4), 499–508.

Carby, H. (1992). The multicultural wars. *Radical History Review, 54*, 7–18.

Carnoy, M. (1989). Education, state, and culture in American society. In H. Giroux & R. McLaren (Eds.), *Critical pedagogy, the state and cultural struggle* (pp. 3–23). Albany, NY: State University of New York Press.

Coard, B.L. (1971). *How the West Indian child is made educationally sub-normal in the British school system.* London: Beacon.

Code, L. (1991). *What can she know? Feminist theory and the construction of knowledge.* Ithaca, NY: Cornell University Press.

Crook, K., & Truscott, D. (2007). *Ethics and law for teachers.* Toronto: Nelson/Thomson Canada.

Cummings, J. (1986). Empowering minority students: A framework for intervention. *Harvard Educational Review, 56*(1), 18–36.

Derman-Sparks, L., & Ramsey, P.G. (2006). *What if all the kids are white? Anti-bias multicultural education with young children and families.* New York: Teachers College Press.

Egbo, B. (2009). *Teaching for diversity in Canadian schools.* Toronto: Pearson.

Feuerstein, R. (1979). *The dynamic assessment of retarded performers.* Baltimore, MD: University Park Press.

Freire, P. (1970). *Pedagogy of the oppressed.* New York: Seabury Press.

Fullan, M. (1992). *Successful school improvement.* Toronto: OISE Press.

Galczynski, M., Tsagkaraki, V., & Ghosh, R. (2012). Unpacking multiculturalism in the classroom: Using current events to explore the politics of difference. *Canadian Ethnic Studies, 43*(3), 145–164.

Ghosh, R. (2011). The liberating potential of multiculturalism in Canada: Ideals and realities. *Canadian Issues/Thèmes Canadiens,* Spring, 3–7.

Ghosh, R. & Abdi, A. (2004). *Education and the politics of difference.* Toronto: Canadian Scholars' Press.

Giroux, H. (1993). Living dangerously: Identity politics and the new cultural racism; Towards a new pedagogy of representation. *Cultural Studies, 7*(1), 1–27.

Goldberg, D. (1992). The semantics of race. *Ethnic and Racial Studies, 15*(4), 543–569.

Grant, C.A., & Sleeter, C.E. (2009). *Turning on learning: Five approaches for multicultural teaching plans for race, class, gender, and disability* (5th ed.). Hoboken, NJ: Wiley.

Grant, C.A., & Sleeter, C.E. (2011). *Doing multicultural education for achievement and equity* (2nd ed.). New York: Routledge.

Janigan, K., & Masemann, V.L. (2008). Gender and education. In K. Mundy, K. Bickmore, R. Hayhoe, M. Madden, & K. Madjidi (Eds.), *Comparative and international education: Issues for teachers* (pp. 215–248). Toronto: Canadian Scholars' Press.

Jaschik, S. (2013, September). Feeling the heat: The 2013 survey of college and university admissions directors. *Inside Higher Ed.* Retrieved from www.insidehighered. com/news/survey/feeling-heat-2013-survey-college-and-university-admissions-directors#ixzz2s1e1IYMS

Jedwab, J. (2007). Faith in Canadian identity: The nation's evolving religious demography. *Canadian American Research Series, 4*(1), 34–37.

Koch, T. (2001). Disability and difference: Balancing social and physical constructions. *Journal of Medical Ethics, 27*(6), 370–376.

Kymlicka, W. (2003). Canadian multiculturalism in historical and comparative perspective: Is Canada unique? *Constitutional Forum, 13*(1), 1–8.

Lusted, D. (1986). Why pedagogy? *Screen, 27*(5), 2–14.

Lynch, J. (1992). *Education for citizenship in a multicultural society.* London: Cassell.

Manning, M.L., & Manning, L.G. (2009). *Multicultural education of children and adolescents.* Boston: Pearson Education.

McIntosh, P. (1990). White privilege and male privilege: A personal account of coming to see correspondences through work in women's studies. In M.S. Kimmel & A.K. Ferbers (Eds.), *Privilege: A reader* (pp. 147–160). Boulder, CO: Westview Press.

McLaren, P. (1994). White terror and oppositional agency: Towards a critical multiculturalism. In T.D. Goldberg (Ed.), *Multiculturalism*. Cambridge, MA: Basil Blackwell.

Ogbu, J.U. (1978). *Minority education and caste: The American system in cross-cultural perspective*. New York: Academic Press.

Ogbu, J.U. (1994). Racial stratification and education in the United States: Why inequality persists. *Teachers College Record, 96*(2), 264–298.

Ontario. (1993). *Anti-racism and ethnocultural equity in school boards: Guidelines for policy development and implementation*. Toronto: Ministry of Education and Training.

Redman, G.L., & Redman, A.R. (2011). *A casebook for exploring diversity* (4th ed.). Boston: Pearson.

Rothenburg, P. (1990). The construction, deconstruction, and reconstruction of difference, *Hypatia, 5*(1), 42–57.

Seljak, D. (2007). Accommodating religious diversity in Canada. *Canadian American Research Series, 4*(1), 34–37.

Sen, A. (1992). *Inequality re-examined*. Cambridge, MA: Harvard University Press.

Shields, C.M. (2013). *Transformative leadership in education: Equitable change in an uncertain and complex world*. New York: Routledge.

Simon, R. (1987). Empowerment as a pedagogy of possibility. *Language Arts, 64*(4), 370–382.

Statistics Canada. (2008). *Canada's ethnocultural mosaic, 2006 Census*. Catalogue no. 97-562-X. Ottawa: Minister of Industry. Retrieved from www12.statcan.ca/access_acces/archive.action-eng.cfm?/english/census06/analysis/ethnicorigin/pdf/97-562-XIE2006001.pdf

Takaki, R. (1989). *Strangers from a different shore: A history of Asian Americans*. Boston: Little Brown.

Tarrow, N. (1990). Human rights education. *Educational Research Quarterly, 12*(4), 12–22.

Tarrow, N. (1993). Educating for positive peace: Goals, strategies, consequences. Paper presented at the Comparative Education Society Conference, Kingston, Jamaica.

Taylor, C. (1992). The politics of recognition. In A. Gutman (Ed.), *Multiculturalism and the "politics of recognition"* (pp. 25–74). Princeton, NJ: Princeton University Press.

Taylor, C. (1994). *Multiculturalism: Examining the politics of recognition*. Princeton, NJ: Princeton University Press.

Troike, R. (1978). Research evidence for the effectiveness of bilingual education. *NABE Journal, 3*, 13–24.

Van den Berghe, R. (1967). *Race and racism: A comparative perspective*. New York: John Wiley.

Walton Radford, A. (2013). *Top student, top school? How social class shapes where valedictorians go to college*. Chicago: University of Chicago Press.

ACTIVITY 1
"What You See Is What You Get": Challenging the Implicit Expectations of Labels

Purpose
- Explore the diversity of representation in visual media
- Promote critical questioning of visual representations
- Encourage students to challenge stereotypes, prejudices, and biases
- Deconstruct concepts of identity and difference by asking students to reflect on how they see themselves and how they are seen by others

Description
Whereas personal expectations and assumptions are shaped by our own experiences, it is important to be cognizant of how our perceptions are framed by our worldviews and come to affect our actions. Likewise, it is necessary to reflect on how representations in visual media—art, advertisements, television programs and films, and even clip art used in class presentations—influence the way that we perceive reality.

In this activity, you will direct your students to examine their own implicit associations with certain labels. Students will need some paper as well as tools for drawing, such as crayons or markers, to complete the activity. Once the students are ready, prompt the class to draw what comes to mind as they envision a particular epithet. This can be done either verbally or with pre-printed handouts. Suggestions for drawing prompts include labels representative of specific traits (e.g., *genius, superhero, athlete, nerd*), professions (e.g., *teacher, doctor, firefighter, scientist*), or dichotomies (e.g., *good teacher/bad teacher, good student/bad student*). Based on curricular needs or time demands, you may choose to focus the activity around close examination of just one epithet or the interrelationships between multiple labels. Students may be given only a few minutes for sketching, in order to gauge their immediate reactions, or extended time to complete the activity for homework or as part of a project.

After students have completed their drawings, ask them to share how they illustrate typical characteristics of individuals identified by such labels. It is likely that certain trends will emerge from the various depictions and that there will be much consistency between the drawings. After this preliminary discussion, you should begin asking questions to challenge the implicit expectations of your students. Depending on the epithets chosen, you may draw attention to the diversity, or lack thereof, in the genders, races, and (dis)abilities represented in the drawings.

You can also ask students to consider traits that they did not illustrate because they deemed them irrelevant to the task; for instance, did students subconsciously assume a particular sexual orientation for the *athlete*, a particular religious background for a *scientist*, or a certain socio-economic background for a *genius*?

As discussion of the drawings continues, introduce the concepts of identity and difference, explaining that these terms relate not only to how we see ourselves but also to how we see each other. Ask students to consider the consequences of their implicit expectations and how they could result in stereotypical, biased, or prejudiced attitudes and behaviours.

Curricular Connections

Social Studies: Modify the activity to serve as an introduction to a lesson on a historical figure who redefined expectations for a person in his or her role, such as a ruler or political leader.

Fine Arts: Inspire students to create artwork in a particular medium that meaningfully challenges people's implicit expectations of its primary subject.

Science: Share with students theories of evolution that attempted to classify people according to physical and cultural traits and how they were debunked historically; explore how scientific advancements led to more accurate understandings of genetic similarities and differences.

Drama: Discuss the roles of protagonists and antagonists as they are depicted on students' favourite television programs; share GLAAD's annual Where We Are on TV report (available at www.glaad.org), which breaks down the diversity of characters' sexual orientations, genders, and races.

Chapter 2

HISTORY OF MULTICULTURAL EDUCATION IN CANADA

Geneviève's parents are from Quebec, Maria's family is anglophone, and Eve belongs to a First Nations group from the Yukon. Until recently, Geneviève, Maria, and Eve were close friends. These days, however, they are not on speaking terms. It all started in history class. Maria and Eve got into an argument about who the real heroes of Canada were. While Maria insisted that they were the original European pioneers, Eve maintained that the Native people were the true heroes. Further along in the course, a conflict also developed between Geneviève and Maria. This time it was about the French-English issue in Canada. While Geneviève saw the English as exploiters, Maria thought that the French should stop seeing themselves as a separate nation. Geneviève tried to get Eve on her side of the debate, but Eve protested by adding that both European cultures had exploited Native peoples and their resources. The conflict grew so intense that the three friends stopped talking to each other. The girls' teacher was unaware that a conflict along ethno-lingual lines had developed in her class.

- Why do you think the three girls identify so strongly with their different perspectives on historical events?
- To what extent does culture shape our identities and worldviews?
- Do you think it is possible for different cultural perspectives to be represented equitably in educational curriculum? If so, how?

INTRODUCTION

Many cultures have existed in Canada for centuries. The original inhabitants were Aboriginal people of various nations. The first European settlers were the French and the English in the provinces of Quebec and Ontario, respectively. Later, immigrants from Western Europe, then Eastern and Southern Europe, and more recently from countries of Asia, Africa, and Latin America, settled across the country. Canada continues to be one of the world's major immigrant nations and is the first country in the world to have a multicultural policy. The perception of Canada as a multicultural nation is often associated with immigration movements. Moreover, policy initiatives dealing with the changing nature of Canadian society were a result of the development of French nationalism in Quebec in the 1960s, as well as the assertive demands of other minority ethnocultural groups. In the 2006 Census, Canadians were able to self-identify as having one or more ethnic origins. (The most recent 2011 Census collected data related to population and language, but did not inquire specifically about respondents' ethnic origins.) While over 32 percent of individuals identified as "Canadian," about half of these respondents also identified with other ancestries. The next most commonly reported ethnic origins were English (21 percent), French (16 percent), Scottish (15 percent), Irish (14 percent), and German (10 percent). All other ethnic origins were reported by less than 5 percent of respondents—with about 4 percent identifying as North American Indian and just over 1 percent identifying as Métis. Counting both single and multiple responses, the province of Quebec, interestingly enough, contained the largest proportion of respondents (in terms of its own demographic population) who identified as Canadian (66 percent), French (29 percent), and Arabs (3 percent) (Statistics Canada, 2008). Furthermore, as of 2011, nearly 20 percent of Canada's population self-identified as representing a visible minority, a categorization that does not include people of Aboriginal descent (Statistics Canada, 2013).

The official recognition of the social reality of diversity came with the policy of Bilingualism within a Multicultural Framework, announced by Prime Minister Pierre Trudeau in 1971. Multicultural policy was meant to help all cultural groups develop the capacity to grow and contribute to Canada, to assist minority groups in overcoming cultural barriers to participate fully in Canadian society, to promote inter-group relations, and to provide facilities to minority groups for language learning. Bilingualism within a multicultural framework was an attempt by the Canadian state to establish a flexible basis for unity and a comprehensive nationhood.

A decade later, the Canadian Charter of Rights and Freedoms (1982), part of the Canadian Constitution, mentioned multiculturalism in Section 27: "This Charter shall be interpreted in a manner consistent with the preservation and enhancement of the multicultural heritage of Canadians." The focus of the subsequent Multiculturalism Act of 1988 was mainly on equality measures for all Canadians. Of its nine principles, eight deal with equity issues; only the ninth refers to culture. The act provides a framework that enables immigrants and those who do not "belong" to the dominant culture to come to terms with society by giving them the opportunity to combat racism and discrimination, seek social justice, and develop a social structure in which openness to diversity is the norm.

ENGLISH CANADA

A major problem with federal multicultural policy is in its implementation in education, which is a provincial responsibility. Whereas multiculturalism once fell under the jurisdiction of the Canadian Multiculturalism Council and a Multiculturalism Doctorate (established under the secretary of state in 1973) and there has been a minister responsible for the policy since 1972 (the Minister of Canadian Heritage, as of 1996), this has not guaranteed the policy's implementation across Canada. The lack of federal control over education has limited Ottawa's ability to ensure multicultural education in schools. The result has been an uneven distribution of multicultural programs in the various provinces.

Multicultural education has evolved through several phases. Multiculturalism is a radical change from early practices in which immigrant groups were assimilated into the dominant culture. Multicultural education began with the observance of "multicultural days," which tended to emphasize the "exotic" elements of ethnic cultures. Empirical studies show, however, that information about different groups does not necessarily lead to greater tolerance and integration (Moodley, 1981).

The next phase involved the study of cultures other than that of the dominant English and French: the cultures of Asia, Africa, and Latin America. Eventually, ethnic content was introduced into the curriculum (by including ethnic minorities in curriculum material as well as removing stereotypical portrayals) and minority-culture teachers were hired. These measures were aimed at developing a sense of identity and positive self-concept in ethnic minority students. Heritage language classes were offered in some provinces to enable ethnic groups to maintain their languages.

Despite these shifts, minority ethnic students did not, in fact, have the same opportunities as the students of the majority groups because the Eurocentric curriculum and culture of the schools still marginalized or excluded them. Also, the racism and discrimination experienced by some minority students in the schools further limited their learning opportunities.

Only recently has any attention been paid to strategies and equity programs aimed at integrating other groups into the dominant framework. The debate has moved to redefining multicultural education in terms of creating the "just" society for which it was proposed. Equality and equal opportunity have been added to widen its meaning.

The next phase in the development of multicultural education involved attempts to broaden the base of school knowledge by incorporating into the curriculum worldviews different from the traditional male, middle-class, Eurocentric bias. One relatively recent trend espoused by some educators is anti-racist education based on critical pedagogy, which emerged over the last few decades and is based on the ideas of John Dewey (1916), Paulo Freire (1970), and Antonio Gramsci (1971), as well as feminist theorists such as Carol Gilligan (1982), Patty Lather (1991), and Carmen Luke and Jennifer Gore (1992), among others. Critical pedagogy deals with questions such as how knowledge is produced and whose knowledge is taught in schools. It is concerned with the impact of Eurocentric knowledge on students of difference. It rethinks the purpose and function of schooling in terms of the empowerment of students as well as teachers. It connects knowledge to power, and learning to empowerment. School is seen as a site for equality and social justice that challenges racism, sexism, and classism. Thus, anti-racist education draws on these principles, but with more specific focus on combatting hate and extremism. Attempts at anti-racist education gained prominence in a few Canadian provinces, such as Ontario and British Columbia, and in urban areas—though such developments are more recent in Canada as compared to England, where this type of program has been practiced for some time.

In 1975, Saskatchewan was the first Canadian province to endorse the federal policy of multiculturalism. The western provinces of Alberta, Saskatchewan, and Manitoba have made efforts to provide linguistic choice by offering instruction in Cree, French, Ukrainian, Russian, German, and Hebrew. Nova Scotia, whose long-established black population experienced racial segregation in schools until the 1950s, has a well-developed policy of intercultural education. British Columbia and Ontario may be at the forefront of educational changes for multiculturalism due to their large non-white populations. British Columbia has a sizable Asian population and continues to attract a large number of Asian immigrants. In Ontario, which attracts the majority of immigrants to Canada, almost 50 percent of the population is made up of non-white ethnocultural groups. It has also reported the largest number of racist incidents. Ontario adopted a multiculturalism policy in 1977, and more recently instituted an anti-racist policy. In addition to providing several important curriculum guidelines over the last three decades, and a policy on race and ethnocultural equity (1987), the Ontario government produced guidelines for policy development and implementation of anti-racism and ethnocultural equity in school boards in 1993. Amendments to the Education Act in 1992 require school boards in the province to implement anti-racism and ethnocultural equity policies. School boards have responded with various programs and policies, the most significant ones related to race relations, student placement, teacher recruitment, curriculum, school/community relations, and heritage language programs.

Over the past decade, key issues related to multicultural education in

English Canada have sparked much media and public debate over the purposes and practices of education. One notable development is the Toronto District School Board's establishment of Africentric alternative schools, which are designed to empower students of African descent through culturally relevant curriculum and pedagogy. In New Brunswick and later in Ontario, proposed reforms to sex education that suggested less conservative treatment of gender issues and sexuality were met by such strong opposition from religious and family groups that they were ultimately abandoned. Along similar ideological lines, the passage of Bill 44 by Alberta's legislature in 2009 required schools to inform parents or guardians about any instances where classroom instruction or activities might include subject matter dealing with religion or sexuality, and granted parents permission to pull their children out of class when such lessons were implemented. Clearly, educational reforms in English Canada demonstrate the divergence between liberal and conservative values across different Canadian provinces.

QUEBEC

Quebec is home to roughly 25 percent of Canada's population. Whereas census information collected at the start of the 1990s (Statistics Canada, 1994) characterized the province as populated overwhelmingly by people of French origin (75 percent), more recent demographic information suggests a shift in Quebeckers' perceptions of their own heritage. In fact, the most recent census, which allowed respondents to select multiple responses to describe their own ethnic origins, reports that over 60 percent of Quebec residents self-identified as "Canadian" or "*Canadien*," while only 30 percent identified as having French origin; under 2 percent identified themselves specifically as Québécois (Statistics Canada, 2013). Then again, in terms of language and religion, over 80 percent of Quebec residents reported that they speak French most often at home and over 83 percent identified as Roman Catholic.

In the 1960s, the continued dominance of English as the language of social and economic power in a predominantly French province gave rise to French-Canadian nationalism, which rejected both federal bilingualism as well as multiculturalism. The Quiet Revolution in Quebec began with the election of the Liberal government of Jean Lesage in 1960. It was a bloodless revolution that limited the influence of the clergy and introduced modernizing reforms in education. It was a reaction not only to the dominance of the Catholic Church, but also against corruption and outmoded ways; at the same time, it was a revolt against the economic and cultural domination of Quebec by English-speaking Canadians. The slogan *maîtres chez nous* ("masters in our own house") embodied the new French-Canadian aspirations.

Before the Quiet Revolution of the 1960s, the Duplessis government did not encourage immigration for fear of changing the nature of French Quebec and minimizing the importance of French language and Quebec culture. Immigration was a matter of joint jurisdiction between the federal and provincial governments under the British North America Act (1867). However, with falling birth rates, immigration became necessary and the Quebec government demanded greater autonomy in immigrant selection. In 1991, the McDougall-Gagnon-Tremblay agreement gave special powers to Quebec in selecting immigrants. Quebec administers its own immigration programs with different selection criteria from those of the federal government. This was made possible by agreements with the Government of Canada on immigration (in 1975 and 1978), with the aim of choosing immigrants who are more likely to adapt to the francophone milieu.

The Quiet Revolution included rapid expansion of the educational system. This challenged Anglo domination and the linguistic and ethnic discrimination against French Canadians in their own province. While bilingualism was symbolically significant for the survival of the French language in other parts of Canada, it was not sufficient to increase the socio-economic power of the French in Quebec. The federal policy of multiculturalism was unacceptable to Quebec because equal status for all cultures implied that French culture was equal to other cultures. French Canadians form only 2 percent of the North American population, and their legitimate concern for cultural identity and survival in a predominantly English-speaking continent prompted linguistic legislation. In 1974, French was made the official language of Quebec. In 1977, Bill 101 gave further prominence to French in everyday life, work, and education; all children, with a few exceptions (such as those of British parentage), would have to be schooled in French. The legislation raised the question of individual rights of non-francophones versus the collective rights of francophones. The concern of immigrant families is that schooling in French will limit the educational and employment opportunities of their children in a continent where 98 percent of the population use English.

Bourhis (2008) uses the term "vitality" to describe how a language community behaves "as a distinctive and collective entity within multilingual settings" (p. 127). He notes that in terms of socio-structural domains such as demography, institutional support, and status, the current vitality of Quebec's anglophones is undeniably in decline, both in greater Montreal and beyond. As an illustration of this, Floch and Pocock (2008) use the term "brain drain" to describe the phenomenon of young, well-educated, and upwardly mobile anglophones in Quebec increasingly pursuing economic opportunities outside the province, and thus contributing to "a net loss of endogenous human capital for Quebec, a society in search of the international immigrants needed to alleviate the demographic and know-how decline of the province" (p. 58). It is unsurprising, then, that some francophones have also felt uncomfortable with the language policies of the Quebec government. In 2000, for instance, 10 francophone families filed a lawsuit over Bill 101. These families, calling themselves "Citizens for Open Schools," were not only disturbed about the falling standards of English teaching in the French schools, but also considered Bill 101 to be an infringement of their basic rights. In their lawsuit, the petitioners invoked Quebec's Charter of Human Rights and Freedoms. The group believed that in an attempt to preserve French language, Bill 101 dictated who should go to the French schools and who should not; thus, Quebec's language laws created two classes of citizens based on the most arbitrary of standards.

Intercultural Education

In 1978, *La politique québécoise du développement culturel* outlined the Quebec government's policy of stressing the value of diversity in building a common society through the medium of French. In 1990, the government of Quebec introduced a policy statement on immigration and integration in recognition of the pluralistic reality of Quebec society (Quebec, 1990). It underscored the need for immigration to counter the demographic decline, reverse the aging of the population, and revitalize the economy through a larger labour market and increased consumption.

The influx of non-French groups into Quebec threatens the survival of the French language because non-whites do not have French culture. This presents a challenge to the Quebec government, which wants to create a pluralistic but French-speaking society.

The three main objectives of the 1990 policy statement were to make French-language teaching more accessible, to encourage full participation by immigrants and cultural communities in Quebec society, and to develop inter-group relations among all Quebeckers. These goals are similar to those of the federal multicultural policy: "Despite the general agreement in Québec that Québécois and Canadian approaches to cultural pluralism are somewhat different in *practice* … there is no profound difference between Canadian multiculturalism and Québec interculturalism: both overlap in significant ways, especially in their philosophically and politically liberal approach" (Leroux, 2010, p. 108–110).

Interculturalism means that Quebec will be pluralistic in outlook within a francophone society. Multiculturalism means that the rest of Canada will be pluralistic within an English-speaking society—but because English is the default language, there is no need to legislate schooling in English. The role of education in bringing about the new social order of interculturalism is significant. The schools are to reflect the francophone vision by preparing students of all cultural communities in the French language to develop a new common identity. It is worthwhile to note that "skepticism about multiculturalism in Québec has little to do with the popular perception that multiculturalist policies encourage isolationism among immigrant groups and, in this way, put in place disincentives to integration. Instead, Québec's opposition to multiculturalism is grounded in the belief that the Canadian government's policy of multiculturalism is a betrayal of Québec's historical status within the Canadian federation and undermines Québec's grounds for seeking greater political autonomy from Canada" (Waddington et al., 2011).

Quebec was the first province in Canada to have a charter of rights and freedoms that gives *de jure* protection to minority educational rights (Chartre des droits et libertés de la personne, 1975). The Ministry of Immigration and Cultural Communities was set up in 1981 to look after issues relating to immigrant and immigrant communities. In the 1980s, several documents (Quebec, 1981, 1983, 1988) addressed the education of cultural communities in Quebec, focusing on discrimination and immigration. According to these documents, the integration of these "cultural communities" was to be facilitated through "intercultural education," although an official intercultural education policy had not yet been formulated. An advisory council of the Ministry provided advice on equal opportunity for cultural communities, and programs were developed with the Ministry of Education's Direction des Services Éducatifs aux Communautés Culturelles. The Quebec Charter of Human Rights and Freedoms was amended in 1985, followed by a Declaration on Ethnic and Race Relations in 1986. In 1989, the Ministry of Education began to offer workshops to help practicing teachers understand and deal with the multicultural students whom they teach. The Superior Council of Education issued documents in 1983, 1987, and 1993 stressing "intercultural education" and its importance for respecting the diverse cultural, racial, and ethnic groups that make up Quebec society. In the 1990s, school boards started developing policies in this regard.

By 1991, non-French, non-English students made up 35 percent of the school population of the four Montreal Island school boards (McAndrew, 1993). Traditionally, the Catholic school system was mainly French, while the much smaller Protestant system was English. Quebec has been a multicultural society for over a century, yet, historically, education in both the English and French sectors has been assimilationist. Immigrants to Quebec either sent their children to English schools for economic and social prestige or were directed to that sector due to the confessional system, which divided the responsibility of education between the Protestant and Catholic churches (Laferrière, 1980). The Protestant system admitted all religious and ethnocultural groups but did not address their particular educational and cultural needs. Some consideration was given to a special school for Jewish education. Catholic schools were restricted to Catholic students (largely French) and did not have to deal with the issue of diversity.

The report of the Committee on Quebec Schools and Cultural Communities (Quebec, 1985) indicated that intercultural education programs in schools focused largely on teaching the French language. There are four types of language classes for students. These are

- *classes d'accueil,* or welcoming classes for new immigrants, designed (since 1969) for developing French proficiency;
- *centres d'orientation et de formation des immigrants* (COFI), which provide adults with basic ability in the French language (although often not enough for them to pursue advanced university courses);
- *program d'enseignement des langues des origines* (PELO), a heritage languages program for allophone students offered mainly in primary schools. Nearly 7,000 students participate in 17 languages (Quebec, 2009); and
- trilingual ethnic schools, privately operated but publicly funded (up to 80 percent of the total costs) for maintenance of heritage languages.

These programs are predominantly publicly funded but are managed privately. Heritage language programs are criticized for being segregationist and insular in nature. Results of the COFI (language teaching for immigrants) have at best been limited. The participants of the program have been unable to get an adequate grasp of the language within the short period of instruction. PELO (heritage language) on the other hand may at best be good for the self-esteem of some immigrant children but does nothing for interaction among different groups. The program involves minimal instruction and is not directed at other linguistic groups, including French: "The program is less popular than might be expected, owing to the resistance of public school teachers and to the choices of highly committed allophone parents, who would rather enroll their children in private trilingual schools" (McAndrew, 2010, p. 297). It is thus only immigrant children who are the main participants of the program.

The 1990 policy statement on immigration and integration (Quebec, 1990) points out that "traditional Quebec society advocated a uniform cultural and ideological model" for all Quebeckers (p. 17). In 1977, however, Bill 101 forced large numbers of different cultural communities into French schools by requiring all children in Quebec to be educated in French. The exceptions to this were temporary residents, Native people, or children with one parent who had received his or her primary education in English in Quebec or with a sibling in an English school. This forced new immigrants into the French school system, which was unprepared for this sudden influx.

The English system had always had a culturally diverse population but pursued an assimilationist policy until the end of the 1980s. The French system, which had been very homogeneous, was now faced with a tremendous diversity of cultural communities. By the beginning of the 21st century, non-French school children in Montreal had increased to about 50 percent of the student population (Henchey & Burgess, 1987). By 1990, about 40 percent of the students in French-language CEGEPs (Collèges d'enseignement général et professionnel—pre-university colleges) hailed from cultural communities (Quebec, 1990, p. 55). With the declining population of the *Québécois de souche* (original Québécois who came from France), the presence, in some French schools, of up to 90 percent allophones (non-French, non-English) from as many as 85 cultural backgrounds and 20 religious groups has been a source of concern to many people. The issues are not only racial tensions but also the fear that too many other cultural communities threaten French culture.

Because of Bill 101, the French Catholic school system is no longer totally Catholic and the English Protestant school system is increasingly French. By 1989, there was a shift in the allophone student population from the English to the French sector. Whereas in 1979, allophones made up 73 percent of the English system, by 1989 they composed only about 35 percent of the English sector, while their numbers jumped to 65 percent in the French system. A new Education Act, Bill 107, became effective in 1989, and linguistic school boards (school boards based on the French or English language) have replaced the Catholic and Protestant school boards. Quebec is divided into separate territories served by French and English boards; four school boards (those serving the Montreal and Quebec City areas) retain the right to remain confessional within the linguistic boards. This new form of division is aimed at diminishing the traditional religious base and strengthening French language in Quebec.

Policy Debates

The lack of a functional interculturalism policy until 1998 was significant. Although there is still no official legislation on interculturalism, the implementation of the *Plan of Action for Educational Integration and Intercultural Education, 1998–2002* (Quebec, 1998, p. 9), was another step in the francization of education. Under this plan, all educational institutions at all levels (primary and secondary schools, colleges and universities, and adult and vocational education programs) were required to conform to the "basic" educational policies that advanced the francization of a multi-ethnic Quebec (Quebec, 1998, p. 4). Although the document instructed all CEGEPs to increase the number of immigrant students, it also reaffirmed that these students must master the elements of a common framework of learning and acquire a common set of values, namely French (Quebec, 1998, p. 5).

Several initiatives in the 1990s and 2000s were aimed at increasing cultural community representation in curriculum material, hiring minority staff, and developing school-community relations. In 1991, the Ministry of Education began intercultural training programs for educational personnel. The Ministry of Higher Education and Sciences supports some training initiatives for CEGEP teachers in Montreal. A 1997 policy document, *A School for the Future: Educational Integration and Intercultural Education,* places special emphasis on the involvement of parents in the education system of the province (Quebec, 1997, p. 22). The Ministry of Education also conducted a study on the prospects of adult education for the parents of immigrant/refugee children to help their children become integrated in the Quebec school system (Quebec, 1998, p. 6). While the implementation of such programs has been an important step in the right direction, there has not been enough emphasis on discrimination and equality issues, nor has any Quebec school board proposed anti-racist education. In general, intercultural education in Quebec has focused on remedial education for cultural communities rather than on developing interaction among all students.

Beginning in about 2005, media reports of incidents of cultural clash in Quebec seemed to become increasingly prevalent. Particularly noteworthy news stories included a Sikh boy who was prevented from attending school because he wore a kirpan, or ceremonial knife, interpreted by administrators as a weapon; a Montreal-based Orthodox Jewish congregation that offered to pay for the windows of a local YMCA to be frosted, so that women who were exercising would be blocked from public view; and the filing of complaint by the Mouvement laïque québécois (Quebec Secular Movement) against the City of Laval to discontinue the inclusion of a non-denominational prayer at public council meetings. In early 2007, the small town of Hérouxville issued a municipal code of conduct that included explicit provisions against the violation of women's rights, including prohibition of stoning, female circumcision, or burning women alive. As such, it became increasingly "difficult to ignore how the arrival of the Hérouxville Code of Conduct on the public stage mobilized a large section of Québécois society to debate issues related to cultural accommodation, racial difference, and national identity" (Leroux, 2010, p. 113).

Before the end of 2008, two provincial government–sponsored commissions released reports on harmonization practices in Quebec. The first, chaired by Bergman Fleury (2007), focused on issues of reasonable accommodation within schools; the second, chaired by Gérard Bouchard and Charles Taylor (2008) under appointment by Premier Jean Charest, went beyond the context of schools to look into Quebec society's position on reasonable accommodation. It comprehensively collected the opinions of Quebec residents through 13 university research projects, over 30 focus groups, nearly 60 meetings with experts and civil leaders, and a full month of public hearings throughout the province—which yielded over 900 briefs from Quebeckers. The Bouchard-Taylor report concluded that perceptions of an accommodation "crisis" in Quebec society (and schools) were inaccurate and significantly distorted, stemming from public misinformation largely influenced by incomplete media coverage. It also stressed that only a small number of accommodation requests resulted in any legal action, that there was no domino effect in cases in which an individual or group was accommodated, and that opinions and perceptions of accommodation were largely aligned between French Canadians and other ethnic groups, as well as between urban and rural Quebec residents.

In 2008, the Government of Quebec introduced a new immigrant integration policy with the goal of educating potential overseas immigrants about shared Quebec values and asking newcomers to sign an agreement affirming respect for these values upon entry into the province. In 2013, the governing political party introduced Bill 14 to make amendments to Quebec's French language charter. This legislation would have removed certain exemptions that allowed English education in special cases, required large workplaces to operate in French for all business purposes, and empowered language inspectors to seize anything deemed to be in offence of the language charter. A few months after a highly publicized incident informally called "Pastagate," in which an inspector of the Office québécois de la langue française (Quebec Board of the French Language) warned the owner of an Italian restaurant against using non-French words on his menu, the focus on Bill 14 was largely abandoned in favor of a push for an even more controversial piece of legislation: Bill 60, or the Quebec Charter of Values. This new charter would amend Quebec's existing Charter of Human Rights and Freedoms by asserting Quebec's secular values and establishing a commitment to neutrality of religion on the part of all state personnel. It would be operationalized by implementing limits on the wearing of religious symbols by provincial employees and by making it mandatory to have one's face uncovered as a stipulation for providing or receiving governmental services. As it would directly affect all levels of education, the charter notably earned condemnation from Quebec's human rights commission, the English Montreal School Board, and all of Quebec's universities (Authier, 2014).

With the charter as a primary focus of its platform—reflecting its sovereignist agenda—the party in power, Parti Québécois, called an election in early 2014 in an attempt to increase representation in the National Assembly. Because of its resounding defeat in the polls, an indication of weakening support for the separatist movement, the proposed charter was not passed.

Given the importance of French-English tensions, it was perhaps unavoidable that intercultural education has primarily been dealt with in the context of Quebec nationalism rather than on its own merit. Leroux (2010) describes the inherent contradiction within Quebec interculturalism as a response to Canadian multiculturalism:

One effect of the discourses of difference unique to Québec is the common-sense belief that respect for and acceptance of differences are fundamental national values. This apparently progressive position, one that rests on an assumption that differences are given, natural social phenomena, was widespread during the Bouchard-Taylor Commission hearings. However, this liberal rationale conceals the complex operation of power at work in the very production of, in this case, "cultural" difference. The very use of the concept of cultural difference in the Commission's creation (e.g., in its official title [the Consultation Commission on Accommodation Practices Related to Cultural Differences]) points to an imaginary norm against which difference is measured and through which the norm is itself produced. (p. 119)

ABORIGINAL PEOPLES

It is generally recognized that Canada's Aboriginal peoples have suffered immeasurable destruction in human and spiritual terms. They have experienced intolerance, discrimination, and racism from the non-Native population, and the formal education system has had devastating effects on them. A history of disastrous educational practices and socio-economic policies for Native peoples has resulted in poor education, unemployment, poverty, high crime rates, alcoholism, substance abuse, and suicide. Yet education also holds the promise of a change that can help restore pride and self-confidence among the Native population and enable them to be equal partners in Canadian society. However, this would involve a shift in attitudes: from viewing Aboriginal culture and values as barriers, to building their culture and values as the cornerstone for developing strong identities, faith in their future, and equality of access and participation. Policy alternatives for Aboriginal educational reform must also keep in mind the reality of 21st-century urbanization, which finds one-half of all Aboriginal peoples now living in a city and most Aboriginal children attending provincially run, off-reserve schools (Richards, 2006).

As the original inhabitants of this land, Canada's Native people date back thousands of years. Some, like the Inuit of Labrador, can be traced back 9,000 years. During colonization, war and disease reduced their numbers. Canada's Aboriginal people consist of over 550 First Nations, Inuit, and Métis groups. In the 1600s, when the French were settling the land around the St. Lawrence River (now Quebec), Native people were partners in the fur trade that the colony depended on for survival. With colonization, Native groups were seen as obstacles to colonial expansion. They were put into compact communities, or reserves, where they were converted by missionaries and taught Euro-Canadian ways; "the extinction of Indians *as Indians*" was the "ultimate end" (Harper, 1945, p. 127). The Natives lost control of their socio-political structures, as colonial strategies effectively eroded the majority of their institutions.

The Aboriginal peoples of Canada do not want to be part of "ethnic Canada" because they are not immigrants; nor do they consider themselves to be visible minorities, although they experience a high degree of racism. One of the major reasons for the reluctance of First Nations to become part of the federal multicultural policy is that, due to the settlement policies of successive governments, there has been a clash of interests between Aboriginal and immigrant communities. It was, in fact, First Nations land on which a number of immigrant settlements were authorized, thus bringing the Natives in direct economic and ideological conflict with the immigrant communities. As Regnier (1995) puts it, "To associate with immigrant constituencies, aboriginal groups run the risk of supporting [a] policy that does not sufficiently address, and ultimately pre-empts, their concerns" (p. 76). To these groups, any association with ethnic or cultural minority status would mean giving up their claims and position on issues of sovereignty, land, and rights, as well as treaty obligations (Regnier, 1995). Verna St. Denis (2011) summarizes it most eloquently:

> What happens to Aboriginal teachers and Aboriginal content in Canadian public schools is a microcosm of what happens at the political level in regards to Aboriginal people. The prevailing and prevalent policy and practice of multiculturalism enables a refusal to address ongoing colonialism, and even to acknowledge colonialism at all. This leads to the trivializing of issues, to attempts to collapse Aboriginal rights

into ethnic and minority issues, and to forcing Aboriginal content into multicultural frameworks. All of these practices deny the reality of Canadian colonialism and reduce efforts for Aboriginal sovereignty and education. The experiences of Aboriginal teachers teach us that just as the Canadian national space is not neutral, so are school spaces not neutral. Dominant cultures regard efforts to address inequality and diversity as a rejection of, and even an intrusion into, broad understandings of self and nation, and so they therefore resist and resent Aboriginal knowledges and history. (p. 315)

Aboriginal peoples of Canada assert that they are "citizens plus" and that their rights supersede all subsequent rights granted to other groups (for example, through multiculturalism policy). In fact, a major criticism of multiculturalism by Native scholars is its defence of public education as a neutral cultural space, which suggests "that it would be wrong to privilege Aboriginal history, knowledge, and experience in the teaching of ... Canadian history and social studies" (St. Denis, 2011, p. 306).

Any real and long-term change will require education to be more reflective of and responsive to Aboriginal interests. Educational policies and curricula must reflect the "aboriginal locations within the historic constructions of Canada's cultural mosaic" (Regnier, 1995, p. 77). Howard and Widdowson (2013) argue that the separate Native studies, in their overreliance on traditional methods and approaches, are actually detrimental to the future of Aboriginal education in Canada because they segregate Aboriginal students from their mainstream peers: "Instead of hiding the educational deficits in Aboriginal education with 'culturally sensitive' initiatives, there needs to be an honest recognition of the developmental differences between modern education and preliterate traditional enculturation. Once this is acknowledged, evidence-based Aboriginal educational policy development can begin" (p. 307).

Native Education in Canada

Education was the vehicle of Native assimilation in 19th-century Canada. The education of Native children was aimed at socializing the young generation with European, Christian, and capitalist values and aspirations. It denigrated First Nations cultures and society in an attempt to remake them in the colonizers' image. Assimilation advocate Duncan Campbell Scott, head of the Department of Indian Affairs from 1913 to 1932, even spoke out on education and intermarriage as the "great forces [that] will finally overcome the lingering traces of native custom and traditions" (Archibald, 1995, p. 348).

The pressure to assimilate did not, however, lead to integration. Rather, it led to the development of an underclass, which was the direct result of redefining Aboriginals as culturally "deprived." In schooling, as in society, the inequalities meted out to the Native population kept them in their underprivileged position.

The education of Non-Status Indians and Métis was neglected for decades because of the confusion between provincial/territorial and federal governments over jurisdiction and responsibility. For Status Indians, after Confederation in 1867, assimilation policy was better organized through residential schools. The federal Department of Indian Affairs and several religious denominations administered the industrial residential schools. These schools were located far from the children's homes to limit contact with parents, and children were sent away for 10 or more months of the year. Native languages and culture were stifled. Rudimentary academic subjects were taught, but the emphasis was on trade skills for boys and domestic science for girls. The schools were overcrowded and ridden with disease and numerous other problems.

Parents initially co-operated with these institutions in the hope that they would help their children cope with the new way of life; however, disillusioned and pained by long separations, disease, and death, they became hostile. It was evident that their values and beliefs were being undermined, that their children had become strangers, and that the family unit was being destroyed. It was obvious that their children's academic achievements remained at low levels and led to unskilled jobs. Most of all, Native children now felt neither part of the Euro-Canadian life nor comfortable with their parents' old ways. They were unable to compete in the dominant society and were unsuited for life on a reserve. Parents began to demand schools on their reserves, which resulted in the establishment of day schools. But the lack of qualified teachers and appropriate curricula resulted in poor quality schools. Once again, these schools tried to force on students goals and lifestyles that were not part of their emotional and spiritual heritage.

After World War II, there was a shift in policy on Native education. Financial problems resulted in a policy of "integration," which meant that Native children would attend public schools (as opposed to segregated schools) and were to be treated in the same way as other children. This was done through an amendment to the Indian Act whereby provinces were to take over Native education while the federal government maintained financial responsibility. The underlying objective, however, remained the assimilation of Native people through formal education within an alien, hostile, and conquering culture.

The history of the education of the Native population by missionaries and governments is characterized by a clash of cultural values. Natives seek harmony with nature and community and emphasize a collaborative orientation. In contrast, the dominant group values exploitation and control of nature, and ruthless competition within a capitalistic and individualistic orientation. Native people have a special relationship with the land, and their identity and self-respect are linked to that relationship. They have highly developed community and group values of cooperation, respect for elders, and an oral tradition of sharing their cultural heritage. Today, their education involves a struggle to maintain their heritage and to survive as distinct people just as their ancestors struggled to survive colonization and occupation. However, the significant changes in their way of life as part of a modern society and the development of the North, where non-Native communities have displaced traditional practices, pose challenges to an education in which Native and non-Native groups must learn to respect reciprocal rights and freedoms.

With increasing immigration, the assimilationist educational policy toward Aboriginal peoples and immigrants was challenged and general curricula materials were examined for stereotypes. Native groups did not accept the policy of multiculturalism because it ignored their treaty and Aboriginal rights. Several studies have indicated the extent to which Native peoples have been stereotyped in textbooks as backward, lazy, cruel, unscientific and superstitious, dirty, and alcoholic. Historical facts have been distorted and interpreted to suit the colonizers. This has resulted in changes in textbooks to provide a more accurate portrayal of Native history and culture, with more school time designated to learning about Canada's original peoples. However, any real and long-term change will require education to be more reflective of and responsive to Aboriginal interests. Educational policies and curricula must reflect the "aboriginal locations within the historic constructions of Canada's cultural mosaic" (Regnier, 1995, p. 77).

In 1973, the federal government accepted demands by the National Indian Brotherhood for Native control of Native education. This was a response to problems identified by provincial groups of First Nations peoples across Canada. The resulting policy involves greater community control in administration and curriculum content and pedagogy, more parental involvement, increases in the number of First Nations teachers, and training in Native culture for non-Native teachers through pre-service and in-service courses (Archibald, 1995). The active involvement of First Nations people in curriculum development and control of education is considered essential to making Native children proud of their heritage and helping them develop self-esteem. It is also essential to eliminating the long-standing distrust between the First Nations and the government.

Most Aboriginal schools have adopted the provincial curricula with added cultural content; however, a number of serious problems remain. Aboriginal youth who had developed an attitude of resistance to schools had to be reoriented. In addition, while some bands considered the teaching of English (and French) to be more import-ant, others wanted more weight attached to teaching Native languages. While some of the obstacles, such as high dropout rates, shortage of qualified Aboriginal teachers, and lack of effort aimed at structural change, still remain, a number of important advances can be attributed to Aboriginal control of their own education. One of the most important advances in Native control of education has been the abil-ity of schools to establish a Native identity among Aboriginal communities, which has been essential for positive change beyond schools. The most notable example is the Alkali Lake Reserve in British Columbia, which had an alcoholism rate of 100 percent and now has a sobriety rate of 95 percent. The reserve then went on to correct the problems related to sexual abuse in the community (Regnier, 1995, p. 83).

A recent study by the C.D. Howe Institute (Richards, 2008) found that although the populations of Canadian Aboriginal groups are growing much faster than those of non-Aboriginals—especially in the west, where approximately 1 in 13 people is Aboriginal—outcomes for high school graduation for students who go to school on a reserve are dismal, dipping under 40 percent in some parts of Canada. While educa-tional attainment levels have actually improved in contrast to those of past generations, the advances of non-Aboriginal groups have been much faster and, subsequently, have contributed to the widening achievement gap. Adding urgency to the issue is the fact that the next generation of students will include an even greater proportion of Aboriginal children, reaching as high as 1 in 4 in Manitoba and Saskatchewan.

From an economic standpoint, businesses must realize that the integration of Aboriginal people into the labour force is crucial in overcoming the labour supply shortage that is currently developing in Canada, but this cannot happen without significant long-term investment in education (Sharpe & Arsenault, 2009). At the same time, the Canadian government's role must not be relegated solely to that of a "funder" without ethical liability; rather it must "work, hand in glove with [Aboriginal groups,] to help build their educational capacity and institutions so that they are able to deliver an effective educational program to their students, comparable to provincial and territorial offerings" (Standing Committee on Aboriginal Peoples, 2007). Moreover, the needs of Aboriginal Canadians can only be met within a holistic framework of education, one that values informal learning and community bonds within First Nations, Inuit, and Métis communities (Canadian Council on Learning, 2009).

It is evident that Native empowerment will only come with ownership of the institutions that affect their lives, education being the most important. The development of band-controlled schools on reserves is not without challenges, due to a lack of qualified First Nations teachers and suitable curriculum material. With respect to public schools (in which about 50 percent of Native children are enrolled), power-sharing at the board level and increased Native culture and history in the regular curriculum seem to be immediate possibilities for developing respect and co-operation in the multicultural milieu of urban schools.

In the past few years, Canada has arguably made great strides in improving relations with Aboriginal peoples. In a report issued by the Minister of Aboriginal Affairs and Northern Development, Stephen Harper's government credited itself with bringing forth "a shift in Canada's relationship with First Nations, exemplified by the Prime Minister's historic apology to former students of Indian Residential Schools, the creation of the Truth and Reconciliation Commission, the launch of the Specific Claims Tribunal, and the endorsement of the United Nations Declaration on the Rights of Indigenous Peoples" (Government of Canada, 2012). Indeed, actions such as Harper's 2008 apology, which acknowledged the "profoundly negative ... lasting and damaging impact [of residential schools] on Aboriginal culture, heritage and language," (Harper, 2008) certainly suggest progress—at least in an ideological sense. In claiming the "burden" of this "sad chapter in our history" (Harper, 2008) as the responsibility of the government, the apology conveys the country's determination to move forward. Likewise, Canada's endorsement of the Declaration on the Rights of Indigenous Peoples in 2010 indicates a new commitment to protecting the individual and collective rights of Aboriginal people. This is particularly true because Canada (along with Australia, New Zealand, and the United States) originally voted against the declaration when it was passed in the UN General Assembly due to its perceived incompatibility with the Canadian Charter, on the grounds that it would grant preferential rights to Aboriginals over non-Aboriginals and could reopen historically settled land claims.

More specifically in regards to education, the Canadian government has created partnerships with First Nations regional organizations and provincial ministries of education to launch new programs intended to improve student outcomes, such as the First Nation Student Success Program (2008) aimed at on-reserve educators. In 2011, the First Nations Joint Action Plan, a partnership between Aboriginal Affairs and Northern Development Canada (AANDC) and the Assembly of First Nations (AFN), was launched with the goal of improving "long-term prosperity for First Nations people and all Canadians" (Aboriginal Affairs and Northern Development Canada, 2011). The plan outlined a joint engagement process to make recommendations on how to ensure quality primary and secondary education for children living on reserves. Early in 2012, over 170 Chiefs met with the governor general, prime minister, and Cabinet members in Ottawa at the inaugural Crown–First Nation Gathering. In the event's proceedings, the parties not only declared support for Kindergarten to Grade 12 educational reform, but also targeted an end goal of financial self-sufficiency for

First Nations, all in an effort "to go beyond the Joint Action Plan and set the context for change" (Prime Minister of Canada, 2012).

Around the same time, a national panel created as part of the plan completed a cross-country tour of meetings and roundtable discussions with elders, provincial officials, teachers, parents, students, and other stakeholders interested in improving Aboriginal education. The panel published a report that recommended both repealing the residential schools provisions of the Indian Act as a conciliatory measure and drafting a new "child-centred" First Nation Education Act, founded upon the right of all Aboriginal children to quality education. The act, formally renamed the First Nations Control of First Nations Education Act (FNCFNEA), was tabled in Parliament as Bill C-33 in April 2014, pledging $1.9 billion in "sustainable funding" over several years to introduce a more structured educational framework permitting First Nations groups to include their own languages, culture, history, and perspectives in developing curriculum—but with conditions for maintaining provincial standards ofaddress issues related to teacher certification, school accreditation, curriculum, assessment, and accountability (First Nation Education Act, 2014). Mendelson (2009) explains why the act has been a long time coming: "Each time a First Nations multischool organization needs to be recognized by federal authorities, a separate piece of federal legislation is required. There is inconvenience, cost, and delay in this for a government, but ... the critical problem is that there is no legislation that recognizes First Nations' right to control their own education and to set up the organizations that allow them to do so effectively" (p. 28). As an act of Parliament, FNCFNEA ostensibly supersedes the Canadian government's obsolete and colonialist authority over First Nations schools in favour of Indigenous peoples' own authority over them. However, a number of First Nations groups have criticized the act on the basis of its failure to provide First Nations peoples with actual jurisdiction over education and to acknowledge earlier treaties.

While the primary focus of the federal government's actions discussed thus far has primarily been on-reserve schools and, therefore, within the scope of primary and secondary education, access to post-secondary education for Aboriginal students also remains a pressing issue. To this end, the Association of Canadian Deans of Education (ACDE) launched the Accord on Indigenous Education in 2010. With a 61-instutition membership, ACDE "recognized the role it could play as an association for educators in order to push for improvements in Indigenous education" (Maclean's, 2010) and drafted guidelines to infuse universities with indigenous values. By making the environment more welcoming, the curriculum more inclusive, pedagogy and assessment more culturally responsive, and research more culturally respectful, the accord envisions how "Indigenous identities, cultures, languages, values, ways of knowing, and knowledge systems will flourish in all Canadian learning settings"

(ACDE, 2010, p. 4). Critics, however, point out that such a lofty goal, though admirable, ensnares indigenous identity (a very diverse and broad concept in itself) within the confines of the restrictive Western university system: "The entire Accord on Indigenous Education is written from the point of view of the gatekeepers and their well-intentioned efforts to widen the doors and widen the perspective of Euro-Education, in order to lend some of their legitimacy to Indigenous issues and allow more Indigenous students to participate in credential-earning" (Rasmussen, 2011).

CONCLUSION

The education of minority groups in Canada was first characterized by a policy of assimilation. The pluralistic nature of society has not been acknowledged by the provincial education systems until much more recently. There are considerable variations in provincial policies on multicultural education. Ontario and British Columbia, in particular, as well as Nova Scotia, Alberta, Manitoba, and Saskatchewan have given attention to the development of multicultural education policies.

• In Quebec, language legislation in 1977 forced a large number of children from many cultural communities into French schools. The problems caused by a sudden influx of different ethnic groups into the French education system led to the need to consider the educational problems and language difficulties of different cultural communities through the concept of intercultural education—the accommodation of diverse populations within the context of a francophone Quebec. In 1998, a new intercultural policy further emphasized increased cultural community representation in curriculum materials and staffing, and the development of community-school relations. The policy also reaffirmed that education must remain within the framework and values of the French language. The last decade has witnessed significant controversy stemming from language and education policy debates in Quebec, as the diverse members of Quebec society have come into conflict over their visions for the province's future.

A long history of discrimination and neglect has resulted in the marginalization of Native education in Canada. The National Indian Brotherhood has identified self-determination in Native education as the only way to break the cycle of poverty and dependency. An agreement for Native control of their own education has been made with the federal government, resulting in the proposal of the First Nations Control of First Nations Education Act in 2014.

REVIEW QUESTIONS

1. Why is multicultural education desirable and necessary for Canada?
2. How has multiculturalism been perceived as controversial in Canada and around the world? Do you think that it is still controversial?

3. In what way is the concept of multicultural education radically different from a policy of assimilation?

4. What are the main differences in the educational policies of English and French Canada?

5. In what ways has the traditional education system failed Native groups in Canada?

6. Why have the education policies of both the Province of Quebec and Native groups rejected the policy of multiculturalism?

7. What has been the effect of the Canadian Multiculturalism Act of 1988 on Canadians' perceptions of heritage and identity?

REFERENCES

Aboriginal Affairs and Northern Development. (2011). *Canada–First Nations joint action plan.* Retrieved from www.aadnc-aandc.gc.ca/eng/1314718067733/1314718114793

Archibald, J. (1995). To keep the fire going: The challenge for First Nations education in the year 2000. In R. Ghosh & D. Ray (Eds.), *Social change and education in Canada* (pp. 342–357) (3rd Ed.). Toronto: Harcourt Brace.

Association of Canadian Deans of Education (ACDE). (2010). *Accord on indigenous education.* Retrieved from www.csse-scee.ca/docs/acde/acde_accord_indigenousresearch_en.pdf

Authier, P. (2014, January 23). Concordia University defends its stance against charter at hearings. *Montreal Gazette* [online]. Retrieved from www.montrealgazette.com/news/Concordia+University+defends+stance+against+charter+hearings/9423606/story.html

Bouchard, G., & Taylor, C. (2008). *Building the future: A time for reconciliation.* Quebec: Commission de consultation sur les pratiques d'accommodement reliées aux différences culturelles.

Bourhis, R.Y. (2008). The English-speaking communities of Quebec: Vitality, multiple identities and linguicism. In R.Y. Bourhis (Ed.), *The vitality of the English-speaking communities of Quebec: From community decline to revival* (pp. 127–164). Montreal: CEETUM, Université de Montréal.

Canadian Council on Learning. (2009). *The state of Aboriginal learning in Canada: A holistic approach to measuring success.* Retrieved from www.ccl-cca.ca/pdfs/StateAboriginalLearning/SAL-FINALReport_EN.PDF

Crown–First Nation Gathering. (2012). *Next Steps.* Retrieved from crownfirstnationgathering.com

Dewey, J. (1916). *Democracy and education: An introduction to the philosophy of education.* New York: Macmillan.

First Nation Education Act. (2014). *Canada's Economic Action Plan.* Retrieved from actionplan.gc.ca/en/initiative/first-nation-education-act

Fleury, B., et al. (2007). *Inclusive Québec schools: Dialogue, values, and common reference points*. Quebec: Minister of Education, Recreation, and Sport.

Floch, W, & Pocock, J. (2008). The socio-economic status of English-speaking Quebec: Those who left and those who stayed. In R.Y. Bourhis (Ed.), *The vitality of the English-speaking communities of Quebec: From community decline to revival* (pp. 35–62). Montreal: CEETUM, Université de Montréal.

Freire, P. (1970). *Pedagogy of the oppressed*. New York: Seabury Press.

Gilligan, C. (1982). *In a different voice*. Cambridge, MA: Harvard University Press.

Government of Canada. (2012). *Government of Canada progress report (2006–2012)— With strong resolve: Advancing our relationship with First Nations peoples and communities*. Retrieved from www.aadnc-aandc.gc.ca/DAM/DAM-INTER-HQ/STAGING/texte-text/ap_fn_cfng_rep_1327192143455_eng.pdf

Gramsci, A. (1971). *Selections from prison notebooks*. New York: International Publishers.

Harper, A.G. (1945). Canada's Indian administration: Basic concepts and objectives. *America Indigena, 5*(2), 119–132.

Harper, S. (2008). *Statement of apology—to former students of Indian residential schools*. Retrieved from www.aadnc-aandc.gc.ca/DAM/DAM-INTER-HQ/STAGING/texte-text/rqpi_apo_pdf_1322167347706_eng.pdf

Henchey, N., & Burgess, D. (1987). *Between past and future: Quebec education in transition*. Calgary: Detselig.

Howard, A., & Widdowson, F. (2013). Running the gauntlet: Challenging the taboo obstructing Aboriginal education policy development. In F. Widdowson & A. Howard (Eds.), *Approaches to Aboriginal education in Canada: Searching for solutions* (pp. 288–317). Toronto: Brush Education.

Laferrière, M. (1980). Language and cultural programs for ethnic minorities in Quebec: A critical review. *Multiculturalism, 4*(2), 12–17.

Lather, P. (1991). *Getting smart: Feminist research and pedagogy with/in the postmodern*. New York: Routledge.

Leroux, D. (2010). Québec nationalism and the production of difference: The Bouchard-Taylor Commission, the Hérouxville Code of Conduct, and Québec's immigrant integration policy. *Québec Studies, 49*, 107–126.

Luke, C., & Gore, J. (Eds.). (1992). *Feminism and critical pedagogy*. New York: Routledge.

Maclean's. (2010, June 1). Deans sign accord on Aboriginal education. Macleans.ca. Retrieved from www.macleans.ca/education/uniandcollege/deans-sign-accord-on-aboriginal-education

McAndrew, M. (1993). *The integration of ethnic minority students 15 years after Bill 101: Some issues confronting the Montreal Island French language public schools*. R.F. Harnie Program on Immigration and Ethnicity Working Papers. Toronto: University of Toronto.

McAndrew, M. (2010). Immigration and diversity in Quebec's schools: An assessment. In J. Rudy, S. Gervais, & C. Kirkey (Eds.), *Quebec questions: Quebec studies for the twenty-first century* (pp. 287–304). New York: Oxford University Press.

Mendelson, M. (2009). *Why we need a First Nations Education Act.* Ottawa: Caledon Institute of Social Policy.

Moodley, K. (1981). Canadian ethnicity in comparative perspective. In J. Dahlie & T. Fernando (Eds.), *Ethnicity, power and the politics of culture* (pp. 6–21). Toronto: Methuen.

Prime Minister of Canada. (2012). *Crown–First Nations Gathering outcome statement.* Retrieved from pm.gc.ca/eng/news/2012/01/24/crown-first-nations-gathering-outcome-statement

Quebec. (1978). *La politique québécoise due developpement culturel.* Québec: Le minister d'Etat au Développement culturel.

Quebec. (1981). *Autant de façons d'être Québécois; plan d'action du gouvernement du Québec l'intention de communautés culturelles.* Québec: Ministère des Communautés culturelles et de l'Immigration.

Quebec. (1983). *Au Québec pour bâtir ensemble; enoncède politique en matière d'immigration et d'intégration.* Québec: Ministère des Communautés culturelles et de l'Immigration.

Quebec. (1985). *L'école Québécoise et les communautés culturelles: Rapport du comité* (Chancy Report). Québec: Ministère de l'Éducation.

Quebec. (1988). *La valorisation du pluralisme culturel dans les manuels scolaires.* Montréal: Conseil des Communautés culturelles et de l'Immigration du Québec.

Quebec. (1990). *Let's build Quebec together: A policy statement on immigration and integration.* Montréal: Ministère des Communautés culturelles et de l'Immigration du Québec.

Quebec. (1997). *A school for the future: Educational integration and intercultural education.* Québec: Ministère de l'Éducation, du Loisir du Sport.

Quebec. (1998). *Plan of action for educational integration and intercultural education.* Québec: Ministère de l'Éducation, du Loisir du Sport.

Quebec. (2009). *Évaluation du programme: Programme d'enseignement des langues d'origine (PELO).* Québec: Ministére de l'Éducation, du Loisir du Sport.

Rasmussen, D. (2011). Some honest talk about non-indigenous education. *Our Schools/Our Selves, 20*(2), 19–33.

Regnier, R. (1995). Warrior as pedagogue, pedagogue as warrior: Reflections on Aboriginal anti-racist pedagogy. In R. Ng, P. Staton, & J. Scane (Eds.), *Anti-racism, feminism and critical approaches to education.* Toronto: OISE Press.

Richards, J. (2006). *Creating choices: Rethinking Aboriginal policy.* Aurora, ON: C.D. Howe Institute.

Richards, J. (2008). Closing the Aboriginal/non-Aboriginal education gaps. *Backgrounder, 116.* Retrieved from www.cdhowe.org/pdf/Backgrounder_116.pdf

Sharpe, A., & Arsenault, J.F. (2009). Investing in Aboriginal education in Canada: An economic perspective. Retrieved from www.cprn.org/documents/51980_EN.pdf

Standing Committee on Aboriginal Peoples. (2007). *Reforming First Nations education: From crisis to hope*, 41st Parl., 1st sess.

Statistics Canada. (1994). *1991 Census highlights*. Catalogue no. 9G-304E. Ottawa: Minister of Industry, Science and Technology. Retrieved from publications.gc.ca/collections/collection_2013/statcan/rh-hc/CS96-304-1994-eng.pdf

Statistics Canada. (2008). *Canada's ethnocultural mosaic, 2006 Census*. Catalogue no. 97-562-X. Ottawa: Minister of Industry. Retrieved from www12.statcan.ca/access_acces/archive.action-eng.cfm?/english/census06/analysis/ethnicorigin/pdf/97-562-XIE2006001.pdf

Statistics Canada. (2013). Immigration and ethnocultural diversity in Canada: National Household Survey, 2011. Catalogue no. 99-010-X2011001. Ottawa: Minister of Industry. Retrieved from www12.statcan.gc.ca/nhs-enm/2011/as-sa/99-010-X/99-010-X2011001-eng.pdf

St. Denis, V. (2011). Silencing Aboriginal curricular content and perspectives through multiculturalism: "There are other children here." *Review of Education, Pedagogy, and Cultural Studies, 33*(4), 306–317.

Waddington, D.I., Maxwell, B., McDonough, K.M., Cormier, A., & Schwimmer, M. (2011). Interculturalism in practice: Québec's new ethics and religious culture curriculum and the Bouchard-Taylor report on reasonable accommodation. In T. Besley & M.A. Peters (Eds.), *Interculturalism, education, and dialogue* (pp. 312–329). New York: Peter Lang.

ACTS

Canadian Charter of Rights and Freedoms, s. 2, Part I of the *Constitution Act, 1982*.

Canadian Multiculturalism Act, R.S.C., 1985, c. 24 (4th Supp.) (1988).

Chartres des droits et libertés de la personne, L.R.Q., chap. C-12. (1975).

ACTIVITY 2
"On the Street Where You Live": (Re)visiting Your Neighbourhood on a Multicultural Walking Tour

Purpose
- Help students become aware of multiculturalism in their immediate surroundings by examining historical influences on the formation of their community
- Validate the local context as a legitimate site of culture and knowledge production
- Develop an accessible, low-cost alternative to traditional field trips
- Engage students by promoting learning as it occurs outside of the classroom

Description

When working in a school, you may find that arranging a typical field trip to a cultural site such as a museum or art gallery requires a significant amount of resources: admission fees, transportation costs, trip insurance, permission slips, recruitment of volunteers, and much more. But while travelling to an off-site cultural landmark can certainly be valuable for students' knowledge growth and acquisition of cultural capital, it is not always necessary for a field trip to showcase culture in such an institutional way (i.e., by viewing collected artifacts housed artificially in a building).

In this activity, you are challenged to design a field trip that consists of a walking tour of cultural sites in the immediate vicinity of the school. The tour should begin and end at the school itself, with four or five stops along the way. The stops on the field trip do not need to be places typically visited by schoolchildren on field trips; rather, they can include less conventional destinations such as outdoor sculptures or street signs or even sections of a local grocery store.

The field trip will need to be designed for a particular grade level and should consistently incorporate a theme or topic relevant to multiculturalism in some way; the field trip might help students recognize difference, challenge stereotypes, or become more cognizant of connections between local and global contexts. For instance, a field trip with stops at key intersections might involve drawing attention to the names of individuals after whom the streets are named, recounting stories of their involvement in the neighbourhood, and critically examining their inclusion through the lens of gender or ethnic diversity. A field trip to the grocery store could consist of stops that highlight the foods that have become staples of students' diets and then exploring the global trajectory of these foods before they arrive in the local store. By focusing on the local neighbourhood as a significant cultural site itself—one worth visiting and exploring—the field trip avoids presenting knowledge as objective or packaged. In doing so, it encourages students to develop critical awareness of their surroundings and environment.

The field trip should be designed in the format of a presentation to the school board; it may be necessary to include a map of the walking tour, an explanation of the field trip theme, a description of each of the walking tour stops, and talking points or discussion questions to engage students at each site.

Curricular Connections

Social Studies: Help students develop cartographic skills by asking them to map out the field trip and examine concepts such as territory issues, spatial organization, scale, legends, and symbolic representation.

Mathematics: Turn the field trip into a scavenger hunt that directs students to collect relevant quantitative data to be analyzed statistically upon return to the classroom.

Science: Design the field trip to examine native and non-native plant life, and discuss the benefits and challenges of introduced species within the ecosystem; allude to immigration as a similar process in human communities.

Music: Challenge students to create a playlist by selecting pieces of music that are representative of each visited site, as if scoring the soundtrack for a short film or advertisement.

Chapter 3

A FRAMEWORK FOR A REDEFINED
MULTICULTURAL EDUCATION

Ms. Rodriguez was not always excited about seeing her Grade 11 math class during fifth period. Not only was the class right after lunch, when all the students would come back bursting with energy, but half of it was made up of varsity hockey players, who could not wait to get to practice immediately afterward. One athlete in the class, Felix, had quit the team a few weeks earlier, and his performance in Ms. Rodriguez's class had been noticeably deteriorating ever since. The teacher also observed that Felix was much quieter lately and hardly ever participated anymore. She assumed he was intimidated by his former teammates, who sometimes snickered when Felix said anything aloud. But he was looking rather sickly too, as if he was not getting enough sleep. One day in class, Ms. Rodriguez caught Felix with his mobile phone and asked him to put it away. A few minutes later she was startled by the desk that Felix overturned as he rushed out of the classroom. She vowed to call his parents that evening, but Felix came back to see her at the end of the day to apologize and explain why he was so upset. He had recently broken up with his girlfriend after admitting he was gay, and word had gotten out around the school. On top of this, Felix told his parents about his sexuality and his dad kicked him out of the house because he did not approve. So when a former teammate sent him hateful text messages while he was in class that day, Felix freaked out. He told Ms. Rodriguez that he was thinking about dropping out of school.

- If you were the teacher in this situation, how would you respond?
- Do you think that Ms. Rodriguez has an ethical responsibility to encourage Felix's self-concept and well-being?
- Is it possible for teachers to empower students by remaining objective and neutral, or without sharing their own moral and democratic values?

INTRODUCTION

In the four decades since the implementation of Canada's multicultural policy, education stakeholders have made efforts to transfer its spirit from policy into pedagogy. This has involved revision of curriculum, as well as teacher education and professional development. At the same time, scholars have debated about what the term "multiculturalism" originally meant and about what it means today. Kymlicka (2003) argues that multiculturalism is "a victim of its own success" (p. 8) because the concept has permeated the consciousness of Canadian society to such an extent that the term itself has lost meaning. He intimates that even when critics propose alternatives to multiculturalism, they continue to build upon "the twin pillars of multiculturalism: the rejection of assimilationist policies and the acceptance of a duty to accommodate. The word multiculturalism may be unfashionable, but those twin assumptions are more widely accepted than ever before, and indeed are often simply taken for granted" (p. 8). The term means different things to different people and this confusion has led to problems operationalizing multiculturalism in education. It is easy to think of multiculturalism in terms of different ethnic cultures and to focus on a "museum approach," which views culture as static and treats it as an artifact that can be brought into and out of contexts and interactions, rather than as a component of identity that is always present and ever evolving. This avoids the need to deal with power issues and the complexities involved in equity issues for people who are different from the "norm." This is why inclusion, from the perspective of a redefined multicultural framework, is predicated on the right to difference.

Working with a broad and inclusive conceptualization of multiculturalism, we can understand that multiculturalism and multicultural education fundamentally encompass similar concepts, such as diversity, interculturalism, human rights and social justice, anti-racism, anti-bias education, culturally responsive pedagogy, critical pedagogy, peace education, environmental education, and community activism. Rather than distinguish these concepts from one another, it is more important to understand that they work towards the same goals. All of these approaches aim to protect human dignity and promote the equitable treatment of all people and our shared world. Grant and Khurshid's (2009) comparative examination of multicultural education found that its operationalization in different countries around the world was complex, multi-layered, idiosyncratic, and ever transforming, but its intent to support students and teachers in their struggles for better educational opportunities remained the common thread. If we think of culture in relation to the politics involved in recognizing and labelling "difference," then we should feel comfortable using the term "multiculturalism" to promote the full spectrum of difference within cultural components of identity: race/ethnicity, gender, class, sexual orientation, (dis)ability, religion, etc. Thus, multicultural education involves all the pedagogical theories, approaches, and methods that help all individuals, whether they identify with dominant or subordinate cultures, work towards the complementary goals of inclusioi the right to be different.

Redefined multicultural education must reflect changes in curriculum, teaching strategies, and school culture, as well as policy and administrative issues. This chapter deals with the *content* of the curriculum. It discusses some ways in which administrators and teachers can create and support strong programs with a practical and progressive outlook. Specific classroom concerns, including the hidden curriculum, evaluation, and discipline, are dealt with in later chapters.

Pedagogy must be developed around identity and meaning—the politics of difference (that is, the social, historical construction of difference and the power this implies). This can be done in various ways (Welch, 1991). First, in teaching, school knowledge and practices must be linked to race, ethnicity, gender, and class experiences because these factors combine to shape identity in complex and contradictory ways. Second, the historical development of concepts such as racism, sexism, and classism needs to be dealt with to reveal how asymmetrical power relations create different conditions for different groups and individuals. Third, the way in which differences within and between groups result in social hierarchy through school structures must be understood. The idea is to construct knowledge in which multiple voices and worldviews are legitimated so that new patterns of relating are formed.

A REDEFINED EDUCATIONAL FRAMEWORK

Education is not simply a matter of accumulating knowledge and skills; it involves acquiring "conceptual schemes"—forming links and understanding ideas. Being educated is to *connect,* to be able to raise one's knowledge beyond the level of a collection of disjointed facts and to understand the "reason why" of things. Knowledge "characterizes the way one looks at the world" (Martin, 1985, p. 72). Knowledge is thus different from mere information or data (i.e., facts); it implies internalized ideas that allow one to pattern information into an insight.

To be educated is to have a voice, which implies knowledge as well as power (McDonald, 1988, p. 472). To be educated is to have the ability to influence one's personal and social environment. That is empowerment. As mentioned in Chapter 1, empowerment is legitimating the multiple voices of students. Teachers cannot give voice to students; being educated means claiming a voice for oneself. This involves not so much struggling to speak but being able to alter the nature and direction of that speech (hooks, 1989).

According to Freire, "Besides being an act of knowing, education is also a political act. That is why no pedagogy is neutral" (in Shor & Freire, 1987, p. 13). School mirrors the real, the power play, the hierarchy in society, and education should illuminate that reality. Different socio-cultural positions transmit different worldviews, and some are more powerful than others (Connell, 1989). Reality is socially constructed and can be reconstructed. For example, students must question the stereotyped, negative images of Canada's indigenous population and aim to rebuild historical reality with perspectives that are not just those of the conquerors. Similarly, the image of India as a poverty-stricken country is formed in students' minds through the curriculum and the media; the stereotype needs to be demolished and rebuilt through a process of analysis that goes to the roots of the country's historical development. A picture would emerge of an India that is undoubtedly poor (although rich in heritage), but whose colonization is linked to the industrialization of Britain on the one hand and its own economic underdevelopment on the other.

Knowledge is not value-free, even in science and mathematics, especially in the applied areas (for example, engineering, medicine, agriculture, and defence technology). In science and math some truths can be objectively verified, such as Newton's law of gravitation or the laws of thermodynamics. However, even the objective truths of science have evolved through a tortuous history of socially constructed knowledge. For example, for many centuries before Copernicus, the earth was regarded as the centre of the universe. The discoveries of Copernicus, Galileo, and Kepler laid the scientific foundation for the knowledge that the earth is only a planet revolving around the sun in one of many universes.

Education not only involves intellectual development, it is also concerned with affective and ethical issues. In this regard, a multicultural education that advocates mere tolerance of differences is problematic. Multicultural education must involve respect for differences, not just tolerance. Of course, respect for cultural differences should not become extreme relativism—differences must be seen within the context of human rights. While people may not agree with a position, they must, nevertheless, learn to understand it as reflecting a moral point of view; in this way, people who disagree can learn from each other's differences (Gutman, 1992).

There is no simple recipe for a comprehensive multicultural curriculum. Because science and math are generally not thought to be conducive to multicultural teaching, several of the examples that follow have been purposely chosen from those fields. The idea is not to prescribe curriculum but to outline a philosophy that recognizes the importance of social responsibility and human interdependence.

Reconceptualizing Knowledge

Traditional knowledge involves the experiences and perspectives of historically dominant groups. Powerless groups have either been generally excluded or portrayed negatively in the curriculum. The ultimate aim of multicultural education is to look at the curriculum in a different way and to reconceptualize the way knowledge has so far been organized. New ways of thinking and conceptualizing raise fundamental questions: Have school curricula excluded the knowledge and experiences of women and other minority groups because they are not worthy of representation? What knowledge is of most worth? Who decides worth?

Postmodern theory questions the validity of Eurocentric knowledge as being the exclusive reference point for judging all learning; as Giroux (1991) states, "There is no tradition or story that can speak with authority and certainty for all of humanity" (p. 231). A Eurocentric viewpoint ignores the contemporary and historical contributions of most of the world's peoples, especially those who live in Africa, Asia, and Central and Latin America. It is no longer acceptable to, for example, prescribe only European literature while ignoring the classics from non-Western countries. This does not imply that European literature should not be prescribed. The idea is that it should not be the only contribution to the literary canon, as works from other cultures are just as worthy.

Sins of omission cannot be rectified through minor inclusions of information about neglected groups, nor can sins of commission be reversed by changing how certain groups are described. For example, adding token references to school texts about Canada's various ethnocultural groups still maintains the dominant culture bias of the curriculum. Simply incorporating this information does not address the sense of alienation and loss felt by such groups. In addition, the appended material on the heroes and experiences of other groups is usually selected and interpreted by the dominant group. Superficial inclusion—sometimes called the three *S* approach (saris, samosas, and steel bands), or the static museum approach (culture as artifact)—merely incorporates elements of different cultures (multicultural education through cultures). This approach naively assumes that the solution lies in knowing about, or even learning to appreciate, each other's cultures. It is a simplistic solution to structural and individual discrimination.

Racial, gender, and class bias is still common in textbooks even after more than a decade of attempts to address the problem. Given today's budgetary realities, teachers may still have to deal with biased textbooks and media material. Rather than pose a problem, this may offer an opportunity for classes to conduct a critical examination and bring in diverse materials. However, the teacher must be able to critically assess the existing material. Bias of omission involves failure to depict a multiracial and multicultural society in which women and the working class play a substantial part. In each subject area, the following basic question must be kept in mind: What can we learn about the daily lives, histories, and achievements of women? Of other cultures? Of ordinary people in Canada and other parts of the world?

This question can be applied to each subject area: science, math, history, social studies, literature, and languages. Art, music, drama, and physical education can also become much more interesting from a multicultural perspective. Even subjects with focused vocational goals can be taught from a multicultural viewpoint. The process of infusion in redefining multicultural education can be accomplished in the following ways:

- It is often difficult to obtain accurate representations of events that include women and ethnic groups because of past racist and sexist practices. Historical analysis will give meaning to contemporary events. Why, for example, have men traditionally occupied the administrative positions in the education profession in which women form the majority? While the presumed explanation may be women's lack of ability, the reasons for this inequality lie in a history of discrimination. An investigation into this topic will involve research, which in itself will be a valuable learning experience for both students and teachers.
- Minority perspectives are built not only on success stories and histories, but also on the daily lives, problems, conflicts, joys, and sufferings of ordinary people.
- Multiple perspectives (the experiences and visions of various groups of people) involve correcting stereotypes and omissions. For example, the lack of women's perspectives in the sciences devalues women's ability and credibility.
- Racism and sexism (through language, interpretation, and pictures) in textbooks and media are harmful and must be discussed. For example, exclusionary language that uses the male pronoun (him/his) to represent all of humanity gives both male and female students a distorted vision of who they are in the hierarchy of social structure.

While inclusion and multiple perspectives are more easily achieved in the humanities and social sciences, science and math courses are often dismissed as being inappropriate for incorporating other experiences, including those of women, who have traditionally been excluded from the study of mathematics and natural sciences. It is argued that science and math are multicultural by nature because they are value-free and neutral and, therefore, universally valid. Yet knowledge in science is created by scientists who ask questions that are not value-neutral. For example, the basic physics of atomic fission is value-free; however, whether this knowledge is used to provide much-needed electrical energy or to make atomic bombs is a decision made by applied scientists whose research funds depend on following the agenda of power elites. Similarly, our knowledge of bacteria and viruses can be applied to alleviating diseases or creating weapons of biological warfare. This means that science cannot be seen as value-free; it "is not something in the sky, not a set of eternal truths waiting for discovery. Science is a practice. There is no other science than the science that gets done" (Young, 1987, p. 18).

Harding (1994) identifies three central questions for addressing the multicultural aspects of the natural sciences: (1) To what extent do the origins of modern science go back to non-Western origins? (2) Do other cultures have indigenous forms of science that are valid? and (3) In what ways is modern science European–North American? Scientific discoveries have been made in many different cultures, especially in the past, and "Western science" has developed more recently from many contributions. This does not negate the need to acknowledge the role and impact of non-Western cultures, as modern science has failed to make explicit the extent to which it has borrowed from these cultures. This lack of recognition has resulted in the trivialization of the achievements of other scientific traditions. Further, the development of science in the West was related to European expansion and colonialism, which had the effect of suppressing the scientific traditions of the colonized cultures. Moreover, the areas in which science and technology developed were those that were important to the colonial (neo-colonial) powers.

Although science and math have contributed much to developing and maintaining stereotypes and prejudiced attitudes towards females and ethnic groups, these subjects offer many opportunities to challenge such assumptions. In biology, for example, it is possible to explode the myths of race and gender propagated by traditional scientific inquiry. Despite attempts by a few scientists to provide "scientific" rationales for racial and gender differences in intelligence, such viewpoints are generally regarded as marginal, flawed, and devoid of rigorous scientific standards. Biology teachers can use modern research to dispel myths that certain biological characteristics can be related to intellectual, social, psychological, or moral traits. Teachers can design activities that involve research to demonstrate, for example, that there is as much variation within groups (e.g., boys/girls, Negroid/Mongoloid/Caucasoid) as between groups in the usual measures of intelligence and ability.

Teachers should infuse all science and math courses with experiences relevant to various groups through the study of the contributions of women and world cultures to the development of these fields. Teachers should also demystify these subject areas by relating them to the lives of ordinary people. The Eurocentric bias in mathematics, for example, has a subtle effect on students' attitudes. A historical approach to math and science would recognize different cultural heritages, involve the contributions of other civilizations, and provide information that would help remove the Eurocentric bias. For example, among the basic contributions to mathematics, the earliest known demonstrations of Pythagoras can be found in an ancient Chinese text, *Chou Pei* (first millennium BC), and in *Sulbasutras* (ca. 800–500 BC) from India (Nelson, Joseph, & Williams, 1993, p. 13). Another interesting example is the story of the now-universal system of numeration that developed in India about 2,000 years ago (Nelson et al., 1993, p. 20). The concept of zero as a full number came from India in the fifth century AD. So important is this concept that complex calculations (e.g., for travelling into space) could not have been made without it. Different ways of computing, such as the Vedic multiplication system, which is still taught in India, can be tried in class and would make math classes more interesting (for examples see Nelson et al., 1993; Lee, Menkart, & Okazawa-Rey, 2006; Galczynski, Tsagkaraki, & Ghosh, 2012).

The destructive effects of textbook stereotyping in terms of gender, race, ethnicity, culture, and class have been amply documented. Departments of education and publishers of school texts have developed guidelines aimed at making curriculum materials more diverse. However, older books are sometimes still in use, and the implementation of these guidelines is not complete.

Critical Pedagogy and Meaning-Making

Critical thinking is an umbrella term for a variety of approaches that share reasoning as a central concern; it is based on a view of the curriculum that stresses interaction among students, teachers, and learning materials (Thornton, 1994). The purpose of the critical thinking approach is to help the student move from a narrow way of thinking to a more global perspective. Because it is an open-ended approach, it is difficult to specify exactly what the outcomes of this approach will be (Cornbleth, 1985). Critical pedagogy, which is focused on the promotion of critical thinking, must not only expose the social, cultural, and economic inequalities created by complex relations of power, but also involve fundamental transformation of the epistemological and ideological assumptions that define what counts as knowledge and where/who it comes from (Apple & Au, 2009). Identifying schools as sites of both knowledge transmission and knowledge production, Guilherme (2002) equates critical pedagogy with cultural politics, stressing how "it is indispensable to use pupils' experiences of their more restricted cultural circles, of the larger society into which they integrate, and of other cultures they come into contact with" (p. 20). Thus, in blending the language of critique with the language of possibility, education must simultaneously draw on the pedagogies of reflection, dissent, difference, dialogue, empowerment, action, and hope.

Teachers must help all students define their own worlds, speak their languages, and reflect on their experiences. Students must be able at some point to relate the curriculum to their daily lives and cultures. Stressing unfamiliar aspects and concepts can be alienating rather than reinforcing. Students cannot relate to knowledge that appears totally unreal to them because of the distance from their own cultures. A redefined multicultural education seeks to span this gap through learning experiences that ease the tension between school culture and home culture. For example, students could study Shakespeare, but also the literature of other countries. Not only are there exceptional Canadian writers of non-English origin, but there is an abundance of excellent writers from other countries, some of whom are Nobel laureates (for example, Rabindranath Tagore, Naguib Mahfouz, Gabriel Garcia Marquez, and Kenzaburo Oe). Likewise, the increasing use of information technology and multimedia approaches creates new vehicles for the teaching of critical thinking. However, students need to learn to be selective when confronted with such a vast knowledge base.

Dewey (1916) stressed the relationship between student experience, critical thinking, and learning. According to him, knowledge must permit students to "experience a meaning" in situations, not replace theoretical knowledge with practical work. School should be a vehicle for uniting mind and body, reason and emotion, self and other. Great educators from other cultures, such as Rabindranath Tagore, also emphasized the unity of mind and body, as well as the need for aesthetics in children's daily lives (Chakrabarti, 1993).

Providing opportunities for minority children to become knowledgeable about their own and other students' cultures enriches the curriculum for everyone and ensures full participation. It is more important for first- and second-generation immigrant students to deal with their present lived experiences as members of minorities in their communities than it is to relate to a homeland that they or their parents have left behind. This means that different students will develop different understandings. For example, racism means something different to a black child than it does to a Jewish child. It also means that students will not "possess" knowledge in traditionally accepted forms—for example, students' understandings of socially accepted behaviour may be different from their parents' concepts. Students must question and redefine established knowledge and perspectives both in the school and at home.

In relating the themes of each subject area as much as possible to students' daily lives, it is important not to simply validate whatever students believe. Rather, a critical examination is essential so that they may then reconstruct their own beliefs.

Infusing Curriculum with Diverse Perspectives

All students must be granted equitable access to knowledge if they are to develop the competencies that are essential for success in our globalized world. As Gramsci (1988) points out, if students are to create and participate in a more just society, they need to master the skills and knowledge that enable the dominant group to remain in control. This means that knowledge of the language(s) of learning (in Canada, English and French) and math and science concepts is fundamental for all students. This common core of school knowledge is important for all students so that they have an equal chance to "'make it' within existing realities." Not doing so will "doom them to social marginality: yet another high-minded way of perpetuating the structural inequalities in society" (Simon, 1987, p. 375).

Educators such as Tagore, Dewey, and Freire have stressed the need for children to have the opportunity to value their own experiences, and to feel part of the curriculum and of their education. This does not mean scrapping the prescribed curriculum. It does, however, mean treating that curriculum critically. It is possible to teach languages (of instruction and others), social sciences (including history, geography, environment), math, the physical sciences (physics, chemistry, biology), the arts (art, music, drama), and physical education within a multicultural perspective. The idea is not to rid the curriculum of a male, Eurocentric perspective but to extend it to include other worldviews. Exposure to different cultures and countries, to women's lives, and to the working class will lead to new knowledge. It also means relearning old knowledge and disengaging from some ways of doing things that are no longer relevant. This will lead students to question the subtle, biased nature of traditional school knowledge.

Infusion means permeating the entire school curriculum with the lives, experiences, works, attributes, and dreams of those traditionally left out. The exclusion of women, ethnocultural groups, and working-class children in the curriculum is not an oversight. Gaskell, McLaren, and Novogrodsky (1989) and others point out that this has the effect of marginalizing the histories and perspectives of those left out, and validating those who have pride of place. For example, by ignoring the point of view of Canada's Native people, school history textbooks not only legitimate the English and French versions, but also devalue the experiences of First Nations people.

Multiple perspectives involve many disciplines organized around key concepts and social issues. Human concerns and issues cut across disciplines and should not be compartmentalized. A thematic approach avoids the isolation of one area of understanding from another as in traditional curricula, especially in science, which treats objects as separate from the environment. Integrated study shows the relevance of science to society, the political economy, and the environment.

For example, the theme of waste disposal and recycling involves societal, political, economic, and environmental concerns and issues.

A thematic approach is more likely to develop students' natural curiosity and critical analysis, as well as linguistic and numerical skills. Curriculum topics could be chosen from social issues with which students are concerned. Books are available to introduce students to different geographical skills and multicultural understandings through activity-based units of study (see Bailey, 1991). Several books integrate conceptual understandings in traditions, history, customs, ecology, economy, and geography, emphasizing literacy and language development through experiential learning. Rather than study a particular revolution in history, students could look at the concept of revolution itself.

In the traditional curriculum, disease and starvation are not studied in relation to their political, historical, and economic roots. An alternative approach is to relate famine in Africa to historical and political forces, such as colonialism and dictatorships. When poverty is studied in isolation, the victim is likely to be blamed, thus promoting racist attitudes. In addition, social problems may manifest themselves in one area while their sources lie elsewhere. For example, a problem such as malnutrition may have geographical, historical, political, economic, or sociological sources. An integrated approach to malnutrition is essential if it is to be understood.

The science-technology-society (STS) program proposed by the National Science Teachers Association in the United States in the early 1980s combines social and environmental concerns in the curriculum to deal with science- and technology-related problems in society. The National Council for Social Issues in the United States has developed guidelines for teaching science-related societal issues that require appropriate knowledge and awareness, investigation skills, and action strategies (Lynch, 1992, p. 13). Another approach that crosses disciplinary boundaries is the "expanding environments model," which begins in the lower primary grades in areas familiar to the students' lives (self, family, community) and broadens its focus in the upper elementary grades (nation, world). (For other ideas, see Verma & Purnfrey, 1993 [secondary schools], 1994 [primary schools].)

When working to infuse curriculum with the representation of diverse perspectives, the teacher needs to think about issues of difference, power, and privilege. Current events should be discussed in the classroom to raise students' awareness and understanding of the world around them. The multicultural teacher needs to consider the issues raised in the current events he or she decides to focus on—and then cultivate discussions with students in a manner appropriate for their level of maturity. In a multicultural framework, lessons that broach these issues cannot be taught as separate subjects; rather, they must be skilfully worked into everyday lesson plans (Galczynski et al., 2012, p. 161). This means that teachers need to become adept at modifying curricular content for their targeted grade level, so that their teaching practice fulfills obligations to the approved curriculum and yet promotes meaning-making well beyond it.

Global and Environmental Awareness

It is important to extend concepts and social issues from local to world conditions. This is easily done in several areas, such as the environment, health, economic conditions, political conflicts, migration, and population. Raising global awareness should be related to becoming active—thinking globally, acting locally. This may involve working in school and at home to preserve the ecosystem by recycling, conserving energy and other resources, and reducing waste. Global awareness could also be achieved by questioning the origins and causes of human conditions or the relationships among historical, societal, and environmental issues that currently affect the community and the world. Gandhi expressed the need to incorporate the subtle nuances of global culture in order to become "a global citizen of goodness" (Chakrabarti, 1990, p. 33). In other words, global awareness is the recognition of human beings' fundamental interdependence—that we are connected in suffering as in well-being.

To extend our earlier discussion of poverty, for example, in the traditional curriculum no explanation is given for the "starving millions in the overpopulated Third World." But students need to learn that poverty has its roots in history (slavery and colonialism) and is not limited to Third World countries, and that prosperous countries, which contain one-quarter of the world's population, consume two-thirds of the world's food production. Students should also understand that poverty in poorer countries is related to how land there is used as cash crops for exports to wealthy industrialized countries, which are advantaged by favourable exchange rates. Students could then relate poverty in some parts of the world to affluence in others and compare pockets of poverty and wealth in their own cities and communities.

Students also need to be made aware of where terms such as "Third World" come from, so that they can begin to question the perspectives that these terms represent. For instance, the ranking of "worlds" stems from Cold War divisions, when democratic countries in North America and Europe were identified as "First World"; communist countries such as China and the Soviet Union and its bloc of influence were labelled "Second World"; and any remaining countries, most of which had colonial pasts, were grouped as "Third World." This categorization system certainly implies a global hierarchy, and it entirely excludes subpopulations living beyond the industrial norm; as a result, Aboriginal scholars developed the term "Fourth World" to describe these "other" societies. Categorizations propagated by international agencies such as the World Bank or International

Monetary Fund also involve hierarchies along spectrums of income and development (in terms of gross domestic product), and these specifically relate to financial lending between countries. The globe has similarly been divided between eastern and western hemispheres, in reference to the cultural differences between peoples living in those parts of the world, as well as between the northern and southern hemispheres; this distinction between the Global North and Global South halves the world into industrialized countries that primarily belong to the northern hemisphere and non-industrialized countries that are on or below the equator. In recent years, the terms "Majority World" and "Minority World" have come into more frequent use. These categorizations are more representative of inequitable power dynamics, as they draw attention to the reality that most people in the world live in economically less developed countries. Indubitably, there is an irony here because the majority of the world's population resides in the "Minority World."

Global awareness is predicated upon understanding how biological, historical, and cultural factors are interconnected with the human species. Anderson (in Bennett, 1992) describes this as a world system model: planet Earth shares the global ecosystem, human and ecological organization is based on a global social order, and each human being is a responsible and participating citizen in the world order. Therefore, a redefined multicultural framework must include attention to the environment and ecological problems. As participants in Canadian society and as global citizens, students should be made aware of environmental issues both in their own country and abroad. This involves discovering what issues are of concern in local and global contexts, comparing environmental problems between different contexts, and listening to multiple points of view in regards to the varying ways that environmental and ecological problems may be managed or solved (Grant & Sleeter, 2009). Egbo (2009) stresses that the environment and biodiversity constitute essential knowledge for Canadian students, explaining that "we live in a volatile world that is rife with environmental exploitation and degradation that can result in conflicts. Some of the world's most enduring conflicts can be traced directly to environmental exploitation, destruction of livelihood, and the subsequent population displacement" (p. 107). Indeed, environmental responsibility is an overarching issue for the 21st century, and it is essential to both social justice and well-being (Cornelius-White, 2007).

ESSENTIAL SKILLS

Language

Language learning is a challenge for those whose mother tongue is not the dominant-group language (English or French). Children from other cultures must deal with several different language systems simultaneously. They may speak English or French but, because of differences in social status or dialect, may not employ what is thought of as correct usage. Since standard usage is the language of elites, it is important for students to know and master the elite form of language, not because it is superior but because of its political implications as a tool of power. Gramsci called for "broad scale mastery of language as a foundation for personal and social autonomy" (quoted in Aronowitz & Giroux, 1985, p. 214). As long as standards of achievement are defined by middle-class norms, lack of fluency in the "standard" form of English or French will disempower students. This is because they cannot learn and succeed in any subject in school if they do not know the language of instruction; eventually, this will affect their ability to compete for social and economic rewards.

Given that students need to learn the dominant-group language, the issue is how best to do it. The teacher must validate the student's own language, and not blame or judge them to be deficient for not knowing the dominant-group language. In addition, teachers must recognize that the dominant language is more than just a skill—it is also significant as a tool for power.

Although language learning is a complex process, it is becoming increasingly important for students to learn more than one language. Language learning involves phonology (speech sounds), vocabulary (quantity of known words), grammar (the use of rules, such as word order or syntax, sentence pattern, gender of a noun, and so on), and language pragmatics (appropriate use of language, which is particularly important in culturally diverse situations) (Garcia, Maez, & Gonzalez, 1983). Research shows that knowledge of more than one language does not confuse the understanding of language rules (Garcia et al., 1983), but enhances student performance (Cummings, 1986; Lambert & Tucker, 1972). There is evidence of a positive relationship between first- and second-language acquisition (Ervin-Tripp, 1974). The interdependence hypothesis proposes that academic proficiency in one language makes competence in another language easier, if the second language is seen to have high status. Among the sociocultural variables that help second-language learning, a positive attitude toward the cultural group of the target language (Lambert & Tucker, 1972) and reduced social distance (relative status) between the two cultures (Schuman, 1976) are significant. As such, the goals of multiculturalism align with strategies for language learning.

Bilingualism (ability to speak two languages with equal fluency) is essential, and third-language acquisition (exposure to a language at a later stage) is most desirable. Bilingualism is important because Canada is a bilingual country, and knowledge of two world languages is a definite asset in intercultural communication on a global scale. The most desirable situation is bilingual (English and French) education along with instruction in the student's mother tongue. While the teaching of numerous heritage languages may not be feasible in all schools, students, ideally, should also learn their own languages in school. This has become possible for certain languages (where numbers warrant) in some Canadian provinces.

Language learning is not just important for students. It is also the key to parental involvement. When a student's teacher and parents cannot communicate due to linguistic or literacy barriers, there are negative consequences for that student and for the community. In such situations, the school represents an artificial arbiter of knowledge that is disconnected from the local context.

Research shows a positive correlation between the incorporation of student language and culture and academic success (Cummings, 1983). When student language and culture are seen positively rather than as a disadvantage, students are empowered. Including student language does not necessarily mean teaching it in school—it means valuing the student's language in the context of the school and communicating the value of the student's culture.

Literacy

Literacy is the medium of pedagogy, the cultural marker, the currency in society. While literacy is a comparative concept and is defined differently in different societies, it traditionally refers to the mechanical ability to read and write at a certain level. At the same time, literacy is socially constructed and political (Freire & Macedo, 1987). A critical literacy, therefore, must be defined in very different terms. It is not related to a deficit theory of learning, nor is it primarily a technical skill.

Of course, critical literacy involves reading as well as writing and computation—that is, the learning and efficient use of symbols such as the alphabet and numbers. The difference between traditional literacy and critical literacy lies in the meaning of what is read, in the correspondence between representation (symbol) and external reality. In contrast to the mechanical ability to "read and write," critical literacy does not mean to "walk on the words" (Shor & Freire, 1987, p. 10), but rather to discover connections between text, the context of the text, and the context of the reader. Reading a book is like doing research. Being critical of the text is demanding, but it is also essential. Freire (1970) points out that critical reading is difficult because of the tradition of accepting the written word through the teaching process. Freire goes on to say that literacy is not liberating in itself. Giroux (1988) further clarified that "to be literate is not to be free, it is to be present and active in the struggle for claiming one's voice, history and future" (p. 65).

Illiteracy is costly to society. In response to data from the 2003 International Adult Literacy and Skills Survey, TD Bank Financial Group concluded that in Canada "every 1% improvement in literacy would boost national income by $32 billion" (Alexander, 2007, p. 14). The social cost of illiteracy, however, cannot be estimated. To be illiterate is to be silenced, marginalized, and vulnerable. Literacy empowers powerless groups by giving value to their experiences. In terms of literacy among Aboriginal peoples, Howard and Widdowson (2013) posit that emphasis on Native cultural traditions and Indigenous languages does not improve educational outcomes. Rather, they argue that preservation of the oral tradition can be viewed as the promotion of illiteracy, as it neither prepares Aboriginal peoples for fuller participation in Canadian life nor for economic self-sufficiency.

Information and Communication Technology
In the traditional curriculum, basic skills were confined to the three r's: reading, writing, and arithmetic. Today, the information revolution has extended the concept of basic skills to include computing skills.

Information and communication technologies (ICT) offer great promise in the pedagogical process of educational production and reproduction. Whether one agrees with the importance of technology in education, few can deny that advances in ICT have revolutionized education as they have changed the global political economy. The educational use of ICT has grown at a tremendous speed. As a matter of fact, the communications revolution has come to characterize the "Net generation" (Oblinger & Oblinger, 2005; Tapscott, 2008; Jones, Ramanau, Cross, & Healing, 2010), or millennials with birth years ranging from the 1980s to the early 2000s. The Net generation consists of children who are quite often more knowledgeable about computers than their teachers and parents and are the users rather than viewers of technology.

The uses of information technology for educational purposes are immense. The most common uses of ICT for educational purposes include the Internet, email, listservs, remote databases, the World Wide Web, bulletin boards, Web course tools (webCT), discussion forums, access to electronic journals and virtual libraries, interactive databanks, and, most recently, social media. An unprecedented amount of quality information is now at the disposal of both teachers and students, as well as myriad ways to acquire, share, and reflect on this information. In addition, computer-assisted instruction has increasingly become integrated into conventional schooling, and computer-based training is now an essential part of pedagogical preparation.

Canadian education systems recognize the importance of ICT for education. But while computers and the Internet are widely available at the school level, such access is not equally distributed across classes and ethnocultural groups at the societal level. This disparity between the information-rich and the information-poor is popularly known as the "digital divide" (Hoffman & Novak, 1998). Just as the Industrial Revolution produced new social classes based on the division of capital, the information revolution has created new classes that are deeply divided based on unequal access to information. Even in Canada, where Internet connectivity is fairly ubiquitous, quality access to ICT remains a crucial issue among ethnic and racial minorities, and particularly among First Nations communities in the Far North; likewise, differences in access between men and women, as well as between rural and urban environments, are persistent, if more subtle (Looker & Naylor, 2010).

The digital divide exists both between and within societies. With over 2.7 billion people using the Internet as of 2013, more than two-thirds of the developing world population remains offline (in comparison to about 20 percent of the developed world) (International Telecommunication Union [ITU], 2013). This situation is worst in Africa, where only 16 percent of people are accessing the Internet—and at significantly lower speeds than in other parts of the world (ITU, 2013). This global divide is also reflected at the societal level. Kenneth Keniston (2004) argues that there are really four digital divides: one consists of wealth and class divisions within nations; another consists of the economic divide between rich and poor countries, and includes the enormous disparity in connectivity; a third consists of linguistic and cultural divisions, taking into account the English-language domination over Web information; and the last consists of the new digital elite who are able to reap the benefits of information technology, particularly in knowledge-based sectors of the economy such as biotechnology and pharmacology. The Internet not only reproduces social inequalities, but also accelerates them: "Although inequalities within society have always existed, the Internet created an even stronger division; the higher status members increasingly gain access to more information than the lower status members" (van Deursen & van Dijk, 2014, p. 521).

Yet another aspect of the digital divide involves the gender gap. In the developing world, access to computers and the Internet can be restricted to the upper classes; within these classes there exist gender divisions with respect to access to information technology. The gender gap is more pronounced in the developing world, where 16 percent fewer women than men use the Internet, as compared to only 2 percent fewer in the developed world (ITU, 2013). Then again, the benefits of ICT are not uniformly shared in the industrialized world either. As data from the United Kingdom show, "boys, older children and middle-class children all benefit from more and better quality access to the internet than girls, younger and working-class children" (Livingstone & Helsper, 2007, p. 690). In the United States, another study concluded that women are less likely than men to have knowledge of online terminology and features (Hargittai & Hinnant, 2008). Research does provide some indication, however, that the gender gap may be shrinking. This may be due to the trend of Internet usage among men and women—as well as among older/younger and urban/rural users—becoming more similar through music and video streaming, gaming, and social media (van Deursen & van Dijk, 2014).

While research on the digital divide was originally focused around statistics concerned with household computers and Internet connections, researchers and educators alike should now be more concerned with the quality of ICT usage and development of digital skills. Despite falling costs of computers and Internet access, "gaps in home access to digital media are still substantial, and inequalities in technology usage and outcomes are even greater" (Warschauer & Matuchniak, 2010, p. 219). As some strata of society are more fortunate than others with respect to access to and use of ICT, children from lower classes and minority groups are less likely to have access to computers and the Internet than children from the upper class and dominant cultural groups. While these children might have equal access to computers and the Internet at school, in their homes they are at a disadvantage because they are less likely to have parental guidance with respect to the use of ICT. They are, thus, not in a position to make as much use of these revolutionary technologies as their counterparts from other cultural groups and classes. Hargittai and Hinnant (2008) found that students from higher socio-economic backgrounds and with parents who had higher levels of education used the Internet for more "capital-enhancing" activities, meaning that they were "more likely to visit the types of Web sites that may contribute to improving their life chances and from which their human and financial capital may benefit" (p. 617). Hence, if we are to help students overcome the digital divide, the solution will reside in the "differential ability to use new media to critically evaluate information, analyze, and interpret data, attack complex problems, test innovative solutions, manage multifaceted projects, collaborate with others in knowledge production, and communicate effectively to diverse audiences" (Warschauer & Matuchniak, 2010, p. 213).

Another aspect of information technology that contributes to inequality is the content of information and its potentially divisive tendencies. In the 1990s, English was indisputably the most dominant language on the Internet. Although it is still the most commonly used language on the Web, dramatic increases of content in languages representing BRIC countries (Brazil, Russia, India, and China) have decreased the proportion of English-language content to under 50 percent (Vannini & Le Crosnier, 2012). This dimension is most apparent within the context of the educational use of ICT in multicultural societies such as Canada and the United States. Widespread access to computers becomes less meaningful when one considers that most of the information students have access to is culture- and language-specific. This fact assumes more importance in the context of multicultural education. To expect students in a multicultural classroom to make equal use of the information on the World Wide Web is unreasonable. Even if English has jurisdiction over a small proportion of the Internet in the 21st century, only 5 percent of the world's languages have any presence in cyberspace (Vannini & Le Crosnier, 2012). What is more, many search engines, bulletin boards, news groups, webCTs, and computer software applications still require English. ICT can, therefore, be used as a tool to organize or reorganize identity and thought processes.

It is difficult to deny the fact that information technology and the World Wide Web provide a single language of teaching and learning, and that this language has its own cultural context and a socio-economic ideology. As UNESCO General Director Irina Bokova explains, "In principle, the internet is open to all languages of the world, but only when certain conditions are met, and when the necessary human and financial resources are in place. A multilingual internet is essential for nations, communities and individuals to access, share and use information and resources which are critical for sustainable development and for managing innovation and change" (Vannini & Le Crosnier, 2012, p. 14). The usefulness of ICT for education in multicultural societies thus largely depends on critical thinking about the content made available by technology. As Web content cannot and will not change itself for children who belong to ethno-racial groups and lower classes, it is up to teachers and schools to ensure that these children feel comfortable with the technology and learn to use it for their own benefit. Multicultural education, as redefined in this text, has the potential to create learning spaces in which children from different cultures can learn to use ICT without feeling insecure about their identities.

Minority students cannot afford to be left out of the communications revolution. They cannot disadvantage themselves further by not being a part of the Net generation. Education is a lifelong process and members of disadvantaged groups and classes can gain more by getting on the communications highway than by being bystanders. While the older generation of minority groups might not be computer-literate, the new generation has the chance to correct their disadvantaged status by challenging the system in the "master's language" of zeros and ones. The only effective way to challenge the hegemony of the dominant system is to challenge it from within, rather than from the outside. If minority students want the Web to be more inclusive and reflective of their own cultural ethos, they will have to learn to use it first.

In terms of ICT literacy, social media is also important. This is because it is the method of communication with which young people are quickly becoming most familiar. In addition, use of social media offers instant access to democratic participation. Social movements around the world, including the revolutionary wave of non-violent and violent demonstrations and protests in North Africa referred to as the Arab Spring, have utilized social media as part of civil resistance and mobilization strategies.

The challenge for policy-makers is to provide as much access to information technology as possible, especially for people who do not have the resources. While the federal government's "Computers for Schools" initiative (which has distributed refurbished computers to schools, libraries, non-profit organizations, and Aboriginal communities since 1993) is good in this respect, more computer and Internet access in public places, such as cybercafés or kiosks, can go a long way to promoting the use of ICT. The greatest challenge for policy-makers is to derive maximum benefits from the communications revolution while minimizing the harmful ramifications of the digital divide.

Critical Thinking

The "essence of critical thinking is informed skepticism" (Cornbleth, 1985, p. 13). Critical thinking involves questioning rather than accepting given knowledge. Freire (1970) calls the method in which the teacher deposits in students' minds knowledge that is accepted without question the "banking approach." In contrast, in being taught how to think critically, students learn to discover and create knowledge, to think and value for themselves; "the emphasis is on reasoning and valuing processes [rather] than mastery of a specified body of content" (Thornton, 1994). Both process and content are important to the development of critical thinking; however, the focus of teaching must be on the *how* of instruction, rather than *how much* (Jenness, 1990).

Teachers and students must never accept the myth of value-free knowledge as claimed by educational institutions. Not only is there a hierarchy of knowledge (for example, science is often deemed more valuable than the humanities), but curricular content is also political in all subject areas (see Chapter 1). An inquiry orientation is best suited to understanding how knowledge is created and for what purposes; the values and assumptions underlying the text; and the dynamic and changing nature of knowledge. This involves understanding how power is constructed and how it works, how to resist oppressive power (which is contrary to democratic values), and how to gain power. Such empowerment allows students to locate themselves in history and to critically appropriate or seize cultural and political codes from their own and other cultures.

Students must be involved in questioning the knowledge they encounter—that is, in reformulating, reconceptualizing, and reorganizing knowledge so that they are not passive consumers of data. Critical thinking means reconsidering prejudices and labels, structures and hierarchies, through multiple perspectives. It involves the ability to identify and confront bias—for example, why are certain groups excluded from and stereotyped in texts?

An essential aspect of critical thinking is to motivate students to learn on their own and to be creative. Passionate involvement in learning is the incentive for knowing. Students are less motivated when they are asked to memorize knowledge than when they are included in the exploration for knowledge and the search for answers.

Social studies subjects provide multiple opportunities for developing critical thinking. In geography, for example, students can critically examine migration patterns and interdisciplinary concepts such as poverty and food distribution. In the field of history, critical examination involves looking at social history, including the role of other ethnocultural groups in war and in peace, and why women are excluded from positions of power. This leads to a discussion of the role of ethnic groups and women in building Canada. Such an approach to history raises important questions: How is the development of some countries related to the underdevelopment of others? Who benefits from international migration? What are the roots of racism, poverty, and sexism? What are the historical explanations of class structure? What topics are researched in science, and who benefits most from such research? Why was Marie Curie, a Polish woman who was twice awarded the Nobel Prize for her work as a physicist and chemist, not buried in the Pantheon until 1995 (in contrast to male scientists who had received only one Nobel Prize)? Why are so many women prime ministers from non-European countries?

Humanities and the arts are suitable to discussions of different cultures, social themes, and gender issues. Relating different subjects to each other offers many possibilities for learning. For example, math and fine art can be related through a study of design and geometry. Learning to write should be less abstract and more experiential, with critical discussions about what students write. In literature, students not only can read prescribed texts but should also be encouraged to discuss female authors and well-known literature from other cultures. Questions for discussion could include: Why were female authors obliged to write under male names? Why are authors from non-European cultures (in English or French translation) not normally studied? Why does the prescribed curriculum exclude them?

Traditionally, education has been defined in productive terms—the male domain, the public sphere where rationality and analytic values are predominant. The reproductive process (not necessarily confined to biological reproduction, although it does include child rearing), which has traditionally been the female domain, has been related to feeling and emotion and excluded from education. The values associated with the reproductive process—nurturing capacities (Chodorow, 1978) and the ethics of care and concern (Gilligan, 1982)—are of central importance to society. Feminist thinkers have pointed to the need to redefine education in terms of both kinds of societal processes—to merge reason and emotion, self and other.

The more students participate in learning (as opposed to being passive receivers), the more they feel a sense of control over their own community and the wider world, and the more likely it is that they will become active citizens. Decision-making skills involve students making choices in their own lives, in the community, in national politics, and in the international arena. This includes taking action to remove injustice in individual lives and in the school organization—for example, avoiding racist jokes and standing up for the rights of others. Students need to develop self-expression and conflict-resolution skills, but they must also sharpen their thinking about social issues and understand their responsibilities as citizens.

Intercultural Communication

Communication involves the transmission of meaning through verbal and non-verbal systems. While verbal communication usually refers to language, non-verbal messages involve body movements, eye contact, and physical contact. Metalinguistic awareness—the consciousness of how communication is used—is the basis for discerning diversity in messages. Intercultural communication skills that span cultures and nations are imperative in today's world. The complex interactions of gender- and culture-specific variables make intercultural communication a very sensitive issue. For example, touching someone (especially females) when introduced is offensive in some cultures.

Because acceptable methods of communication vary from culture to culture, "intercultural competence is the ability to interpret intentional communications (language, signs, gestures), some unconscious cues (such as body language), and customs in cultural styles different from one's own. The emphasis is on empathy and communication" (Bennett, 1992, p. 183). Empathy, which is the capacity to understand the feelings or point of view of others, is essential for communicating across cultures. The development of intercultural competence is affected by cultural conditioning and jeopardized by a limited experience of cultures. In such cases, one may be unable to perceive different ways of doing things and to understand why others cannot see things one's way.

Intercultural communication goes beyond studying diverse cultures to an understanding of how reality is defined by people's experiences and shaped by their cultural values. The intercultural person is not restricted by particular cognitive, affective, and behavioural characteristics and is able to move beyond the parameters of one culture (Bennett, 1992). More than developing knowledge, intercultural communication fosters empathy so that we can understand how another person thinks and feels. For example, one may learn about war-torn Bosnia but have no understanding of or feeling about what it is to be a victim of war. The curriculum offers many opportunities to develop empathy; role-playing has been found to be an effective method for doing so.

Hanvey (1975) identifies two dimensions in the development of cultural consciousness: perspective consciousness and cross-cultural awareness. Perspective consciousness is the awareness that one's own worldview is not universally shared, that it is dynamic and changing, and that influences are often not apparent. In education, this implies examination of concepts and assumptions about time, space, and causality. For example, the concept of race has changed over time in Canada and now focuses mainly on non-white people, although this was not always so. An example of causality is found in the reasons given for student failure. Explanations of high failure rates may range from low intelligence to parental neglect. Also, assumptions about student performance could range from the belief that Asian students excel in math and science to the notion that girls do poorly in science classes. Cross-cultural awareness is concerned with obvious as well as subtle diversities in cultures and worldviews, and with an understanding of how one's own cultural practices might look from another vantage point.

Communication also involves conflict resolution. When situations of conflict arise, culture- and gender-based differences among peers can present barriers to resolution. Students must learn to understand the cultural dynamics that influence a conflict situation. A three-step mediation process in such a situation involves

1. defining the problem from both points of view;
2. uncovering the assumptions and cultural interpretations of each side; and
3. creating a cultural synergy by recognizing and accepting the legitimacy of different cultural values but working out mutually acceptable alternatives (Adler, 1986).

Cultural synergy means that the total effect of several cultures working together is greater than the sum of their effects when individual cultures act independently: the whole is greater than the sum of its parts. Cultural synergy is multiculturalism rather than cultural pluralism.

PERSONAL AND SOCIAL DEVELOPMENT

Identity

In multicultural societies, the psychological impact of difference—racial, ethnic, gender, and class, among others—is important to the development of identity for both dominant and minority groups. Identity is developed through inter- actions. If the construction of difference based on irrelevant characteristics is to be reversed, and if positive racial/ethnic and gender identities in all children are to be built through the education process, it is necessary to understand and then confront the issues. This is essential for the development of inclusive attitudes in white, male, middle-class children, as well as culturally diverse children. Group identity means sharing attitudes, behaviour, thoughts, and feelings with members of one's own group, but it also means knowing one's relationship to the dominant group (Carter & Goodwin, 1994).

The issue for schools is how to achieve a psychological balance between a child's cultural identity and appreciation of different cultures in one's commun- ity. Appreciation of one's culture is not the same as ethnocentrism, which implies prejudicial attitudes toward other groups that are thought to have inferior status in terms of attitudes, values, and behaviour. The development of a strong individ- ual identity is the foundation for affiliation with the community.

In terms of fostering national identity and unity, multicultural policy must be recognized as central to the concerns of education and society. Ethnic/racial identity should not be seen as producing contradictions in dominant and minor- ity groups; for example, it is possible for a Ukrainian to identify with Ukrainians as a cultural group and, at the same time, consider him/herself a Canadian. Recent nationwide surveys have concluded that the majority of Canadians now perceive multiculturalism as a symbol of Canadian identity—and fewer and fewer Canadians feel that immigration levels are too high (Dewing, 2013).

The presence of multiple identities indicates that political culture and social culture can coexist (see Chapter 1). Political culture is identified with citizenship education, which involves literacy and critical thinking skills (discussed above) as well as moral and democratic values and human rights (discussed below).

In a postmodern world, moreover, social and national political identities are intertwined with a global awareness. Global identity involves the ability to look at the world as an interdependent system and to make decisions based on concern for the survival of our common planet.

Positive Self-Concept

The traditional curriculum has the effect of eroding the self-concept of students who do not represent the norms of the dominant culture. Students are valued or devalued according to their presence and status in the curriculum. For example, when a student finds no reference point in texts with which she can identify or if her ethnocultural group is portrayed in a negative light, she feels devalued. The effect of traditional pedagogical techniques and content on minority students is to make them feel unworthy and "culturally deprived." The maintenance of dominant-group power in school relations and in society is referred to as "symbolic violence" (Bourdieu, 1979).

Minority status in itself does not produce low self-esteem (Ianni, 1989), rather it is the manner in which minority students are treated in society and the educational system through social interactions and the curriculum that is significant. Schools play an important role in constructing a student's self-esteem and self-concept. This is true for all students. An individual's self-concept is based on experiences. For example, experiences of racism may cause minority students to develop a negative self-concept, while at the same time causing dominant-group children to develop an undue sense of self-importance. Nieto (1992) cites data showing that the higher the level of minority presence in the curriculum, the higher the level of positive self-identification and self-esteem. Another good strategy for developing positive self-concept among minority students is to involve their parents in school activities.

Physical and Mental Well-Being

No amount of educational programs and facilities will be of any use to a student who is not in top physical and mental condition. As mentioned in Chapter 1, poverty is especially damaging to students because ill health and unhealthy living conditions put them "at risk" in terms of school achievement and completion. Others develop patterns of resistance, such as alienation, drug use, and violence. Problem children are socially created (Holt, 1982); a large number come from minority racial/ethnic groups and the working class. Students' mental health is related to their experiences of alienation from the content and process of schooling, as well as of institutional and individual racism, sexism, and classism.

Adaptability to Change

"Change is not necessary to life," said Alvin Toffler in *The Third Wave* (1980), "it is life." Traditional education offers few alternatives to the outmoded thinking of the Eurocentric, white, male model. In today's global village, the educational system must change before it can produce students who can make changes in their own lives. Global economic and technological competition makes ability to change imperative as a precondition for survival. Teachers and students together must seek alternative ways of seeing and doing things. Just as the computer has revolutionized our manner of writing, retrieving information, and creating graphics, so we must radically change our way of thinking about knowledge and people.

Empowerment

The basic aim of education is empowerment—the freedom and ability to control one's destiny. Research on "locus of control" (Lefcourt, 1976) indicates that in order to become empowered, people need a sense of control over what they are doing so that they can achieve and act.

Shor and Friere (1987) point out that in an individualistic society empowerment is embodied in a new sense of self and self-worth as individuals become aware of their own rights and capacities. Schools need to develop skills in all students, but minority students, in particular, need to be empowered because they are more likely to develop negative self-concepts. Empowerment can be brought about through decision making, critical thinking, and communication skills, along with a strong identity and positive self-concept.

MORAL AND ETHICAL DEVELOPMENT

Values

Moral values establish the principles that guide choices and form the basis on which to assess one's own and others' lifestyles and worldviews. Values are socially constructed conceptions of the desirable and, as such, involve emotions that influence behaviour. They have no basis in objective facts, although they do maintain certain patterns in society. It is important to remember that not all values are moral and ethical—democratic principles, for example, are also values. Moreover, values are not rules, nor should they be confused with behaviour. Racism is a behaviour, and zero tolerance of racism is a rule or a norm. The values that underlie zero tolerance of racism are justice and respect for others. The rules change with time—for example, until recently, there were no rules against racism or sexism. Rules change because society changes and old rules become obsolete and threaten societal peace and stability.

In a postmodern world, particularly in multicultural societies, it is the responsibility of schools to be involved with moral issues relating to racial, gender, and other forms of discrimination. These moral issues are respect, trust, and compassion.

The implications of values in education are significant. Children have values when they come to school even if they cannot articulate and define them. Teachers must design a process (discussed in Chapter 6) in which students will *develop* a sense of their own values. The task of education is to "provoke the values into consciousness" (Hague, 1993, p. 169).

Each person's set of values cannot be thought of in structural terms, that is, in terms of degree of good and bad. Rather, value judgment is a process that is constantly changing and dynamic and involves relationships and communication. Value clarification is a reflective process in which students are confronted with other peoples' values and have to re-examine their own. It involves two aspects: first, reasoning or cognitive understanding, and second, caring and the development of feeling through understanding. Justice is not a purely cognitive concept—it involves an emotional response.

Hague (1993) reminds us that "moral education is that part of values education that especially teaches people to care" (p. 179); thus, the challenge to the teacher is to let students experience fear and disappointment, hurt and confusion. The 3 c's of caring, concern, and connection are values that can be developed through the curriculum; however, this is a difficult task that requires careful planning and sensitivity on the part of the teacher (see Chapter 5 for details). For example, learning about slavery is one thing, but being able to feel its injustices (not merely reason it out) is imperative in order to prevent something similar from happening again. Goodfield (1981) demonstrates that feeling and connection can also become part of the process of scientific discovery. For instance, in addition to studying the causes and effects of AIDS, students need to learn to care about those who have the disease. Martin (1985) points out that today's world is filled with unconnected, uncaring, and emotionally impoverished people. Co-operation, feeling, and concern must be targeted competencies in any school subject, along with rationality and independent judgment. For example, there will be little hope for future generations if the development of caring and concern are not part of educating today's children about our environment.

Values such as human dignity, equality, justice, and freedom are universal ethical values that form the basis of democratic values. A personal commitment is necessary to pursue these ethical values for society's good. What happens if such a commitment is not made?

An education that neglects the ethical questions of democracy is irresponsible and can be described as miseducation (Martin, 1985). In a democratic society, the notion of cultural citizenship involves the right to be different and the right to belong (Reyes, 1994). This means that differences of gender, class, and ethnicity cannot be used to confer inequality of status. According to the legal definition of the term "citizenship," all citizens must receive full status with no allowance for second-class rank.

Human Rights and Social Justice

Some moral concepts are not specifically based on values but arise from rights and obligations. A common framework of such concepts for the education system is suggested by the principles enshrined in the Universal Declaration of Human Rights, the Canadian Charter of Rights and Freedoms, and provincial human rights codes. The Universal Declaration of Human Rights was adopted by the United Nations General Assembly on December 10, 1948. This document, first drafted by Canadian John Humphrey with the help of Eleanor Roosevelt, is unique in world history because it consists of 30 articles that reaffirm civil and political rights, which have long been regarded as fundamental to human freedom (such as equality before the law), while at the same time proclaiming new rights related to economic, social, and cultural areas now recognized as essential to human dignity. The Canadian Charter of Rights and Freedoms (1982) builds on the Canadian Bill of Rights (1960) and earlier human rights codes of the 1940s. The Charter consists of rights—both individual and collective—and freedoms. Equality rights are set out in Section 15 of the Charter.

Because issues of equal rights for all are a common human concern, they are an aspect of multicultural education. Multiculturalism is not only a commitment to rights, but also to freedoms and responsibilities. Schools must be involved in teaching students what rights and freedoms they have, as well as their responsibilities and obligations. The understanding that rights involve responsibilities is essential and will empower students (see Canadian Human Rights Foundation, 1986).

Comprehension of rights and principles is essential, but not sufficient. This is because knowledge of rights is a cognitive process—it involves understanding. It does not necessarily develop the emotional, feeling, and caring aspects—the affective domain. Further, knowledge of the historical and social context is essential to any meaningful understanding of rights.

While some values and principles are considered universal, others are culture-specific. On the other hand, rights are denied to several groups in the name of cultural relativism. For example, the wearing of religious headgear (hijab) by Muslim girls on soccer teams has become an explosive issue over the last few years. The questions involved in this issue are what the headgear represents, and whether the wearing of headgear makes a difference to participation in the sport. There is debate, particularly in Quebec, over whether this represents a religious symbol or symbolizes female subordination. Clearly, in a democracy where there is religious and sexual equality, the first is acceptable while the second is not. Arguments that focus on standardizing how students look in order to avoid attracting attention to differences are not educationally sound. Students must, and do, get used to differences in appearance.

This, however, does not mean that everything can be allowed in the name of cultural importance. McLeod (1992) points out that human rights codes sometimes clash with cultural practices. For example, female circumcision is a cultural practice that violates universal human rights. In such cases, rights must be upheld even if the practice is endorsed by a particular culture. Azmi, Foster, and Jacobs (2010) point out that practice and expression of human rights in Canada and around the world has become increasingly complex since the turn of the 21st century: "There are times when the claim to a right of one individual or group directly affects the claim to the human rights of another group. Such competing rights claims can be played out in many places, from the classroom to workplaces, to the international stage, wherever individuals or groups actively claim the recognition of rights that may interfere with the access to rights of others" (p. 5).

The public is often made aware of the intersection between competing rights through the media, as in early 2014, when news of a male student's religious accommodation request (to be excused from a group assignment in which he would need to interact with female peers) was denied by his professor at York University. In such cases, the focus should be not on how to address the conflicts of competing rights, but rather on how to reconcile these rights in equitable ways. At the same time, human rights claims are delimited by majoritarian values, meaning that we must sometimes consider what is most just for our society collectively than for specific individuals or groups. When Canadian courts have been asked to resolve similar conflicts between gender and religious rights, religious and privacy rights (sometimes related to sexual orientation), and disability and property rights, the most important deciding factors were related to the unique context of each situation (Azmi et al., 2010).

Averting Extremism

Schools can be alienating to certain students—particularly those who represent minority groups, but also for those who identify with majority groups. This alienation manifests in different ways, but withdrawing from participating in the classroom or being drawn towards activities that valorize the student can lead to dangerous consequences, such as suicide, violence, and extremist actions. These phenomena are increasing at an alarming rate in many countries, most notably the United States.

Given that religious extremism leading to violence and terrorism is an increasing global threat, there is an urgent need to explore the role of education in challenging beliefs before they become radicalized. Currently, such issues are not being addressed within Canada's formal education system. Failure to do so has prevented students from developing the ability to critically analyze extremist views in order to counter radicalization, which can potentially threaten human security and peace. There is an urgent need to explore the role of formal education in challenging religious extremism before beliefs become radicalized. Not all fundamentalists are extremists nor do all extremists engage in terrorism that leads to violence aimed at large numbers of people. Fundamentalism, extremism, radicalization, and terrorism are stages in the development of political, religious, or ideological belief that build on one other. The role of education is to short-circuit the evolution.

Moghaddam (2005) uses the metaphor of a narrowing staircase to describe the path to the extreme act of terrorism, progressing from fundamentalism to extremism to radicalization and finally terrorism. The staircase narrows as it goes higher, as fewer and fewer people are persuaded to climb to the top and commit acts of violence. The terms "fundamentalism" and "extremism," while often used interchangeably, are not the same. Originally, fundamentalists were Protestants in early-20th-century America who sought to preserve the distinctiveness of their religion. The modern connotation of the term is that of intolerance of "the other"; all religions have fundamentalists. Davies (2009) argues that fundamentalists may be predisposed to extreme positions. Since fundamentalism in and of itself need not be a social or a security threat, the problem is the shift to extremism. Extremism then, is the rejection of other perspectives. Radicalism is the stage at which this state of mind leads to a moral hierarchy, in which extreme positions are justified on moral grounds. Except in rare cases, extremism and radicalism do not lead to terrorism and violence, although all terrorists are extremists. Terrorism is most extreme; it is "a tactic.... [It is] the level of anger and hate that drives people to join [terrorists] ranks. It is that anger and hate which must be addressed" (Elworthy & Rifkind, 2006, p. 27).

Since education plays a significant role in the socialization of youth, schools are important sites for exploring and influencing the propensity for violence. Literature indicates that low levels of education and impoverished backgrounds are not characteristics of incarcerated extremists and terrorists. This implies that they spend a long time in school. Unlike the policies of several powerful countries, however, the Canadian government's national security policies fail to mention education's role in the development of resilient communities that would ensure public safety and harmony. Furthermore, educators lack the skills and knowledge necessary to deal with controversial and contentious issues, such as terrorism in the classroom and in the school environment. Canadian teachers have yet to be trained to deal with issues of national security and even to recognize potential terrorist threats among their students, despite the fact that there have been several cases where Canadian youth have been involved in terrorist activities. Research indicates that teachers avoid such topics in class because they are uncomfortable and unsure how to establish ground rules for discussion.

CONCLUSION

A non-racist, non-sexist curriculum would depict reality, showing people as they are, women in both traditional and non-traditional roles, and different visible minorities in both professional and non-professional roles. When children see the world as it is, they must challenge existing inequalities; for example, the fact that most women are restricted to certain occupations and minority ethnic groups still occupy the lower rungs of the societal ladder. In 1965, John Porter described Canadian society as a hierarchy based on ethnicity, class, and gender. In 1990, Lautard and Guppy found no substantial changes to that structure. There is no evidence that this hierarchy has ceased to exist in the 21st century, either. This is why students must learn to talk about and challenge racism, sexism, and class discrimination. They must see the world from diverse perspectives—those of women, different ethnic groups, and working-class students—so that these groups are no longer silenced or considered inadequate and can claim a space, an education, for themselves. The challenge is to recognize the importance of difference and yet cross the borders difference creates, reject stereotypes, and incorporate different experiences.

REVIEW QUESTIONS

1. How is education political?
2. What are the key elements of the redefined multicultural education framework presented in this chapter? What are the goals of this framework?
3. Can knowledge be objective? How is it constructed?
4. Why must students be encouraged to think critically about the definition of "knowledge"?
5. Why is identity development important for students?
6. What does it mean to have "voice" in education? Can teachers "give voice" to students?
7. At what point in a child's schooling should teachers start encouraging them to think critically about what they are learning?
8. What are some implications of critical pedagogy for multicultural education? How can moral or ethical issues pose a challenge to multicultural education?

REFERENCES

Adler, N. (1986). Cultural synergy: Managing the impact of cultural diversity. *The 1986 annual: Developing human resources.* San Diego, CA: University Associates.

Alexander, C. (2007). *Literacy matters: A call for action.* N.p.: TD Bank Financial Group. Retrieved from en.copian.ca/library/research/litmat/litmat.pdf

Apple, M.W., & Au, W. (2009). Politics, theory, and reality in critical pedagogy. In R. Cowen & A.M. Kazamias (Eds.), *International handbook of comparative education* (pp. 991–1007). Amsterdam: Springer.

Aronowitz, S., & Giroux, H. (Eds.). (1985). *Education under siege.* South Hadley, MA: Bergin & Garvey.

Azmi, S., Foster, L., & Jacobs, L. (Eds.) (2010). Balancing competing human rights. *Canadian Diversity* (special issue), *8*(3), 5

Bailey, C. (1991). *Start-up multiculturalism: Integrate the Canadian cultural reality in your classroom.* Markham, ON: Pembroke Publishers.

Bennett, C. (1992). Strengthening multicultural and global perspectives. In K. Moodley (Ed.), *Beyond multicultural education: International perspectives* (pp. 171–200). Calgary: Detselig.

Bourdieu, P. (1979). Symbolic power. *Critique of Anthropology, 4,* 77–85.

Canadian Human Rights Foundation. (1986). *What are human rights: Let's Talk...* Montreal: Canadian Human Rights Foundation.

Carter, R.T., & Goodwin, A.L. (1994). Racial identity and education. In L. Darling-Hammond (Ed.), *Review of research in education* (pp. 291–336). Washington: American Educational Research Association.

Chakrabarti, M. (1990). *The Gandhian dimensions of education.* New Delhi: Daya Publishing.

Chakrabarti, M. (1993). *Tagore and education for social change.* New Delhi: Gian Publishing.

Chodorow, N. (1978). *The reproduction of mothering: Psychoanalysis and the sociology of gender.* Berkeley, CA: University of California Press.

Connell, R.W. (1989). Curriculum politics, hegemony, and strategies of social change. In H.A. Giroux & R.I. Simon (Eds.), *Popular culture: Schooling and everyday life* (pp. 117–130). Toronto: OISE Press.

Cornbleth, C. (1985). Critical thinking and cognitive processes. In W.B. Stanley (Ed.), *Review of research in social studies education: 1976–1983* (pp. 11–63). Washington, DC: National Council for the Social Studies.

Cornelius-White, J.H.D. (2007). Environmental responsibility: A social justice mandate for counseling. *Journal of Border Educational Research, 6*(1), 5–15.

Cummings, J. (1983). *Heritage language education: A literature review.* Toronto: Ontario Ministry of Education.

Cummings, J. (1986). Empowering minority students: A framework for intervention. *Harvard Educational Review, 56*(1), 18–36.

Davies, L. (2009). Educating against extremism: Towards a critical politicisation of young people. *Erziehungswissenschaft/Revue Internationale De L'education, 55,* 183–203.

Dewey, J. (1916). *Democracy and education: An introduction to the philosophy of education.* New York: Macmillan.

Dewing, M. (2013). *Canadian multiculturalism.* Publication no. 2009-20-E. Ottawa: Library of Parliament. Retrieved from www.parl.gc.ca/Content/LOP/ResearchPublications/2009-20-e.pdf

Egbo, B. (2009). *Teaching for diversity in Canadian schools.* Toronto: Pearson.

Elworthy, S., & Rifkind, G. (2006). *Making terrorism history.* London, UK: Rider.

Ervin-Tripp, S.M. (1974). Is second language learning like the first? *TESOL Quarterly, 89*(2), 111–127.

Freire, P. (1970). *Pedagogy of the oppressed.* New York: Seabury Press.

Freire, P., & Macedo, D. (1987). *Literacy: Reading the world and the word.* South Hadley, MA: Bergin and Garvey.

Galczynski, M., Tsagkaraki, V., & Ghosh, R. (2012). Unpacking multiculturalism in the classroom: Using current events to explore the politics of difference. *Canadian Ethnic Studies, 43*(3), 145–164.

Garcia, E., Maez, L., & Gonzalez, G. (1983). Language switching in bilingual children: A national perspective. In E. Garcia (Ed.), *The MexicanAmerican child: Language, cognition and social development* (pp. 56–73). Tempe, AZ: Arizona State University.

Gaskell, J., McLaren, A., & Novogrodsky, M. (1989). *Claiming an education: Feminism and Canadian schools.* Toronto: Our Schools/Our Selves Education Foundation.

Gilligan, C. (1982). *In a different voice.* Cambridge, MA: Harvard University Press.

Giroux, H. (1988). Literacy and the pedagogy of voice and political empowerment. *Educational Theory, 38*(1), 61–75.

Giroux, H. (1991). Postmodernism as border pedagogy: Redefining the boundaries of race and ethnicity. In H.A. Giroux (Ed.), *Postmodernism, feminism, and cultural politics* (pp. 217–256). Albany: State University of New York Press.

Goodfield, J. (1981). *An imagined world.* New York: Harper & Row.

Gramsci, A. (1988). *Gramsci's prison letters: A selection.* London: Swan/Edinburgh Review.

Grant, C.A. & Khurshid, A. (2009). Multicultural education in a global context. In R. Cowen & A.M. Kazamias (Eds.), *International handbook of comparative education* (pp. 403–415). Amsterdam: Springer.

Grant, C.A., & Sleeter, C.E. (2009). *Turning on learning: Five approaches for multicultural teaching plans for race, class, gender, and disability* (5th ed.). Hoboken, NJ: Wiley.

Guilherme, M. (2002). *Critical citizens for an intercultural world: Foreign language education as cultural politics.* Clevedon, UK: Multilingual Matters.

Gutman, A. (1992). Introduction. In A. Gutman (Ed.), *Multiculturalism and the "politics of recognition": An essay by Charles Taylor.* Princeton, NJ: Princeton University Press.

Hague, W.F. (1993). Teaching values in Canadian schools. In L.L. Stewin & S.F.H. McCann (Eds.), *Contemporary educational issues: The Canadian mosaic* (2nd ed.). (pp. 161–180). Toronto: Copp Clark Pitman.

Hanvey, R. (1975). *An attainable global perspective.* New York: Centre for War/Peace Studies.

Harding, S. (1994). Is science multicultural? Challenges, resources, opportunities, uncertainties. In D.T. Goldberg (Ed.), *Multiculturalism* (pp. 334–370). Cambridge, MA: Basil Blackwell.

Hargittai, E., & Hinnant, A. (2008). Digital inequality: Differences in young adults' use of the internet. *Communication Research, 35*(5), 602–621.

Hoffman, D.L., & Novak, T.P. (1998). Bridging the racial divide on the Internet. *Science, 280,* 390–391.

Holt, J.C. (1982). *How children fail.* New York: Delta/Seymour Lawrence.

hooks, b. (1989). *Talking back.* Boston: South End Press.

Howard, A., & Widdowson, F. (2013). Running the gauntlet: Challenging the taboo obstructing Aboriginal education policy development. In F. Widdowson & A. Howard (Eds.), *Approaches to Aboriginal education in Canada: Searching for solutions* (pp. 288–317). Toronto: Brush Education Inc.

Ianni, F.A. (1989). *The search for structure: A report on American youth today.* New York: Free Press.

International Telecommunication Union (ITU). (2013). *The world in 2013: ICT facts and figures.* Geneva, Switzerland: ITU, ICT Data and Statistics Division. Retrieved from http://www.itu.int/en/ITU-D/Statistics/Documents/facts/ICTFactsFigures2013-e.pdf

Jenness, D. (1990). *Making sense of social studies.* New York: Macmillan.

Jones, C., Ramanau, R., Cross, S., & Healing, G. (2010). Net generation or Digital Natives: Is there a distinct new generation entering university? *Computers and Education, 54*(3), 722–732.

Keniston, K. (2004). Introduction: The four digital divides. In K. Keniston & D. Kumar (Eds.), *IT experience in India: Bridging the digital divide* (pp. 11–36). Thousand Oaks, CA: Sage.

Kymlicka, W. (2003). Canadian multiculturalism in historical and comparative perspective: Is Canada unique? *Constitutional Forum, 13*(1), 1–8.

Lambert, W., & Tucker, R. (1972). *Bilingual education of children: The St. Lambert experiment.* Rowley, MA: Newbury House.

Lautard, H., & Guppy, N. (1990). The vertical mosaic revisited: Occupational differentials among Canadian ethnic groups. In P.S. Li (Ed.), *Race and ethnic relations in Canada* (pp. 189–208). Toronto: Oxford University Press.

Lee, E., Menkart, D., & Okazawa-Rey, M. (2006). *Beyond heroes and holidays: A practical guide to K–12 anti-racist, multicultural education and staff development* (3rd ed.). Washington, DC: Teaching for Change.

Lefcourt, H.M. (1976). *Locus of control: Current trends in theory and research.* New York: John Wiley.

Livingstone, S., & Helsper, E. (2007). Gradations in digital inclusion: Children, young people and the digital divide. *New Media and Society, 9*(4), 671–696.

Looker, E.D., & Naylor, T.D. (Eds.). (2010). *Digital diversity: Youth, equity, and information technology.* Waterloo, ON: Wilfrid Laurier Press.

Lynch, J. (1992). *Education for citizenship in a multicultural society.* London: Cassell.

Martin, J.R. (1985). Becoming educated: A journey of alienation or integration. *Journal of Education, 167*(3), 71–84.

McDonald, J.R. (1988). The emergence of the teacher's voice: Implications for the new reform. *Teachers College Record, 89*(4), 471–486.

McIntosh, P. (1990). White privilege and male privilege: A personal account of coming to see correspondences through work in women's studies. In M.S. Kimmel & A.K. Ferbers (Eds.), *Privilege: A reader* (pp. 147–160). Boulder, CO: Westview Press.

McLeod, K.A. (1992). *Multicultural education: The challenges and the future, report 4.* Toronto: Faculty of Education, University of Toronto.

Moghaddam, F.M. (2005). The staircase to terrorism: A psychological exploration. *The American Psychologist, 60*(2), 161–169.

Nieto, S. (1992). *Affirming diversity: The sociopolitical contexts of multicultural education.* New York: Longman.

Nelson, D., Joseph, C.G., & Williams, J. (1993). *Multicultural mathematics.* Oxford: Oxford University Press.

Oblinger, D., & Oblinger, J.L. (Eds.). (2005). *Educating the net generation.* Boulder, CO: Educause.

Porter, J. (1965). *The vertical mosaic: An analysis of social class and poverty in Canada.* Toronto: University of Toronto Press.

Reyes, P. (1994). Cultural citizenship and social responsibility: A call for change in educational administration. *UCEA Review, 35*(1), 11–13.

Schuman, J.H. (1976). Affective factors and the problem of age in second language acquisition. *Language Learning, 25,* 209–239.

Shor, L., & Freire, P. (1987). *A pedagogy for liberation: Dialogues on transforming education.* South Hadley, MA: Bergin & Garvey.

Simon, R. (1987). Empowerment as a pedagogy of possibility. *Language Arts, 64*(4), 370–382.

Tapscott, D. (2008). *Grown up digital: How the net generation is changing your world.* New York: McGraw-Hill.

Thornton, J.S. (1994). Social studies near century's end: Reconsidering patterns of curriculum and instruction. *Review of Research in Education, 20,* 223–254.

Toffler, A. (1980). *The third wave.* New York: Morrow.

van Deursen, A.J., & van Dijk, J.A. (2014). The digital divide shifts to differences in usage. *New Media and Society, 16*(3), 507–526.

Vannini, L., & Le Crosnier, H. (Eds.) (2012). *Net.lang: Towards the multilingual cyberspace.* Caen, France: C&F Éditions. Retrieved from http://net-lang.net//externDisplayer/displayExtern/_path_/netlang_EN_pdfedition.pdf

Verma, G.K., & Pumfrey, P.D. (Eds.). (1993). *Cultural diversity and the curriculum: Cross-curricular themes and dimensions in secondary schools* (Vol. 2). London: Falmer Press.

Verma, G.K., & Pumfrey, P.D. (Eds.). (1994). *Cultural diversity and the curriculum: Cross-curricular themes and dimensions in primary schools* (Vol. 4). London: Falmer Press.

Warschauer, M., & Matuchniak, T. (2010). New technology and digital worlds: Analyzing evidence of equity in access, use, and outcomes. *Review of Research in Education, 34,* 179–225.

Welch, S. (1991). An ethic of solidarity and difference. In H.A. Giroux (Ed.), *Postmodernism, feminism, and cultural politics* (pp. 83–99). Albany: State University Press of New York.

Young, R.M. (1987). Racist society, racist science. In D. Gill and L. Levidow (Eds.), *Anti-racist science teaching* (pp. 16–42). London: Free Association Books.

ACTIVITY 3
"It All Keeps Adding Up": Enumerating the Benefits of Privilege

Purpose
- Explore the relationships between cultural factors perceived as societal differences
- Observe the inverse relationship between the disadvantages of subordinate groups and the privileges of dominant groups
- Help students understand how social norms create interlocking hierarchies that often serve as barriers to educational and life opportunities
- Develop empathy in students by encouraging them to reflect over their own and others' positionality in terms of these hierarchies

Description
This activity is designed to complement "White Privilege: Unpacking the Invisible Knapsack," (1990), an excerpt from Peggy McIntosh's landmark essay "White Privilege and Male Privilege." The full text of the article can usually be accessed through a simple Web search, and permission for reproduction can be obtained from the Wellesley Centers for Women (www. wcwonline.org). Students should be familiar with McIntosh's work prior to engaging in this extension activity.

Informed by a feminist perspective, in her essay McIntosh explores how society is structured in a way that disproportionally benefits men. Her reflection on positionality and power dynamics led her to the realization that analogous power structures exist in terms of skin colour as well, such that unfair societal advantages are afforded to white people (and typically reinforced through education). To illuminate her point, McIntosh recounted the daily effects of her own white privilege by brainstorming a list of 50 everyday interactions and situations in which her whiteness entitled her to special treatment, in contrast to the experiences of individuals who represented racial minorities.

During this activity, ask your students to use McIntosh's list as a model and similarly delineate the daily effects of another type of societal privilege. Students should consider privilege in terms of a politicized difference other than race: gender, class, sexual orientation, religion, (dis)ability, or any cultural component of someone's identity that deals with relationships of power. Moreover, students will need to identify what societal norm is assumed in terms of their selected factor and how privilege is granted to those who belong to the dominant group. If working individually, students might be asked to list 10 daily effects; if working collaboratively, each small group might be asked to draft a list as long as McIntosh's—or perhaps challenged to come up with as many items as possible within a designated time period. Taken together, the students' lists will exemplify McIntosh's notion of interlocking hierarchies within our society, and the instructor may lead a class discussion on how various privileges (e.g., male, heterosexual, middle-class, and able-bodied privilege) may have complementary or contradictory effects.

You may also ask your students to write or orally present a brief introduction to explain their perspective on the topic selected. Students may identify themselves as part of the dominant group (and think about the privileges they have) or as part of a minority group (and think about the privileges they do not have, in contrast to the dominant group). For more focused class discussion, you can restrict the parameters of the activity to highlight a specific context, such as a school setting.

Curricular Connections

Language Arts: As part of a poetry unit, make allusions to existing works that explore themes of identity and difference; allow students to draw from their own lists in order to inspire lines of original poetry.

Drama: Prompt students to take an existing fairy tale or other well-known work and recast the main character in a way that exposes him or her to the daily effects of difference.

Mathematics: Design a finance lesson that highlights class issues by requiring students to role play and budget for privileged experiences such as buying goods, planning a vacation, or paying for university studies.

Physical Education: Modify the activity's context to address competition between professional or national teams within a particular sport; discuss the concept of fair play and draw connections between economic factors and a team's likelihood of winning.

Chapter 4

THE SCHOOL ENVIRONMENT

Bimla, a Grade 5 student in Mr. Zaremba's class, feels confused these days. This confusion is a result of the discrepancy between what she is being taught by her mother at home and what she is learning at school. Bimla has always loved going to school, but now she feels isolated. Most of the ideas discussed in the class either clash with what her mother and grandmothers tell her or are, at best, irrelevant. Nobody at school discusses issues that are raised at home. This affects Bimla in two ways. When everybody is giving their opinion in the class she has nothing to contribute, as certain topics are never discussed at her home and she cannot identify with them. When her family is discussing "important stuff," she again feels alienated because these things seldom come up at school. On top of all this, Bimla faces a third source of confusion: the media. Most of the notions about being cool that are shown on television are not accepted either by her school or her family. Bimla is beginning to think that life is tough, and maybe it is all right if she does not do so well at school. After all, her mother expects her to get married and look after her husband as soon as she finishes high school, and at school she is just another "Indian" girl.

- What kinds of messages do you think Bimla picks up from the hidden curriculum of her school?
- In what ways do you think a teacher might be able to ameliorate some of the effects of culture clash?
- To what extent does culture affect our educational and life opportunities?

INTRODUCTION

Schools contribute to students' educational difficulties in both subtle and blatant ways through the total school environment. This realization has focused attention beyond curriculum content and method to a wide range of issues in the culture of the school. A redefined multicultural education suggests potentially significant changes in the total school environment.

This chapter deals with the context of the school and the many components involved in a child's school experience. The context is important because a student's education is not limited to the formal school curriculum. The manner in which the environment affects the student has implications for academic achievement and the quality of educational experience, as well as the development of self-concept and identity.

The school culture also includes the co-operation and involvement of parents. In monocultural education systems, linguistic minority parents tend to be excluded from participating in their children's education. In a truly multicultural education framework, parents are partners with teachers and school administrators.

Subtle and complex issues are involved in change. As an organization, the school is a system of shared experiences whose meanings are created by people. When any group or groups do not share these meanings, the system develops problems. All school personnel—administrators, teachers, and support staff— are involved in solving problems and reducing conflicts when they arise. The present education of administrators and teachers emphasizes functionality and prevention of conflicts—in other words, it trains them in the management of the system. Multicultural education, on the other hand, demands that administrators (in particular) be leaders rather than merely managers, and that they change organizational structure and culture, rather than merely manage it. Schools should be organized for the needs of children, not for the benefit of educational administrators. This change from a management style to a leadership style demands an emancipatory leadership that incorporates all of the actors in the education system and makes them part of a proactive decision-making process.

Change is directed by policy, which is made by bureaucrats and administrators. Policies are formal means of implementing and directing change in society and its institutions. As such, policy-making is highly political. In Canada, both federal and provincial government policies, along with those of school boards, determine goals and imprint a vision of society on education. These system-level goals tend to focus on the economic needs of society without attention to how students in the school system are ultimately streamed into "male" and "female" fields of study, or professional and vocational areas. Ideally, these goals should also be based on the values of human dignity, justice, and social responsibility.

Systemic policies should support equity programs and strict controls for discrimination, but work to internalize values of justice and equality should be done at the local level. It is policies formed at the institutional or school administration level that will determine the school environment and the relationships that form the basis for success or failure.

SCHOOL CULTURE

Ethnographic research in many Canadian schools reveals that students who are different in one or more ways from the dominant group experience a "chilly climate" in school. This hostile climate results when some students are excluded from the content and method of learning, as well as from the culture of the school through messages that they are unimportant and have second-class status. A diverse school population does not make a school multicultural; in fact, the environment could very well be monocultural. Several studies (Gaskell, McLaren, & Novogrodsky, 1989; Giles, 1977; Kozol, 1991) have pointed to the structure and environment of the school, rather than student differences, as the cause of learning problems. The subjective experiences of students are determined by the objective organization of schools. When student experiences are negative, student achievement is affected. The problem of failure is not as much in the child as it is in the values, ethics, and vision of the school environment (Giroux, 1992; Reyes, 1994). Educators are morally responsible for both the successes and the failures of their students.

Many school cultures put the blame on students of difference, which places a burden on them to change. A redefined multicultural education is aimed at integrating diversity into the organization by seeing diversity as an asset, rather than a problem. It involves a broader framework in terms of not only content, but also structure and culture.

The Hidden Curriculum

The most enduring lessons learned in school spring from the subtle interactions between student and teacher, student and student, and student and administration. The hidden curriculum consists of the implicit messages transmitted by the teaching process and the school environment. This concept draws on Dewey's idea of "collateral learning," which suggests that we develop certain attitudes as an indirect by-product of the learning process. The formal curriculum includes messages embedded in the written text, illustrations, and media; the physical setting through arrangements of lighting and space, such as seating; and school culture through the organization of student groups, language use, time, roles and relations, and policies and procedures. These messages are not only hidden from students, but also remain invisible to others involved in education.

Implicit meanings are often more powerful in effect than the official agenda. While conservative theorists see the hidden curriculum as necessary to maintaining the social order, radical theorists see it as reproducing relations of exploitation and inequality. Critical pedagogy views the ideological messages as shaping and forming the content of knowledge. These messages are linked to identity development, self-concept, and dignity, and to ideas of social justice and what is right. This is what simultaneously affirms the dominant-group student while devaluing and disparaging students who are different from the dominant group. The messages teach students their position in the social hierarchy, what kind of person is valued, what type of learning is important, what type of work is socially rewarded, who has authority, and what matters and what does not. The exclusion of some kinds of knowledge conveys a subtle message of preference, perpetuating the structural inequality of different groups while validating the cultural superiority of the dominant group. Minority students may not be able to pick up the implicit skills, such as behaviour patterns, necessary for school success. Subtle messages that give meaning to differences based on gender, race/ethnicity, and class make school life complex and contradictory for children from other groups. Students tend to resist a worldview that devalues them. It is essential for teachers to have strong associations with parents to negate the effects of the hidden curriculum. A redefined multicultural education focuses on altering the messages of the hidden curriculum to validate identity and self-concept in all students.

Culture Clash

One cause of alienation and the failure of culturally diverse students is the experience of discontinuity that results from the clash between the home culture and the dominant-group school culture. Policy initiatives that have been developed to reconcile this fundamental tension between home and school deal with developing strong links with parents and community members through organizations, volunteer work, and involvement in school and classroom activities. Parents of minority ethnic/racial and working-class children tend to be excluded from the educational experiences of their children due to culturally embedded perceptions of and communication difficulties with school administration and teachers. To bridge the communication gap between the school and parents, it is essential to establish trusting relations and a shared responsibility to pursue a common vision to reinforce academic, behavioural, and social objectives. If parents are reluctant to come to the school, parent-teacher meetings could be held elsewhere. Attention should be paid to the need for cultural and linguistic translators for some, and the assistance of community leaders should be sought. Fullan (1992) suggests four different forms of parental involvement: at school, at home, through school governance, and through community service.

In all policies, support from the top is critical to success. Policies must be regularly reviewed and assessed for effectiveness. But inclusivity encompasses more than the structural changes discussed above. It includes school culture—the informal patterns of ideas and actions that give meaning to and represent the dominant worldview.

The high educational achievement of some Asian groups in the United States and Canada has caused speculation regarding minority groups and school success. Cultural adaptation theories focus on the values, beliefs, and behaviours of certain groups to explain their success in North America. Based on the motivational studies of McClelland (1961), a variety of factors, such as cultural identities and community ties and attitudes, have been suggested as contributing to "achievement orientation." Ogbu (1978) explains the success of some groups by pointing to the positive relationship between ethnic identity and education, supported by a strong home background and a family system that is able to produce and enforce a single-minded pursuit of education as an explanation for success. However, Ogbu (1992) recognizes that students from these groups initially experience difficulties in interpersonal relations due to differences in language, cultural assumptions, behaviour patterns, and cognitive styles. Lewis's (1961) concept of the "culture of poverty" suggests, however, that cultural endowments are determined and perpetuated by the structure of one's environment—that is, cultural values and achievement orientations often reflect the consequences of social inequality more than its causes.

Discipline

Discipline problems arise from student resistance to aspects of school. This is not a result of student inadequacy, but of alienation in an inhospitable environment that fails to meet their needs. The symbolic violence of schools (Bourdieu & Passeron, 1977), which results from an environment of rules, tests, and punishment based on manipulation and subordination, causes a "performance strike" (Shor & Freire, 1987, p. 125). This takes the form of passivity and rebellion: refusing to perform and do homework, using bad language, missing classes, dropping out literally or figuratively (passivity), using drugs and alcohol, and engaging in crime. Passivity is not a natural condition of childhood; it is provoked, and can produce aggression. Oppositional identities also cause performance strikes. Oppositional identities are negative self-concepts that result from competing pressure from peer groups that disapprove of behaviours seen to be in conflict with group identity. The aspiration to be academically successful, for example, is often in conflict with ethnic identity (for example, "acting white"), which is influenced by images and messages in the school curriculum and culture, and teacher as well as peer expectations. This results in behaviour that is disruptive to achievement.

Classrooms that promote the active involvement of all students are democratic in nature. A liberating education and democratic classroom do not mean non-interference, a *laissez-allez* (let go) attitude, or lack of teacher authority; it does, however, mean establishing the teacher as a person of integrity, intellect, and authority, as "freedom needs authority to become free" (Freire, in Shor & Freire, 1987, p. 91), but not an authoritarian. The challenge is to establish a delicate balance between freedom and control, to poise authority with being laissez-faire, to be democratic but responsible, and to be directive of the process but not of students.

It is absolutely necessary to create a framework of clear, precise rules of behaviour so that students can make intelligent choices within the rules, accept responsibility for their own actions, shape their own destiny, and care for others. The teacher has more experience making judgments, is more developed intellectually, and has more power. To make liberatory education possible, it is necessary to acknowledge that teachers and students are in different "locations." While this does not imply the need to control the students, overlooking discipline problems and keeping silent has no value and can have disastrous consequences.

Teachers can face student antagonism and manipulation (although the root of the problem often lies elsewhere). Establishing direct eye contact may help, but opening lines of communication with the student is essential. Authority must be exercised when needed and be perceived by students as fair and necessary. Freedom and authority go together.

Banks (1981) points out that some degree of conflict is inevitable in the classroom and that the probability of conflict is greater in multicultural ones. Since conflict cannot be avoided, teachers should develop the knowledge and skills needed to identify points of potential conflict, minimize them, and channel them toward constructive purposes rather than let them disrupt teaching and learning. For example, brighter students who become disruptive because they are bored can be channelled into tutoring their peers. Banks identifies three types of conflict: (1) procedural conflicts, which are disagreements over process (that is, over how things should be done); (2) substantive conflicts, which arise from differing goals (what should be done and why); and (3) interpersonal conflicts, in which values, attitudes, and beliefs clash (differences in behaviour and communication styles). All three types, especially the third, may be influenced by cultural differences. In order to mediate, teachers need to understand the socialization of students and how it may be at variance with the school culture.

Bullying and Cyberbullying

Historically speaking, bullying behaviours, whether they occur in or outside of school, have been overlooked or ignored because they were considered part of normal child development. Both individual factors, such as race and gender, and school-level factors, such as classroom management and disciplinary policy, influence when and where bullying occurs—as well as to whom and by whom.

Racial bullying and victimization have been found to be more strongly related to individual factors than to school-level factors, though instances of racial bullying were lower in schools with higher teacher diversity (Larochette, Murphy, and Craig, 2010). Yet a focus on the individuals involved in bullying situations can distract from larger issues related to the culture and climate of the school (Elias & Zins, 2003). After a meta-analysis of school bullying intervention programs, Merrill, Gueldner, Ross, and Isava (2008) concluded that such programs are more likely to alter knowledge, attitudes, and self-perceptions than to put an end to actual bullying behaviour.

Bullying in all its forms must be recognized as a social justice issue. This is because "youths involved in bullying—whether perpetrating, witnessing, or being victimized—face inequitable access to school-based resources and opportunities aimed at academic growth and empowerment" (Polanin & Vera, 2013, p. 303). Multicultural educators are an essential part of bullying prevention and intervention because they encourage students to become more tolerant and accepting of those who are seen as different. For instance, students who are bullied because of their (perceived) sexual orientation may be offered interventions that focus on providing protection and eliminating bullying behaviour. But we must realize that "dominant understanding of LGBTQ students' school experiences has been shaped by discourses that reduce 'the problem' to bullies [alone].… Within this framework, cultural privileging of heterosexuality and gender normativity goes unquestioned, LGBTQ marginalization is reproduced and re-entrenched in new ways, and schools avoid responsibility for complicity in LGBTQ harassment" (Payne & Smith, 2013, p. 1).

If teacher education programs are to better prepare teachers to manage bullying, they need to focus on helping pre-service teacher candidates develop knowledge and skills relevant to dealing with issues at both individual and system-wide levels. Teachers need to gain confidence and courage in order to deal with bullying effectively: "Teachers need reassurances from administrators that they are expected to identify and manage bullying, impose specific consequences, and seek and obtain support from administrators" (Beran, 2006, p. 125). In examining teachers' responses to incidents of bullying, Ellis and Shute (2007) observed that teachers' moral orientation (as in caring-oriented versus justice-oriented) impacted whether their reactions were more focused on sanctioning school rules or on actual problem solving. And while the seriousness of the incident was the most important factor in a teacher's response, how seriously the teacher interpreted the bullying behaviour was not always consistent with how seriously it affected the targeted student.

While many parents set rules for how their children are permitted to use the Internet, research shows that they are largely unaware of the harassment their children suffered or initiated through virtual mediums (Dehue, Bolman, & Völlink, 2008). Especially in comparison to physical bullying, cyberbullying tends to be an individualistic and anonymous behaviour. In fact, victims of cyberbullying do not typically report incidents to adults (though girls are more likely to do so than boys) (Li, 2006). Unsurprisingly, it is those individuals who are perceived as different that are most vulnerable to bullying and cyberbullying. For example, Didden and colleagues (2009) confirmed the widespread prevalence of cyberbullying among students with intellectual and developmental disabilities in special education programs.

Stover (2006) explains that even though cyberbullying takes place virtually, it is still an extension of classic in-school bullying and must be addressed as a school violence issue. Students, teachers, and school officials have found themselves the targets of cyberbullying, and policy-makers are currently racing to establish a clear legal framework to combat its many forms—whether on or off school grounds, on computers or mobile phones, on blogs or social media (Shariff, 2009). It is important to realize that the advent of social media has made cyberbullying incredibly easy for students to engage in. It cannot be dismissed as trivial, even if it simply consists of text messages sent by mobile phone, posts made on Facebook, or tweets distributed via Twitter. A profound example of cyberbullying occurred in January 2014, when a University of Illinois chancellor received a series of racist and misogynistic tweets from students after deciding not to issue a campus-wide snow day. Cyberbullying prevention programs need to incorporate awareness of these varied technological formats in order to simulate more authentic virtual environments that might better engage students in discussion on the topic and help schools address harassment problems (Wright, Burnham, Inman, & Ogorchock, 2009).

Youth suicides in response to cyberbullying have received media attention throughout Canada and the United States. One notable example is that of 15-year-old Amanda Todd, who, prior to her death in October 2012, posted a video on YouTube detailing her experiences of being blackmailed, bullied, and physically assaulted. Her video went viral soon after and sparked efforts to criminalize cyberbullying in British Columbia. In Nova Scotia, the suicide of 17-year-old Rehtaeh Parsons in 2013, stemming from the online distribution of photos allegedly depicting her gang rape by four teenage boys, led to the enactment of a provincial law allowing victims of cyberbullying to sue their perpetrators. But cyberbullying is not limited to high school students: the suicides of Mitchell Wilson, an 11-year-old Ontario boy who suffered from muscular dystrophy and took his life after being physically attacked by a schoolmate, and Tyler Clementi, a Rutgers University freshman who jumped off a bridge after his dorm roommate used a webcam to record him kissing another man, exemplify that students at all levels of education can be targeted. These high-profile cases reaffirm the message that cyberbullying is serious business, with very serious consequences.

As cases of cyberbullying have become well documented in educational research in Canada and around the world, we have learned that culture is an important factor in how different students respond to adult intervention (Li, 2008). For instance, a study comparing cyber-aggression among students found that while higher levels of parental control were linked with levels of cyber-aggression among East Asian students, these students were more likely to engage in proactive cyber-aggression than their peers of European descent, who were more likely to exhibit such behaviour reactively (Shapka & Law, 2013). Similarly, differences between boys and girls have been documented in relation to the effect of bullying on their academic achievement (Konishi, Hymel, Zumbo, & Li, 2010), their motivations for engaging in bullying behaviour and their approaches to cyber-agression (Li, 2006; Shapka & Law, 2013), and their tendencies toward depression or suicide (Bauman, Toomey, & Walker, 2013). Culturally responsive prevention and intervention programs need to address all of these aspects.

SCHOOL STRUCTURE

Restructuring schools for inclusion requires more than allocating resources: it means changing roles and relations from an ethnocentric to a multicultural framework. The following are some ideas for a redefined multicultural school environment.

Administrative Leadership

Leadership implies responsibility, and administrators have a social responsibility to help people connect. Individual school policies should focus on exposing everyone associated with the school to the diversity of perspectives and values, through both the curriculum and school activities. Administrators themselves need to appraise their assumptions and learn to communicate through formal and informal, and verbal and non-verbal means in multicultural settings. Educational leaders must offer school actors—administrators, teachers, and students—multicultural literacy that will allow them to communicate across the borders created by differences in culture, experience, and history (Greene, 1988). They must develop the ability to understand interrelationships and the capacity for respect. They must be evaluated for innovation, proactive leadership, and interpersonal interaction with staff, students, and parents. For example, requests for parental involvement in the school can be proactively aimed at averting discipline problems rather than waiting for such problems to arise and reacting to them after the fact.

Multicultural educators and administrators who represent an ideology of social change and student liberation must go beyond simply managing programs and services to create spaces for trust and to nurture the development of meaningful, participatory, and equitable relationships (Berryman, SooHoo, & Waller, 2010). Madsen and Mabokela (2005) identify the following principles of administrative leadership for creating inclusive schools: understanding and challenging racial boundaries; creating an organizational identity in which the school's image is perceived as inclusive; developing a relationship identity that promotes positive exchanges among followers and constituencies; and developing an adaptive organizational structure to address inter-group differences. As Shields states, "The call is not for educational leaders to become politicians, social workers, humanitarians, or counselors—although we sometimes find ourselves engaged in an element of each of these. The call is for us to take seriously the fact that the playing field is still inequitable, the achievement gaps still unacceptable, the barriers for children from non-mainstream homes often untenable" (2013, p. 127).

Yet structural change typically encounters resistance. There are many reasons for resistance, but underlying them all is the fear of loss: loss of familiarity, loss of turf (power, dominance, organizational influence, and even language), loss of familiar structure (in reward system and accountability), loss of future (success no longer guaranteed by being a white male), loss of meaning (reversal of existing principles), and loss of control. The most basic fear of diversity, loss of control, involves loss of power to manipulate the world (Gardenswartz & Rowe, 1993). In addition, diversity in education is often not a priority because of the belief in a system that appears egalitarian through apparently objective testing. School administration should expect a level of opposition to any change from people involved in education because of the above-mentioned "fears." Getting total environment support through involvement in decision making is all the more necessary.

A change-oriented administration needs to confront participant fears in order to prevent disruptive behaviour from staff, such as absenteeism, anger, complaints, negative attitudes, minimal communication, and declines in performance. Policies must include long-term effort—time, energy, and emotional commitment to change—rather than just the allocation of financial resources. In-service training of teachers, counsellors, librarians, and other staff is imperative.

Staff Diversity

Both systemic and institutional policy must actively promote the recruitment and retention of multicultural staff. This is not merely an issue of under-representation but involves the need to include minority perspectives (female, racial/ethnic, working-class) in administration, teaching, counselling, libraries, and support functions. It is important to consider how diversity of staff affects various factors in the interpersonal relationships of teachers and students. The dimensions of the student-teacher relationship are undoubtedly affected by who the teacher is—and different students within the same classroom may view the teacher differently. For instance, one study found that trust (for the teacher) had a positive effect on the achievement of Native American high school students, even though it did not make a difference for European American students (Fryberg, Covarrubias, & Burack, 2013).

It is not surprising that university-based teacher education programs are not always successful in preparing pre-service teachers for multicultural education. In terms of diversity, teacher education programs do not make enough of an effort to recruit all kinds of teacher candidates, nor do they make enough of an effort to ensure that these candidates are taught by diverse lecturers and instructors. This is fundamentally problematic because "if colleges of education are not able to recruit and retain faculty of color, how will they be able to provide an example of cultural diversity for their teacher education students?" (Irvine, 2003, p. 24). This logic also applies to representations of diversity among staff in elementary and secondary schools, as well as in kindergartens and preschools. When recruiting and promoting staff, administrators should seek out diverse candidates—in terms of race/ethnicity, gender, sexual orientation, (dis)ability, and other cultural factors—so that the school can benefit from the inclusion of many unique and compelling worldviews.

Counselling

School guidance counsellors have a special significance for students of minority groups because it is they who channel the students into specific areas of study, often because parents are unaware of the opportunities and possibilities that are available. The subjects students take ultimately define their life chances in a segregated labour market organized on the basis of class, gender, and ethnicity. Separating students into "male" and "female" fields of study, or professional and non-professional areas, perpetuates the white male model of excellence and devalues others. It also means that various subject areas are given different value based on their suitability for entry into higher-status and higher-paying jobs. Minority students (defined thus by class, race, or gender) must be encouraged to give sufficient thought to their futures in a realistic manner, but they must also be able to dream.

Guidance counsellors must be committed to anti-racist, anti-sexist education;

must recognize students' diversity of values and traditions, abilities, and possibilities; and must not be limited by stereotyped expectations. Cross-cultural knowledge is imperative to the development of counselling, assessment, and placement skills. Subtle systemic and institutionalized racism and sexism must be studied to avoid their unintentional effects. Obvious examples include steering female students toward highly gendered fields of study (which may limit their opportunities), or not informing minority and working-class students about universities in other cities. Counsellors must make specific efforts to counter the harmful effects of societal and school practices.

POLICY AND EQUITY

Equity policy is important to starting off a process of justice and fairness. A zero tolerance policy on harassment is essential to eliminating racial, ethnic, or sexual slurs, jokes, graffiti, and conflicts. The consequences of these negative actions must be understood by all. For instance, zero tolerance would mean that racial jokes would not be tolerated under any circumstances, and would be dealt with severely. Formal mechanisms for complaints—for example, telephone numbers for emergency situations—must be provided. There must be an institutional will to promptly and firmly address issues of racism and sexism. An inclusive-language policy (non-sexist, non-racist) is very important because of the relationship of language to identity and power. For example, the use of male pronouns and words to represent the universal norm excludes female students. An inclusive-language policy would use, for example, "humans" instead of "mankind," "human resources" rather than "manpower," and so on.

Policy-makers must keep in mind, however, that greater equity does not imply a reduction of standards. It is exactly the opposite: equity means commitment to educational excellence. According to Ghosh, "Standards are of utmost importance, but definitions of excellence must represent plurality because the norms in use come out of the particular experiences of those who have the power to define standards and make the rules and are not inclusive" (2012, p. 353).

Multicultural School Climate

A multicultural school climate creates a culture of diversity. It needs to pervade every aspect of the school through a language and attitude of inclusion. It has the following features:

- Recognition of the values and characteristics of a diverse student and staff population, where differences are irrelevant to inclusion.

- A student-centred learning atmosphere that emphasizes information sharing, the questioning of social inequality, and an understanding of discrimination and the ability and will to fight it.
- A co-operative spirit in which school, classroom, and playground spaces and activities are not dominated by students belonging to the majority group, and where co-operative relations between people of diverse backgrounds are encouraged.
- Democratic practice through an inclusive, consultative process and the recognition that individual talents are enhanced, not reduced, by the abilities of others.
- A physical setting that reflects diversity: bulletin boards in classrooms, the library, and the cafeteria could display information in different languages and highlight achievements of exceptional students; a library with a diverse range of magazines and books; universal access to resources such as gym, pool, and playgrounds, regardless of ability; co-operative decisions about how resources are shared; the use of peer tutoring/coaching.
- Extracurricular activities that stress equal access and treatment; clubs, teams, activities, trips, and speakers that reflect a diverse, open-door policy in recruitment and membership; cultural sensitivity in scheduling events (for example, organizing school socials and dances in afternoons in response to some groups that do not allow girls to stay out late at night); inviting parents on field trips.
- Strong, informal parent and community involvement through school events, as speakers and tutors in daycare and language classes. When parents are viewed as partners in the learning process, the strength of the family in minority groups is recognized and the student is validated, rather than marginalized. Schools cannot, and should not, exist in isolation. Studies show that student achievement in reading programs rises significantly with parental involvement.

Sensitivity to Cultural Differences

School administration needs to be sensitive to different customs and languages, allowing for variety in dress, music, and art. Schools should not be limited to the Judeo-Christian calendar, but should acknowledge other religious holidays. School cafeteria menus should, as a matter of policy, offer foods from different parts of the world and demonstrate sensitivity to religious and special needs—for example, a choice of fish and meats other than pork and beef, since Muslim and Jewish students may not eat pork and Hindu students may not eat beef. Some students are vegetarian for religious reasons or by preference. Others may have special medical needs.

Meeting Ability and Language Needs

While there have been tremendous changes in attitude toward intellectually and physically challenged students, school policies based on organizational needs rather than on the needs of students have not disappeared altogether. Minority students are sometimes put in special education classes when they cannot keep up with the rest of the class due to lack of language of instruction, and this is explained as student failure. The segregation of students in special education classes has lifetime consequences for students: not only are they likely to be permanently branded as underachievers, but that stigma negatively affects their self-concept and identity, which, in turn, may be expressed through socially unacceptable behaviour. Current evaluation procedures tend to test what students do not know rather than what they do know.

Second-language teaching is also an important part of multicultural education. Language provides the context in which students relate to themselves, to others, and to socio-cultural and educational environments. Because education is a political act, it is not surprising that, as in the Canadian political system, language has been central to the Canadian educational system. This has been especially so in Quebec.

In Canada, there are two official national languages, and either French or English is the first language of large numbers of Canadians. Many immigrants learn one of these languages as their second language. Since World War II, immigrants with languages other than English or French have made up a sizable proportion of Canada's population. While the term "bilingual" in Canada means the ability to speak in Canada's two official languages, many immigrants are, in fact, already bilingual in the sense that they speak two languages; however, it is their ability to speak one or both of Canada's two official languages that will determine their success in Canadian society. Language is a tool of empowerment and thus the need for second-language education in the overall context of multicultural education becomes paramount.

With the shift in academic and policy focus from assimilation to multiculturalism and the rise of Quebec nationalism, immersion became a viable strategy for second-language teaching. In 1965, a French immersion program was launched on an experimental basis in Quebec. This program aimed at improved French instruction in English schools. The concept of immersion schooling is based on the principle that the second language can best be learned if the student is placed in an environment where only that language is spoken. In other words, languages are best learned in contexts where the person is socially stimulated to acquire the language and is exposed to it in its natural form (Lambert, 1990).

In immersion classes, English-speaking children who have no French language experience in their homes, and little if any in their communities, enter public school kindergarten or Grade 1 classes that are conducted by a monolingual French-speaking teacher. This "early immersion" means that students are taught exclusively in French through Grade 2 and English is introduced only in Grade 2 or 3 in the form of a language arts program for one period a day. By Grade 4, some subjects are taught in English by an English-speaking teacher. By the time students are in Grades 5 and 6, about 60 percent of instruction is in English (Lambert, 1990).

The primary focus of immersion education is subject matter, and learning the language is incidental. The teachers are not language experts but subject specialists. It is argued that placing children in a particular language environment opens their minds to an otherwise foreign and possibly threatening outgroup. They not only learn the other language well, but they also learn to appreciate the other cultural group. Children with immersion experience realize that "effective and peaceful coexistence calls for something even more important—opportunities for both ethnic groups of young people to interact socially on an equitable basis. This is a very sophisticated insight that most adults never attain" (Lambert, 1990).

Immersion programs have been hailed as a success all over Canada as well as in the United States. According to one estimate, in Quebec, enrolment in these programs jumped from 37,835 in 1977–78 to 317,351 in 1997–98 (Rebuffot, 2000, p. 2). Evaluations of immersion programs show positive academic and linguistic outcomes. It has been noted, for example, that French-language proficiency of students enrolled in immersion programs improves considerably.

A second dimension of second-language education is teaching English or French to the children of visible minorities from different ethnic and racial groups, collectively called allophones. Dominant languages are often perceived by minorities as potential threats to their ethnic identity, thus providing a negative motivation to learn second languages. Apart from its implications for education, reluctance to learn other languages also has socio-political ramifications. For instance, research indicates that, as in the case of Canadian francophones, those who were least fluent in English felt the greatest threat to their cultural identity. Those who understood the English language also found it easier to understand the intentions of anglophone Canadians (Lambert, 1990).

Allophones are made to believe that mastering English or French is necessary in order to survive, compete, and possibly even succeed in their new land. As Lambert (1990) puts it, young children are expected to "reprogram themselves in terms of basic language-thought relationships, replacing earlier formed word-thought connections with new ones. They are also asked to become Canadian as quickly as possible by distancing themselves from old country ways of thinking and behaving."

Allophone children often have to balance three language structures in order to make sense of the realities surrounding them. Although it is imperative that allophone children learn the dominant language so that they can acquire the skills with which to challenge the people in power (Gramsci, 1971), the emphasis should not be placed on acquiring language skills (as is usually the case). The primary focus should be on the production of knowledge through the teaching of subject matter.

Second-language instruction should also be sensitive to students' historical and cultural context. Second- (or third-) language instruction should not try to organize or reorganize students' sense of who they are or their relationship to the social world around them; in other words, second-language teaching should not be a power tool used to demean the language and culture of the student. Instead, it should create spaces in which children from different cultural and socio-historical contexts can relate to each other in common surroundings. Teachers must be sensitive to the language and culture of the student and try to refer to words and cultural cues that make the child comfortable and help him or her relate to the language and culture of the second language. Language is a tool of empowerment; teachers must be aware of this fact. Language learning should be both fun and empowering for students.

Participatory Decision Making

Democracy is best learned through democratic participation. All school committees, teams, and organizations should be representative of the diversity of students, staff, and communities. All members must have equal status and equal power to speak and be heard. The tendency of some groups to shy away from participation must be recognized, and attempts made to make them feel comfortable enough to gradually take part.

Lee, Menkart, and Okazawa-Rey (2006) suggest that staff and parents should be encouraged to work both separately and together to uncover and understand how racial and cultural biases are embedded within the organization and governance of the school—by asking questions such as "How is decision-making shaped by race?" and "Who has what kinds of power, influence, and authority?" (p. xi).

Administration must involve all those affected by policy in decision making: teachers, students, and parents. This will develop a sense of ownership and control in these groups and create commitment and enthusiasm regarding policy changes. Shared responsibility implies that control is not vested in appointed positions but in a collective freedom to create and innovate. Students must also be involved in formulating, implementing, monitoring, and assessing policies. A participatory culture develops trust and co-operation. Involving people from diverse backgrounds means including them in the power structure; this can only enrich the experiences of all by including a variety of perspectives.

ACCOUNTABILITY

Like awareness of issues related to the natural environment, awareness of issues related to one's community is also essential. Because Canadian society is multicultural and multilingual, students need to be aware of their communities in order to have cross-cultural understanding and tolerance. Students not only need to know about the historical contributions of different cultural groups to their communities, but also how various cultural groups are helping the community to evolve in the present day. Without community awareness, we would be promoting students' local knowledge gap "as evidence of the existence of a macro-Canadian culture that should obviate all talks about diversity" (Egbo, 2009, p. 110). This is unquestionably in opposition to a redefined framework of multicultural education.

The relationship between the community and the school, in a broader sense, is related to the concept of accountability. Johnson (2007) argues that culturally responsive leaders "need models of how they might challenge the status quo of inequitable assessment practices, incorporate students' cultural knowledge into the school curriculum, and work with parents and community activists for social change in the larger community" (p. 55). Parents and community members cannot look toward the school or teachers as solely responsible for student outcomes. Administrators should work to help facilitate interactions between the school and its surrounding community in hopes of establishing culturally responsive, empowering relationships with diverse parents and community members.

Educators are also accountable for educating all students equally. The current conception of accountability does not include challenging structures of oppression and forms of "pedagogical silencing" (Giroux, 1992, p. 8), which include tracking, or streaming and grouping, and unfair testing of students who are different. Policy changes are involved in accommodating differences. Performance evaluations of staff must include adaptability to change.

An exploratory study conducted by the US labour union, the American Federation of Teachers (AFT), involved observing schools and meeting with educational leaders in countries recognized as educational leaders through large-scale international assessments. After two years of visits spanning the globe from Finland to Japan to Singapore, the study team pronounced that "embedded in the culture of ... countries with strong educational results is a shared responsibility for learning. Not just teachers, but parents, students, school administrators, and governments all do their part to make sure learning happens" (American Federation of Teachers [AFT], 2012, p. 2). As evidence of this, the AFT team recounted how it had observed much professional collaboration both within and between schools in the places they visited. For example, in Shanghai, a "turnaround" system paired lower-performing schools with higher-performing counterparts, so that groups of teachers actually swapped places to promote better educational effectiveness.

The study team also compiled a comprehensive list of lessons learned, all indicative of the respect for public education and for the teaching profession found in the countries visited; ostensibly, these lessons represent prospective directives for Canadian and American policy-makers. They include specific advocacy for the professionalization of teachers, such as

- competitive salaries;
- professional autonomy, particularly as a demonstration of faith in restrictive candidate selection;
- support for ongoing professional collaboration;
- farsighted vision in educational reform ("coherence over time" in policy);
- rooting curricula and standards in consistent, stable educational goals;
- coherence across the system, so that individual schools refrain from implementing improvements in isolation, as small islands of success; and
- involvement of all stakeholders in policy decisions, even teacher unions.

In addition, the AFT study team noted that in the countries they visited, students themselves were heavily factored into the equation of accountability, taking on responsibility for their own learning. Hence, a system of shared accountability "bolsters professionals' efforts and 'balances' accountability—a stark contrast to the mechanistic approach taken by too many [North] American reformers, who primarily seek to assign quantitative 'value' to the actions of teachers, excluding other factors that support or hinder student success" (AFT, 2012, p. 12). Perhaps most intriguingly—and in contrast to the North American accountability trends so prevalent in recent years—the study team added: "In none of [the countries visited] did we hear any mention of ideas ... [such as] expanding charter schools, limiting the union rights of teachers and school employees, dismantling tenure and seniority, using standardized test scores heavily in teacher evaluation, or 'trusteeing' districts and 'reconstituting' schools for poor student performance" (AFT, 2012, p. 11).

Teacher Empowerment

Teachers are the most critical (and mutable) element in education reform, but they can only have a meaningful impact in their students' achievements when they are recognized as professionals. Teachers and other staff must be given a voice in how their work environment will be organized. They must be allowed to function as intellectuals, not treated as technicians (Giroux, 1992). Policy-makers must abandon their attempts to make teaching "foolproof" through standardization of curriculum and deficit-model accountability reforms, and instead set their sights on getting the best—and the best out of—teachers. Educational accountability needs to be redirected from placing blame on teachers for student failure and shifted toward recognizing the expertise of teachers in their professional work, which extends far beyond their students' performance on tests.

Reversing the accountability trends that have disempowered North American teachers in the past few decades can create the conditions for teacher empowerment. Accountability practices can only be validating if they allow those who have the most experience in the classroom to influence educational policy and reform. Moreover, if the status of the teaching profession is elevated by the promotion of teachers' professionalism (Schleicher, 2012), the possibility of attracting all kinds of diverse candidates to careers in education will improve. This is important because, as research suggests, it is easier to pick a good teacher than to train one (Chingos & Peterson, 2011).

CONCLUSION

At present, the learning and emotional environment in schools tends to alienate some students. A redefined multicultural perspective assumes a sensitive administration and inclusive policies. Inclusivity is a mindset, a perspective. Institutional policy must focus on changing the structure and culture of schools to include all children—female and male, from diverse racial and ethnocultural groups, and of various abilities—so that their educational experiences will be happy. Inaction reaffirms the status quo. Structural and policy changes are essential. At the same time, we must understand that implementing a redefined multicultural framework in schools and making policy changes are just steps in advancing society in the direction of equity. As Diane Ravitch (2013) puts it, "there is no example in which an entire school district eliminated poverty by reforming its schools or by replacing public education with privately managed charter and vouchers. If the root causes of poverty are not addressed, society will remain unchanged" (p. 225).

REVIEW QUESTIONS

1. How can structural changes in a school or school system make school culture more inclusive?

2. How does the hidden curriculum promote certain messages with respect to racial, class, and gender differences? Identify examples from your own school experiences.

3. Can you think of ways in which students get into trouble because of their ethnic, class, or gender background? How do schools tend to deal with these issues?

4. Is ethnocultural/racial diversity essential in making a school multicultural? How can other kinds of differences be explored in the classroom to help students begin to understand the politics of difference?

5. Do you think that guidance counsellors may have a racial, class, and gender bias in the way they guide students? Explain why.

6. In what ways are school administrators in your community trying to make the school environment multicultural? What are some recommendations you could make to help them do so?

REFERENCES

American Federation of Teachers (AFT). (2012). Lessons learned from the world's highest-performing school systems. *International update: The AFT at work in the world (special report)*. Retrieved from www.aft.org/about/world/trends/studymissions.cfm

Banks, J.A. (Ed.). (1981). *Education in the 80s: Multiethnic education*. Washington, DC: National Education Association.

Bauman, S., Toomey, R.B., & Walker, J.L. (2013). Associations among bullying, cyberbullying, and suicide in high school students. *Journal of Adolescence, 36*(2), 341–350.

Beran, T.N. (2006). Preparing teachers to manage school bullying: The hidden curriculum. *The Journal of Educational Thought, 40*(2), 119–128.

Berryman, M., SooHoo, S., & Woller, P. (2010). Leading pedagogy: Promoting school reform through teacher leadership and the implementation of a culturally responsive pedagogy of relations. In A. Normore (Ed.), *Global perspectives on educational leadership reform: The development and preparation of "leaders of learning" and "learners of leadership"* (pp. 187–210). Bingley, UK: Emerald Group.

Bourdieu, P., & Passeron, J.C. (1977). *Reproduction in education, society, and culture*. Beverly Hills, CA: Sage.

Chingos, M.M., & Peterson, P.E. (2011). It's easier to pick a good teacher than to train one: Familiar and new results on the correlates of teacher effectiveness. *Economics of Education Review, 30*(3), 449–465.

Dehue, F., Bolman, C., & Völlink, T. (2008). Cyberbullying and traditional bullying in relation to adolescents' perception of parenting. *CyberPsychology and Behavior, 11*(2), 217–223.

Didden, R., Scholte, R.H.J., Korzilius, H., de Moor, J.M.H., Vermeulen, A., O'Reilly M., Lang, R., & Lancioni, G.E. (2009). Cyberbullying among students with intellectual and developmental disability in special education settings. *Developmental Neurorehabilitation, 12*(3), 146–151.

Egbo, B. (2009). *Teaching for diversity in Canadian schools.* Toronto: Pearson.

Elias, M.J., & Zins, J.E. (Eds.). (2003). *Bullying, peer harassment, and victimization in the schools: The next generation of prevention.* New York: The Haworth Press.

Ellis, A.A., & Shute, R. (2007). Teacher responses to bullying in relation to moral orientation and seriousness of bullying. *British Journal of Educational Psychology, 77*(3), 649–663.

Fryberg, S.A., Covarrubias, R., & Burack, J.A. (2013). Cultural models of education and academic performance for Native American and European American students. *School Psychology International, 34*(4), 439–452.

Fullan, M. (1992). *Successful school improvement.* Toronto: OISE Press.

Gardenswartz, L., & Rowe, A. (1993). *Managing diversity.* New York/San Diego: Irwin/Pfieffer & Company.

Gaskell, J., McLaren, A., & Novogrodsky, M. (1989). *Claiming an education: Feminism and Canadian schools.* Toronto: Our Schools/Our Selves Education Foundation.

Ghosh, R. (2012). Diversity and excellence in higher education: Is there a conflict? *Comparative Education Review, 56*(2), 349–365.

Giles, R. (1977). *West Indian experience in British schools.* London: Heinemann.

Giroux, H.A. (1992). Educational leadership and the crisis of democratic government. *Educational Researcher, 21*(4), 4–11.

Gramsci, A. (1971). *Selections from prison notebooks.* New York: International Publishers.

Greene, M. (1988). *The dialectic of freedom.* New York: Teachers College Press.

Irvine, J.J. (2003). *Educating teachers for diversity: Seeing with a cultural eye.* New York: Teacher's College, Columbia University.

Johnson, L. (2007). Rethinking successful school leadership in challenging US schools: Culturally responsive practices in school-community relationships. *International Studies in Educational Administration, 35*(3), 49–57.

Konishi, C., Hymel, S., Zumbo. B.D., & Li, Z. (2010). *Canadian Journal of School Psychology, 25*(1), 19–39.

Kozol, J. (1991). *Savage inequalities: Children in American schools.* New York: Crown Publications.

Lambert, W.E. (1990). *Issues in foreign language and second language education.* Presented at the First Research Symposium on Limited English Proficient Students Issues, US Department of Education, Office of Bilingual Education and Minority Language Affairs, Washington, DC. Retrieved from www.gwu.edu.ncbepubs/

resource/foreign/htm

Larochette, A., Murphy, A.N., & Craig, W.M. (2010). Racial bullying and victimization in Canadian school-aged children: Individual and school level effects. *School Psychology International, 31*(4), 389–408.

Lee, E., Menkart, D., & Okazawa-Rey, M. (2006). *Beyond heroes and holidays: A practical guide to K–12 anti-racist, multicultural education and staff development* (3rd ed.). Washington, DC: Teaching for Change.

Lewis, O. (1961). *Introduction to the children of Sanchez.* New York: Random House.

Li, Q. (2006). Cyberbullying in schools: A research of gender differences. *School Psychology International, 27*(2), 157–170.

Li, Q. (2008). A cross-cultural comparison of adolescents' experience related to cyberbullying. *Educational Research, 5*(3), 223–234.

Madsen, J.A., & Mabokela, R.O. (2005). *Culturally relevant schools: Creating positive workplace relationships and preventing intergroup differences.* New York: Routledge.

McClelland, D.C. (1961). *The achieving society.* Princeton, NJ: Van Nostrand.

Merrill, K.W., Gueldner, B.A., Ross, S.W., & Isava, D.M. (2008). How effective are school bullying intervention programs? A meta-analysis of intervention research. *School Psychology Quarterly, 23*(1), 26–42.

Ogbu, J.U. (1978). *Minority education and caste: The American system in crosscultural perspective.* New York: Academic Press.

Ogbu, J.U. (1992). Understanding cultural diversity and learning. *Educational Researcher, 21*(8), 5–14.

Payne, E., & Smith, M. (2013). LGBTQ kids, school safety, and missing the big picture: How the dominant bullying discourse prevents school professionals from thinking about systemic marginalization or … why we need to rethink LGBTQ bullying. *QED: A Journal in GLBTQ Worldmaking, 1*(1), 1–36.

Polanin, M., & Vera, E. (2013). Bullying prevention and social justice. *Theory Into Practice, 52*(4), 303–310.

Ravitch, D. (2013). *Reign of error: The hoax of the privatization movement and the danger to America's public schools.* New York: Alfred A. Knopf.

Rebuffot, J. (2000, August). The three Ps of Canadian French immersion education: Politics, pedagogy, and perspective. Presentation. McGill University. Montreal, QC.

Reyes, P. (1994). Cultural citizenship and social responsibility: A call for change in educational administration. *UCEA Review, 35*(1), 1, 11–13.

Schleicher, A. (Ed.). (2012). *Preparing teachers and developing school leaders for the 21st century: Lessons from around the world.* OECD Publishing. Retrieved from www.oecd.org/site/eduistp2012/49850576.pdf

Shapka, J.D., & Law, D.M. (2013). Does one size fit all? Ethnic differences in parenting behaviors and motivations for adolescent engagement in cyberbullying. *Journal of Youth and Adolescence, 42*(5), 723–738.

Shariff, S. (2009). *Confronting cyber-bullying: What schools need to know to control misconduct and avoid legal consequences.* Cambridge: Cambridge University Press.

Shields, C.M. (2013). *Transformative leadership in education: Equitable change in an uncertain and complex world.* New York: Routledge.

Shor, I., & Freire, P. (1987). *A pedagogy for liberation: Dialogues on transforming education.* South Hadley, MA: Bergin & Garvey.

Stover, D. (2006). Treating cyberbullying as a school violence issue. *Education Digest: Essential Readings Condensed for Quick Review, 72*(4), 40–42.

Wright, V.H., Burnham, J.J., Inman, C.T., & Ogorchock, H.N. (2009). Cyberbullying: Using virtual scenarios to educate and raise awareness. *Journal of Computing in Teacher Education, 26*(1), 35–42.

ACTIVITY 4

"Rules Make the Winners": Exploring How Different Understandings Affect the Ways We Participate

Purpose
- Encourage students to reflect on their environments and critically question how the status quo is established, who it tends to benefit, and what it takes for change to occur
- Simulate the politics of difference and the compounding effects of privilege and disadvantage
- Debate the fairness of evaluation methods in relation to concepts of equity and sameness
- Help students develop empathy by exploring the effects of discriminatory practices on self-concept and agency

Description

In exploring the politics of difference, we must analyze how power dynamics position the dominant group, in terms of some cultural marker, over subordinate groups—and in doing so, designate members of the subordinate group as the "other." Sometimes the dominant group represents the majority of the population, as in the cases of sexual orientation and (dis)ability; but this is not always true, as in the cases of gender or class. Over time, the disadvantages of the subordinate group and the privileges of the dominant group are compounded and normalized. Because of this, it becomes incredibly difficult, if not impossible, for members of the underprivileged group to challenge the status quo and rise up to a status of parity with their overprivileged counterparts.

In preparation for this simulation activity, you will need to design three short multiple-choice quizzes, each with two different variations: one that is easy and one that is difficult. The quizzes should cover topics relevant to your course so that students will initially pay more attention to the content than the format or instructions. However, the quiz versions you design will be dissimilar in their levels of difficulty for various reasons in each round. In the first round, differentiate the quizzes in terms of how questions and answers are phrased, ensuring that one version is significantly more difficult than the other because it demands more time and concentration from students; you can achieve this by including more text to read and less obvious answer choices. In the second round, use identical test questions but modify the number of possible answer choices so that students with the easy version only need to choose from three options while students with the challenging version must choose from five. In the third round, design the challenging version of the quiz to be on a completely irrelevant topic with which students will not be familiar. By this point, the differentiation of quizzes should become quite obvious because some students will begin questioning the activity and noticing that they are not all being treated in the same way.

As you distribute the first quiz to your students, intentionally select certain students to receive either the easy or challenging version. Depending on your needs, you might distribute the different quiz versions to students based on the expression of a certain characteristic (e.g., gender, eye colour, height), or simply on the order that they arrived to class or where they sit in the room. In this way, students who get the easy quiz version will represent the overprivileged dominant group within a society, while students who take the more challenging version will represent underprivileged subordinate groups.

Explain to your students that they will be taking the quizzes in three rounds, so they will need to pick up the second and third handouts only after completing the previous ones. Leave the second and third quizzes on a table, but arrange the stacks of handouts with the easier versions on top and more difficult versions on the bottom. Instruct your students to work silently and wait patiently for their classmates once they have completed all three quizzes. As the activity continues, the ease or difficulty of the quizzes will be compounded. Students who start with the easy version in the first round will likely finish first, so they will be rewarded with the easier version of the second quiz (and later the easier version of the third quiz). The opposite will be true for students who begin with the difficult version and need more time to finish.

To conclude the activity, begin a discussion with the class and prompt students to share their reactions to the quizzes. Ask those students who took the more challenging versions if they had a sense that the quizzes treated them unfairly. Did they realize that those who benefitted in the first round continued to benefit in subsequent rounds? If any students came to such realizations, did they consider trying to protest? Or did they feel like giving up? Once students have a sense of how the quizzes were differentiated for different populations within the class, ask them to collectively brainstorm how the quizzes might be evaluated. Would it be fairer to grade all the quizzes in the same way or to differentiate the method of evaluation? Throughout the discussion, encourage students to reflect on how the quiz modifications could represent institutional challenges faced by certain cultural groups.

Curricular Connections

Language Arts: Give students a creative writing assignment in which they are asked to take fictional characters from two different literary works and imagine how they would interact if they existed in the same world; explore the concept of tension and how these characters might experience culture clash because of their different perceptions.

Physical Education: Set up a game of volleyball in which you discreetly tell one team to play according to the current rules and the other team to play by pre-2000 rules, when points could only be scored by the team that served and play ended at 15 points; incorporate discussion of what happens when groups of people play by different rules and aim for different goals.

Science: Break up the class into small groups, distribute one simple machine to each group, and then have students compete in a series of technological challenges; discuss how each tool is most appropriate for a specific kind of task.

Social Studies: Engage students in a debate where they must represent different sides of a still-disputed historical event, such as American versus Canadian perceptions of victory in the War of 1812.

Chapter 5

TEACHER EDUCATION AND CLASSROOM INTERACTIONS

Amelia always knew she wanted to be a teacher, so she was ecstatic about starting her first pre-service internship. She realized that Grade 8 students would be a challenge, especially since nearly all of them were taller than her, but she was determined to be authoritative and confident in terms of class-room management. She also hoped that the students would be appreciative of someone young and enthusiastic, at least in contrast to their current teacher, Ms. Caron. But Amelia had not anticipated just how well-received she would be by her new students, particularly the boys. Two of them, Antoine and Nick, even seemed to be flirting with her when they asked about what she did after school. She laughed off such comments because the boys continued to be engaged in their schoolwork, but she took them aside in the hallway a few times to explain how their tone could be inappropriate. Things generally settled down until one day when Nick started asking Amelia if she had a boyfriend in front of the entire class. In that instant, Amelia debated what to say next. She could explain that she was in a serious relationship, which was true, and it might encourage her students to be better mannered. Then again, her partner was a woman and she had not shared personal details regarding her sexuality with any co-workers or administrators. Amelia managed to avoid answering the question before the bell rang to dismiss the class, but she now realized that this situation would likely present itself again in her future teaching career.

- If you were the teacher in this situation, how would you respond?
- To what extent do you expect Amelia's teaching practices to be affected by her personal beliefs?
- How well do you think teacher education programs prepare candidates for the realities of the teaching profession?

INTRODUCTION

Teacher education is a crucial part of a redefined multicultural education. The curriculum initiatives in the school system are important, but no amount of curriculum material can make a significant difference if teachers do not have the knowledge and the proactive attitude necessary to change the status quo. As authority figures for students, teachers underpin the politics of difference.

This chapter discusses the urgent need for changes in teacher education programs and explores reasons why reform is slow. In terms of change, teacher education programs have two problems. First, they are established in university settings where change does not always occur quickly due to bureaucratic procedures, even when education professors have the vision for change. Second, the curriculum of teacher education programs is often defined by government departments of education. This factor makes teacher education programs a product of the prevalent educational ideology, which is determined by the political ideology of the state.

The components of a redefined multicultural teacher education program are derived from an understanding of the kind of teacher we want to produce. Problems arise when teaching is reduced to a prescriptive model: models give formulas "and formulas squeeze the life out of teaching" (Brandt, 1987, pp. 36–37). It is preferable to put forward a set of propositions that provide guidance for directions to be taken and questions to be asked. Multicultural pedagogy does not require teachers to have an expertise of all cultures; this is because its purpose is not to teach about the cultures per se, but rather to promote students' awareness and appreciation of difference and other perspectives. Teachers must strive to expose their students to the full spectrum of difference, in its varied and multi-faceted forms. The following, therefore, is an examination of general teaching practice with a focus on issues specifically related to students who are "different."

REDEFINING TEACHER EDUCATION

If teachers are the key players in the education game, then teacher education programs are of crucial significance. At the heart of the educational endeavour is the individual teacher, whose sensitivity and skills as a professional can enable children of various capabilities and cultures to achieve their maximum potential, or, alternatively, whose inability may (often inadvertently) lead to student failure. School dropout rates and the increase in juvenile crime (National Crime Prevention Centre, 2012) suggest that society, of which schools are a pivotal part, is producing individuals who are alienated. And teachers, often without realizing it, help extend the cycle of underachievement leading to unemployment and poverty from generation to generation. Schools are failing to provide equality of opportunity for children if they do not train teachers to achieve this equality. Inadequate training in multicultural problems means inadequate training in educational problems, for "if education has to become multicultural, teacher education has to become multicultural first" (De Vreede, 1986, p. 6).

Neither social policy for a multicultural society nor the equity provisions in the Charter of Rights and Freedoms that are aimed at eliminating social inequities have been incorporated into teacher education programs. The departure in philosophy from assimilation to multiculturalism in education is a radical shift. Any educational modification requires change in teacher preparation, and transformative change demands a redefinition in the perception of the teacher's role.

The Urgent Need for Change

Why should teacher education be multicultural? The answer is related to the goals of education. In today's world, students must be prepared for democratic citizenship and international communication. Further, in heterogeneous (especially immigrant) societies teachers work with children whose cultural, linguistic, ethnic, community, religious, and intellectual backgrounds are diverse and, therefore, only partially understood. This is particularly the case when teachers represent urban middle-class norms, when their "sense of history and their knowledge about justice and equality for [their] students come, in part, from a biased society" (Grant, 1989, p. 766). The presence of diversity in cultural as well as intellectual terms demands going beyond common-sense measures to very specific training needs.

In the "accepted dominant ideology, [teachers] are technicians who, by virtue of the specialized training they receive in an assembly line of ideas, and aided by the mystification of this transferred knowledge, seldom reach the critical capacity of analysis to develop a coherent comprehension of the world" (Macedo, 1993, p. 194). Furthermore, teachers are removed from a vision and practices that would foster democracy and social justice (Giroux & McLaren, 1986). Not only do teacher education programs neglect to address the moral implications of social inequalities, they portray the classroom as a simple rather than extremely complex site of multi-dimensional forces of conflict and negotiation. Teacher education programs continue to devalue differences through subtle but nonetheless debilitating ways because classroom culture is not seen as socially constructed. Nor do student teachers recognize their role in reproducing inequalities through relations of power. Teaching practice is offered in neutral terms, and there is no attempt to discuss the ideological dimensions of the teaching process.

Transforming teacher education programs cannot be seen in merely quantitative terms. Because teacher education courses and school curricula are overloaded, multiculturalism should not be a course or a discipline simply added to existing programs. Transformation does not mean appending information to different groups in each course, or adding one course in multiculturalism and gender studies to the program. While new knowledge and perceptions are involved, transformation must be seen to be qualitative and fundamental. Multicultural education is a state of mind; it is an attitude, an ideology that permeates every discipline. It is concerned with the objective world of knowledge as well as with the subjective world of feelings and values—the cognitive, affective, and ethical domains (Mukherjee, 1981, p. 120).

What is the best way to structure teacher education programs? It is hardly a matter for debate that the dramatic demographic changes in society and in the role of education should be reflected at all levels of teacher preparation. Yet an examination of teacher education curricula does not indicate a noticeable change in philosophy toward pluralism. A comparative survey of Canadian and Australian universities done in 1993 indicated that very few institutions across Canada (both English and French) had attempted to integrate multicultural components into compulsory courses (Milligan, 1993).

Resistance to Change

Multiculturalism means a transformation, a radical shift in power relations. That is why institutions are slow to change the status quo. Economic conditions also have an effect on the implementation of multicultural programs. The drop in school enrolments across Canada has affected teacher education programs and employment prospects. In addition, there has been a sharp decline in educational expenditures, both at the university and school levels. This is gradually eroding the quality of teacher education programs and ultimately the quality of education in the schools. It is becoming increasingly difficult to allocate the extra resources needed to educate both teachers and a diverse school population.

To some extent, resistance may come from teachers themselves. Teachers are often not equipped to deal with sensitive issues in the classroom—from racism and homophobia to bullying and violence—even though these issues pervade the lives of students outside of school (and sometimes within it, too). One problem is that society and students do not respect teachers who do not impart a given "knowledge." Multicultural education depends on using what children already know and constructing new knowledge and skills, rather than merely imparting organized information. Many teachers may believe in transformative education, but dare not "rock the boat" for fear of losing their jobs in the present economic situation. Deviating from the standard curriculum can be a risky business. Teachers are under pressure from ministries of education to cover prescribed material, and multicultural education is seen as an additional "burden." Teachers are often overworked, have too many students and too many classes, and are subjected to administrative control. There is little time to take evening courses and relearn theory and practice. In addition, there is the fear of making mistakes and losing control in the classroom because of discipline problems. In short, the system offers little incentive for teachers to undertake the changes necessary to make education appropriate for a multicultural society.

Combatting Superficial Change

Teacher education programs in North America have increasingly appeared to be concerned with multiculturalism, but these programs generally do not go to the root issues. In the United States, the National Council for Accreditation of Teacher Education requires that multicultural issues become an integral part of all aspects of the curriculum. The State of California Commission on Teacher Credentialing requires candidates to demonstrate sensitivity, competence, and confidence in teaching students who are different in terms of ethnicity, culture, gender, language, and socio-economic status (Ghosh & Tarrow, 1993). Canada has no national teacher credentialing body. In general, school boards have been more effective than teacher education institutions in taking up the challenge by providing in-service training in multicultural or anti-racist education. A few boards require teachers to have some knowledge of problems related to a multi-cultural school population. However, pre-service teacher education programs in general, both in Canada and the United States, could do much more to equip student teachers with usable skills for working in multicultural classrooms.

Teacher education programs that have traditionally aimed at dealing with a homogeneous student body cannot be effective in a multicultural milieu without radical restructuring. The museum approach to multicultural education, which presents ethnic culture as static, is misleading because it fails to appreciate the evolving nature of culture. For instance, a curriculum may attempt to be more inclusive of Aboriginal perspectives, but it is also important to consider whether it portrays Aboriginal peoples in a contemporarily relevant way. Imagine that you are an Aboriginal student in the classroom: do you recognize the portrayal of your own identity in the textbook, or are you disconnected from it because it does not relate to the way that you actually perceive yourself, your family, and your community? Arshad-Ayaz points out that "in many teacher education programs, culture gets treated as a taxonomy and is used as a checklist to mark the characteristics of a people" (2011 p. 73). Although there may be attempts to incorporate diverse cultures into the curriculum, the representation of these cultures is often limited to an oversimplified, homogenized, and outdated portrayal. It is unsurprising, then, that superficial approaches to multicultural education have led to alienation for both majority- and minority-group students.

Teacher training institutions behave as if student teachers either do not need

or will be automatically prepared to deal with the culturally diverse populations in schools today. The reluctance to respond to changing societal needs has
resulted in a non-active and "colour-blind" policy by teacher training institutions
and, until more recently, by teacher unions, school boards, and schools. This is
due to several factors (Ghosh, 1991):

- Cultural diversity is a politically volatile issue, and teachers have tended to avoid the extremely controversial realities embedded in concepts
  such as racism, prejudice, discrimination, and unequal opportunities and
  treatment.
- This avoidance has inhibited a discussion and study of the issue, causing a lack of understanding of the power dynamics embedded in the
  concept of multiculturalism. This has prevented schools from adequately
  dealing with the problems while hindering the constructive development
  of programs and policy. Not surprisingly, programs have tended to focus
  on a non-racist/non-sexist approach, rather than on an anti-racist/anti-
  sexist strategy, which would uncover systemic and interactional power
  differentials. This has had the effect of neutralizing inequality and
  masking unequal power relations.
- The slowness to respond is also due to the assumption that student
  teachers will pick up the necessary skills and attitudes that will make
  them successful teachers in culturally diverse classes without any direct
  instruction or planned experience (Contreras, 1988).
- The attitude still exists that intercultural education is for culturally different students only, rather than for all students. This argument is flawed
  because it equates cultural difference with deficiency. It is also academically dangerous because teaching programs do not feel obliged to
  commit time and resources to preparing teachers of children who are at
  risk of being miseducated and undereducated (Contreras, 1988).

"Colour-blindness" implies that everyone is treated the same by appearing to
be blind to differences in skin colour (racial and ethnic differences). But human
beings are deeply diverse—not only in their inherent characteristics (ethnicity,
gender, age, physical attributes and aptitudes, and physical and mental health),
but also in their location or "positioning" (place of birth, socio-economic background, etc.)—which results in unequal power relations. The effect of ignoring such differences, in fact, may be unjust and inegalitarian. Studies indicate
that how these differences are constructed has a significant impact on student
achievement and experiences in school, as well as on students' formation of

their own identities. In effect, colour-blindness condones and maintains white privilege and the status quo of unequal power relations. Not to recognize the "location" (Bhabha, 1994) of a person or acknowledge that certain differences have disadvantages is misrecognition. And, as Taylor (1994) points out, non-recognition or misrecognition can inflict harm, be a form of oppression, and imprison someone in a false, distorted, and reduced mode of being. Fairness, not colour-blindness, is a fundamental principle of justice (Appiah, 1996). Difference is seen as a problem and one way to deal with it is to fail to recognize it (Ghosh, 2011).

With the gradual shift in educational ideology, the focus of teacher education has changed from teaching as a craft to teaching as a technical pursuit. In traditional education programs, the purpose of teacher education was mastery of subject content and the technical aspects of classroom management. Student differences were overlooked, devalued, and structurally excluded. With multicultural education, there was a recognition of racial/ethnic and gender differences, but this did not induce much change in teacher education except that jobs in teaching second languages (ESL/FSL) opened up and a few "ethnic group" students were accepted for training to teach ethnic studies. On the whole, teachers were expected to be able to do "cultural" days and displays while concentrating on issues of content and discipline and the transmission of the dominant culture. These kinds of superficial, cure-all approaches present culture as static and disregard local contexts. In contrast, "the exploration for a different kind of teacher education (one that could not be boiled down to a few weeks of 'training') needs to contest the idea that there are methods, strategies, or approaches to teaching that work anytime, anywhere" (Friedrich, 2014, p. 12).

The concept of multiculturalism has significant implications for teacher education. Studies show that teacher expectations influence student performance and that teachers have different expectations based on gender, race, and social class (Rist, 1970; Rosenthal & Jacobson, 1968). Research by psychologists indicates cultural differences in ways of learning and behaving (Cole & Bruner, 1972); however, the results of such research have not yet filtered through to teacher education programs in any meaningful way. A redefined multicultural education must take on a more political tone, and deal with issues of discrimination and racism, human rights, and anti-racist education. Unfortunately, this ideology has not penetrated education in all Canadian provinces to the same extent. It has, however, prompted discussion about how to make teacher education multicultural by focusing on teacher educators themselves (Banks, 1979; Craft, 1981; Gay, 1986; Lynch, 1987).

THEORETICAL PRINCIPLES FOR TEACHER EDUCATION PROGRAMS

A transformed teacher education curriculum would involve the four components that usually make up existing programs (Cremin, 1977): (1) a general education; (2) specialized study in subject areas; (3) professional study dealing with the foundational (social/psychological) context of teaching, as well as with pedagogy and methods of teaching; and (4) practice, which is the focus in professional fields and translates theory into practical action in the classroom. However, teachers need competence not only in the skills outlined above but also in terms of attitudes and values.

The trend in Canadian pre-service courses, especially at the elementary level, is toward breadth of knowledge and versatility (polyvalence in Quebec) rather than an emphasis on one or two subject areas. This would better equip teachers for interdisciplinary approaches to issue-based concepts in school. The increased emphasis on general education focuses on language, culture, and history.

Teacher education institutions must take advantage of information and communication technology as an aid to instruction to prepare future teachers. Personal computers are now part of societal and classroom culture. They offer immense opportunities for learning skills and developing higher-level thinking and learning. Learning through technology, including social media, offers the potential for meeting some objectives of multicultural teaching because teacher and students learn together and can be involved in the process of creating and developing a sense of control and mastery; however, the use of technology must be balanced with the human aspects of education. The issue of access to this technology must be kept within the context of equity for girls and minority and working-class students.

There is no consensus on the precise needs of a multicultural school population, and there is controversy over the most appropriate approach to teaching such a population. This has usually taken the form of preparing teachers for English or French as a second language or teaching minority cultures, religions, and traditions. Satisfying only the language needs of minority students suits the goals of an assimilationist model, not a multicultural one. There is little evidence that teaching about cultures helps eliminate prejudices (Harmingson, 1973; Moodley, 1981; Stenhouse, 1975). The "insertion" approach of offering optional courses on multicultural topics defeats the aim of reaching the entire class, since these courses are usually taken by the few students who are already "converted." Even if made compulsory, special courses would have the effect of marginalizing the subject. Because multiculturalism is a philosophy of education, it must shape all aspects of teacher education. Finally, multicultural teacher education should be provided through pre-service programs for student teachers as well as in-service programs for practising teachers.

What knowledge is essential for teaching in the multicultural context? The raison d'être of teacher education programs is to improve student learning experiences. The literature on the subject identifies both practical and formal knowledge. For instance, Schulman (1986) theorizes three essential forms of knowledge: (1) propositional knowledge, which is obtained from empirical and philosophical inquiry, practical experience, and moral reasoning; (2) case knowledge, which stems from specific events that transform propositional knowledge to practical knowledge; and (3) strategic knowledge, which describes rules spanning professional judgment and practice. A realistic analysis of content emerges from the needs related to the teacher's role in the education process. First, there is the need for theoretical clarification of multicultural education aims and objectives in the school. Second, the responsibility of the teacher extends to establishing a broad framework for curriculum planning that recognizes the pivotal role of teaching as a moral enterprise with immense social consequences. This means "enabling student teachers to reflect critically upon both the craft of teaching and the contexts ... to bring about ... an emancipatory educational process" (Liston & Zeichner, 1987, p. 127). Third, student teachers need to master ways to meet the objectives. This does not mean that they need a manual of clever techniques; instead, it requires a process orientation. How should this be done? How are student teachers to be taught? One significant intention of multicultural teacher education is to help prospective teachers recognize the invisible biases and hidden inequalities in classroom interactions. Ethnographic studies offer a strategy for doing so. In this exercise, students spend time in classrooms to identify the ideological elements of the school curriculum. This leads to examining routine perceptions and interrelationships in school culture, as well as socio-economic and political contexts. Supervision of student teaching can be done in a variety of ways (partnership, horizontal, or peer supervision) that focus on the emancipatory aspects of teaching. Action research and journal writing are other strategies in critical pedagogy that are particularly suitable for multicultural teacher education.

Teaching Objectives

According to Rich, "the primary purpose of teaching is to help children claim kinship with humanity" (1985, p. 722). More specific purposes include developing critical citizenship (Giroux & McLaren, 1986) and enhancing self-concept. This means empowering students to claim a full human identity by developing critical thinking and values, as well as understanding the power relations and skills needed to deal with injustice.

To be able to foster the conditions for student self-empowerment, teachers must themselves be empowered. They need to reflect on the unique perspectives that they bring into the classroom, how they can best share these points of view with students, and how their long-term contribution to the profession may have a lasting effect on hundreds, if not thousands, of children; perhaps the best way for student teachers to think about this is that "it is *you* and what *you* bring—the knowledge, skills, and attitudes you already possess, as well as how you think about and act on 'becoming' a teacher—that will influence the kind of teacher you become" (Grant & Sleeter, 2011, p. 2). Yet empowerment is more than self-confirmation; it is a process by which students will appropriate aspects of the dominant culture (knowledge and skills) with which to define and act in society. Essential skills for teaching include learning about computers to aid instruction and develop higher-level thinking, learning the "culture of power," and recognizing that the rules of power (such as language codes and styles of speaking and behaving) are enacted in classrooms (Delpit, 1988).

Because they are situated in the experiences of the classroom, teachers' voices and perspectives must be engaged in policy-making decisions. They must also be used to engage with students in order bring to their needs and opinions to the forefront of education; "this engagement is required in order to both innovate from within and at the same time not to fall into dogmatic and arrogant traditionalism and racism, idealizing oneself and one's tradition, and rejecting learning from the present and from the outside world" (Niyozov, 2008, p. 157). An excellent model of this has been represented by the Université de Montréal's Centre d'études ethniques des universités montréalaises (CEETUM), which has organized an annual summit on multicultural education in Quebec universities since 2012. These meetings of instructors of post-secondary multicultural education courses are aimed at developing a model of knowledge, intrinsic attitudes, and observable skills required of successful multicultural educators (Larochelle-Audet, Borri-Anadon, McAndrew, & Potvin, 2013).

Understanding Education as a Process

Prospective teachers must first learn to recognize that education is not neutral but political and understand how power dynamics work to construct difference. They must learn to see how power dynamics in interactions tend to exclude and marginalize children of some groups. For example, it is documented that children from low-income families and some minorities have higher dropout rates (Bowman, 1994). Student teachers must recognize that differences have become enshrined in common knowledge and language and that their discriminating effects are taken for granted. To see discrimination only in personal terms at the individual level is to overlook the racism and sexism embedded in institutions and systems. Teachers must understand how schools deal with difference at both the systemic and individual levels through social and pedagogical interaction. Most importantly, they must be aware of how the organization of difference influences the way teachers and students define themselves and each other.

Teacher education has generally been seen as apolitical because teacher education institutions separate the teaching experience from the existence and reproduction of inequalities in society in general, and within the school in particular. Questions regarding the very nature and quality of knowledge and society, and the teacher's role in transmitting the hidden ideology behind this knowledge, make the teaching experience a highly political one. The dominant ideology legitimizes existing school practices and this "strips teacher-education programs of their purported innocence" (Giroux, 1981, p. 149).

Teaching is an ethical activity and education a moral enterprise—a "moral type of friendship" in which students and teachers work together to a common end (Noddings, 1986, p. 509). A sense of caring should guide teachers' thinking and language. Caring must be central to teaching through modelling, interaction, practice, and confirmation (Noddings, 1986). The object must be to bring out the best in students. Students' intellectual development must not impede concern for the formation of values and affective qualities.

Teaching is not an isolated act detached from social obligations. Teachers must help students connect their lives with the larger world and develop conceptual schemes, rather than merely accumulate information. Socio-economic, cultural, and political dimensions are primary categories for understanding contemporary schooling.

Traditional education has been the means of transmitting the dominant culture. Culture is both a lived experience, a set of relations, as well as a commodity that is accumulated—what Bourdieu (Bourdieu, 1973; Bourdieu & Passeron, 1977) has called "cultural capital" in the same sense as economic capital or assets. As a matter of fact, cultural resources are easily translated into economic wealth. Students who are different do not have the cultural capital that schools use as currency (that is, the values of the dominant culture) and are thus at a disadvantage. This means that groups outside the mainstream live in a different world from those on the inside, and are not socialized with the values, beliefs, and aspirations for school learning that are common to school culture. They may emphasize different skills and value other kinds of knowledge according to their concerns. That is why they find it more difficult to achieve by the standards set by the system.

Schools create and perpetuate difference, however inadvertently. Teachers are necessarily confronted with the question of difference because student groups are heterogeneous—in experiences, cultures, and lifestyles, as well as in terms of gender, ethnicity, and race. How they respond to this question is important because of the influence that difference has on how children learn and how they see themselves and others. Studies show that motivators, learning styles, behaviour patterns, and aspirations vary among cultural groups. Failure to recognize this is to perpetuate a system of inequalities. Prospective teachers must recognize that students neither participate equally nor are they treated equally. They must not ignore the powerful influence of the social context that shapes students' individual development.

Student teachers should explore alternatives and create spaces within which students are able to develop their identities and interact with each other. They must recognize similarities in racism, sexism, and class discrimination and foster co-operation between females and males, blacks and whites, and working- and middle-class children. They must challenge such culturally biased procedures as IQ testing and tracking, which separate and ghettoize disadvantaged students.

The traditional school curriculum is slanted in favour of the dominant culture. Student teachers must extend their vision beyond purely utilitarian interpretations of educational goals. When students are seen in terms of human capital investment, education becomes mere training for productivity and profit. Teachers must challenge the hidden dominance of those ideologies that lead to misinterpretations and misconstructions of historical phenomena and events. For example, modern industrial culture is dedicated to a system of values and behaviours in which humans control nature and some cultures dominate others. Teachers shape future citizens, and they need to confront practices that restrict opportunities for some.

Teachers should question the ability of the present system to adequately educate diverse populations. That means challenging policy, practice, pedagogy, and curriculum. It is imperative for student teachers to recognize the effects of the hidden curriculum and analyze unconscious stereotypes and biases.

Knowledge is socially constructed. Who produces school knowledge? Who speaks for society? As Freire (1970) pointed out, knowledge is not an object to be transmitted from the teacher who has the knowledge to the students who do not. Knowledge is increasingly seen as the result of specific social and historical relations rather than as a static entity that is context- and value-free. As such, students should be active knowers at the centre of the learning process, rather than at the receiving end, simply acquiring knowledge as objects. Freire also points out that one reason for the loss of status of the teacher is that she or he is not allowed to be involved in knowledge production, only in its transference.

There is also a need to look at teacher education textbooks in terms of prejudice, bias, stereotypes, and problems of omission or commission. Library resources and teaching materials must be constantly updated.

INTRINSIC ELEMENTS OF MULTICULTURAL EDUCATION PRACTICE

Redefined Norms

Teachers need to redefine standards and norms that are at present derived from white, male, middle-class values and goals. These standards and norms, which marginalize women, different racial and ethnic groups, and the working classes, have crucial implications for academic success and its evaluation. They also influence teacher expectations and attitudes. Demands for excellence, standards, and higher grades have become inseparable from the stated purpose of schooling, the process of teaching and learning, and organizational arrangements that cater to the needs of the norm (Cornbleth, 1986).

Moral Purpose

Teachers must model what they want their students to acquire, thus modelling is central to teacher education. The teacher must be a model in critical thinking and listening and as an active learner. Teachers cannot be neutral about moral issues, because neutrality ignores inequalities and thus perpetuates them. They must demonstrate democratic values if they want their students to develop values of justice and equality. Democracy is best exemplified through democratic methods, not authoritarian classrooms. Participation is learned through experiencing it.

Teachers should have a sense of mission and moral purpose, not just a duty to impart mere technological knowledge. Teachers must question and examine their own values and attitudes and their expectations of students if their teaching is to be effective. They must reflect on their own attitudes and expectations regarding females, racial/ethnic minority groups, and working-class students. They cannot discuss education without examining their own attitudes; teachers must reflect on their own beliefs in order to understand and acknowledge the assumptions that stem from them (Rich, 1985). "Educators need to understand their own levels of racial identity development in order to change their perception and expectations of children" (Carter & Goodwin, 1994, p. 324), especially those who are different from the dominant group. All educators must undertake the task of developing awareness, effective skills, and competence about race and culture. When teachers do not share common experiences and beliefs with students of different backgrounds, their understanding of the world conflicts with students'. This can lead to misunderstanding because of the inability to recognize cultural meanings in interactions (Bowman & Stott, 1993).

Teacher education involves not only intellectual development but also affective and ethical issues. Multiculturalism must be demonstrated as a caring way of life—caring for all students and their well-being is an important concern of teachers. An ethics of caring guides us to ask what effect the teacher's actions will have on the student (Gilligan, 1982; Noddings, 1986), with an aim to strive for excellence and realizing each student's full potential. The object of teacher education is not only to produce teachers who can write lesson plans and behavioural objectives, but who will also make sound decisions for the sake of students (Noddings, 1986). Furthermore, children construct their world and their identities through interactions with adults, and learn best from those whom they perceive as being caring. Teachers must ask themselves, "Is your main responsibility toward society fulfilled by helping students do well on tests, transmitting academic content, preparing your students to help [their country] compete internationally, developing engaging citizens, or breathing life into ideals of equality, freedom, and justice? And what might these ideals and responsibilities actually mean on a day-to-day basis in the classroom?" (Grant & Sleeter, 2011, p. vii).

Communication

Mediating content and context is at the core of the teaching process. Communication is the medium for the process of education, and is the most important requirement for effective teaching (Banks, 1981). Communication styles are complex because they involve cues, both verbal and non-verbal, that are culturally specific. The messages embedded in communication have a profound impact on the student's self-concept. We must demand that our teachers are skilled in interpersonal relations, so that they can communicate with understanding across student-teacher and school-community divides—and tackle head-on student racism and autonomous peer cultures (Gundara, 2009).

The classroom must be recognized not simply as a place for learning, but as a site for resistances and negotiations, conflicts and dialogues. There is a tension between teacher and student that may or may not be creative (McDonald, 1988). It is important to consider the construction of difference and racism/sexism as sources of conflict. The process of critical reflection also offers potential for learning together and giving meaning to multiculturalism.

Student Motivation

The issue of motivation lies at the core of the teaching act. Student motivation cannot be taken for granted. What produces student participation? While theories of motivation and learning are best studied in psychology courses, learning that is empowering and that validates student identity is likely to create intrinsic motivation. Throughout his writings, Dewey emphasized that knowledge should be useful to the learner. All subjects can be situated in the culture, language, experiences, and social context of students. Finding a place in the curriculum where they can anchor themselves also validates students' experiences and strengthens their self-concept and identity. In contrast, ignoring the experiences and history of some students violates their sense of self-respect. While minority students must learn the culture and language of the dominant group, dominant-group students should also learn about minority cultures.

Students are naturally curious when they enter the classroom; unfortunately, education has a long history of subduing and silencing children (Holt, 1982; Kozol, 1991). Students need to be challenged if they are not to be bored. Teachers must find a profile for motivation based on knowledge of the student and his or her cognitive and learning styles. Students become bored and withdraw not because they are deficient, but because they cannot relate or cannot identify with the text, or because their interests, learning styles, and skills are at variance with the teaching.

Achievement motivation also has a direct relation to learning style, and perceived control is closely related to achievement motivation (Parsonson, 1986). Children who feel a sense of control perform better in school than those who feel helpless (Perry & Dickens, 1984). Porter (1965) has suggested that control is influenced by socialization and therefore varies among ethnic groups.

Teachers must be conscious of their questioning styles and non-verbal communication, because their face and voice have a great impact on students. Teachers must themselves be convinced of what they teach. The teacher's enthusiasm for learning and interest in students will perhaps be the most motivating factors. Humour is also an important part of the learning process.

Diverse Teaching Methods

The relationship between classroom discourse and learning is so complex that even a teacher's way of speaking can influence student learning. Teaching only creates conditions for learning to take place; it cannot cause learning. Therefore, teaching and learning are not directly connected; rather, the teaching process is ambivalent and ambiguous. Student teachers must learn and experience the methods they will employ to create the best learning conditions for their students. And their methods will be derived from the guiding principles they develop and implement—principles that should valorize the aspirations and skills of a diverse student population and make learning an exciting personal adventure.

Since knowledge is constructed by the one who learns, teaching means providing the opportunity to learn. Research suggests that children's biological capabilities do not develop evenly, so that there is variability in normal children's development patterns—the younger the children, the greater the differences (Bowman, 1994). In addition to individual differences in the general population, there are cultural differences: the social context of each child further influences development. Learning, thus, is both individual and socio-cultural. The need for diversity in teaching methods cannot be overestimated because they must respond to the developmental needs of each learner.

Teaching methods must be liberatory. The pedagogical conditions for this involve allowing different students' voices to be heard and legitimated, creating classroom conditions for challenging different "languages" and ideological discourses, and examining multiple perspectives. Teaching and learning are meant to bring about confidence and enhanced self-knowledge. The liberatory climate will depend on the ideology and philosophy of the teacher and the methods he or she induces. Teachers need to keep in mind the social context of teaching and the fact that both teacher and students are partners in the learning process.

Differences are not static qualities that can be applied to all members of a particular group; within-group variations can be as important as inter-group ones. Attention must be paid to recognizing the different ways in which students learn (their learning styles). Knowledge of learning styles offers teachers the opportunity to recognize these different ways of knowing and tailor their strategies to build on the strengths of individual students.

Cognitive style—the way in which people perceive and understand their environment—can be either field-dependent (external locus of control, relational) or field-independent (internal locus of control, analytical) according to their socialization (Bagley & Young, 1983; Berry, 1971). Cognitive style is related to differences in culture, socialization, and economic and cultural adaptation. Field independence/dependence is related to parental restrictions; overprotection, for example, leads to field dependence. Due to socialization, more boys than girls are field-independent, and schools try to influence students in that direction so that they develop greater autonomy and better cognitive analysis and structuring; however, field independence is also connected with being more impersonal and psychologically distant. Teachers need to be aware of their own cognitive styles. Field dependence is associated with better social skills, greater interpersonal orientation, a strong interest in others, and emotional openness.

These qualitative differences in how students process the world affect learning styles and school achievement because Canadian schools are set up to reward field-independent styles. Goodenough (1976) stresses that cognitive styles affect the manner in which learning occurs, not how well it occurs. Bagley and Young

(1983) found that socialization, social class, and ethnicity influenced cognitive style, so that Jamaican children socialized in Jamaica, for example, were more field-dependent, whereas Jamaican children who grew up in England were more field-independent. Teachers must therefore be able to recognize cognitive styles if they are to maximize student learning.

Learning styles are specific to individuals. This is further complicated by cultural and socio-economic factors. Huber and Pewewardy (1990) suggest that distinct differences in the learning environment must be acknowledged because of variations in right/left brain hemisphere dominance, field sensitivity, social intuition, communication emphasizing non-verbal cues, and group orientation (i.e., co-operation as opposed to competition). In addition, there are differences in oral/aural versus visual/spatial or tactile/kinetic modalities, and process/problem solving over product orientation (Carter & Goodwin, 1994). While individual differences exist in terms of all of these factors, variations in socialization also result in different but equally valid ways in which students see the world. For example, although there are as many differences within groups as between them, some groups have been identified as displaying variations in motor activity, physical energy, facility in non-verbal communication, oral/aural modalities (Hale, 1982), and mobility processes (Kerekhoff & Campbell, 1977). These differences suggest different teaching methods for different cognitive styles and behaviour patterns.

EDUCATING THE EDUCATORS

None of the above can be achieved if those who teach the teachers are themselves not committed to the needs of a multicultural society and the aims and objectives of an education system for that society. One should ask how educators define legitimate knowledge, and what their attitude and commitment are to producing effective teachers in a multicultural, multiracial society.

Marx once posed the question of who will teach the teachers, and pointed out that "the educator must himself be educated" (Marx, 1942, p. 472). Change in teacher education will not be implemented without the effort of those who teach the teachers. Research has suggested the need for "rejigging" all teacher educators, who are themselves subject to restricted cultural perceptions and who misinterpret the behaviour of their students (De Vreede, 1986; Lynch, 1987; Craft, 1981; Gay, 1986). Teacher educators themselves must be culturally aware, have knowledge of educational needs and human rights principles, and be up-to-date on the most recent relevant literature. "Training the trainers," as it is referred to in the literature, is an important and necessary component of effective teacher education, otherwise "how can teacher education become multicultural with teacher educators that do not have a multicultural education?" (De Vreede,

1986, p. 6). A multicultural teacher education assumes that the educators are willing to reflect on their own teaching effectiveness in order to improve it (Bowman, 1989) and require their students to do the same.

Teacher Expectations

As far back as 1968, Rosenthal and Jacobson's *Pygmalion in the Classroom* showed evidence that student performance was linked to what teachers expected of them. It has been argued that there is a connection between poor performance and teacher expectations that underestimate the ability of black children (Braun, 1976; Cooper, 1979; Rist, 1970). For example, mistaking a student's lack of proficiency in standard English for general lack of ability and intelligence has had disastrous effects. The possibility that differences in race, ethnicity, culture, sex, or class may be the basis of lower teacher expectations indicates how schools perpetuate social stratification.

While teachers are often not aware of the different ways in which they treat students, they may reflect the systemic discrimination of society and school cultures. Studies have shown that subtle and overt forms of discrimination result from teachers' attitudes (Giles, 1977) because their lack of information leads them to make inappropriate assumptions about children of different racial groups. If they operate within a framework of stereotypes (Brittan, 1973; Tomlinson, 1980), teachers may equate minority students and poor performance, with the result that these students are overrepresented in special education and lower-ability groups (Elder, 1981). Teaching in such classes is minimal because teachers spend more time on classroom management and discipline than on academic teaching (Locke, 1988). Cultural differences in interactional styles affect the amount of help given. For example, teachers pay more attention to and expect more from dominant-group males, asking them more questions, and prompting them with the right answers or allowing them more time to give answers. Ethnic minority and working-class students are also suspended from schools more often than majority-group students (Mills, 1975; National Council of Welfare, 1975); this is in keeping with the way race and low socio-economic status are presented as problems in the larger society.

Knowledge alone is not likely to produce the desired expectations without the emotional commitment of teachers who share a belief in the basic tenets of equality, justice, and human rights. Teacher education, then, must aim at producing teachers who are informed, caring, and competent—which, of course, is necessary to promote the ideals of multiculturalism and democracy. In order to enhance cultural sensitivity for teaching effectiveness, consciousness-raising techniques are available. As an example, Locke (1988) proposed the six-level Cross-Cultural

Awareness Continuum to increase levels of awareness. The first level involves self-awareness, as understanding oneself is the basis for understanding others. This involves a process of introspection relating to one's beliefs, attitudes, and values. The second level is awareness of one's own culture by relating the attitudes, values, and language of one's culture to those of another culture. The third level is awareness of racism, sexism, and poverty. Exploration of these issues is essential not only at the personal level, in terms of beliefs regarding children of poor or racially different groups, but also in situational terms. The fourth level involves awareness of individual differences, so that teachers are aware of the uniqueness of the individual while not disregarding culturally specific behaviours. These four levels provide the background from which the teacher is ready to explore the dynamics of other cultures.

The fifth level in the continuum is awareness of other cultures, which involves being sensitive to the verbal and non-verbal language of that culture. Hofstede (1980) has identified four criteria by which cultures differ: power distance, uncertainty/avoidance, individualism/collectivism, and masculinity/femininity. An alternate scheme for analysis is provided by Kluckhohn and Strodtbect (1961), who see cultural differences in terms of time, view of human nature, importance of relationship, human activity, and view of the supernatural. Analysis of cultures through either model will greatly enhance the understanding of other lifestyles and worldviews.

The sixth level in Locke's continuum is awareness of diversity. Teachers must make an effort to know and understand the children in their classroom. Finally, teaching effectiveness is only possible with teaching competence and self-confidence based on a knowledge of sound theories of learning and styles of teaching.

Teaching Practice

According to Lusted, "How one teaches ... becomes inseparable from what is being taught and, crucially, how one learns" (1986, pp. 2–3). The emphasis on the professional and scientific aspects of instruction overlooks the "mystical" element of teaching (McDonald, 1988). While it has a technological component, teaching involves much more than implementing what works in the classroom (Jackson, 1987). This refers to the teacher's voice (the knowledge as well as the power of the teacher), which influences teachers' perceptions of the kind of innovations that fit their work.

Teacher education programs cannot really teach precise techniques but should, instead, attempt to give broad directions. Teaching strategies must move from a process-product model and technological orientation toward what Clifford Geertz

(1973) called the "interpretive tradition." Schulman (1986) develops the concept of interpretive tradition in teaching and learning as a continuously interactive, contextual process in which meanings, understandings, and new perspectives replace the notion of teaching as merely the application of techniques for given ends. It is also important to remember that teaching involves what happens before, during, and after class. Multicultural teaching practice, therefore, can be extended to extracurricular activities. For example, one elementary school teacher in Montreal wanted to promote critical consciousness and resistance in her young students, so she sponsored them in establishing an after-school social justice club (Hayden-Benn, 2011).

Educational objectives are achieved by motivating students to learn. To optimize learning conditions, teachers must first not only understand how cognitive and learning styles differ, but also how their own expectations and behaviour, and the hidden curriculum, mediate the learning process.

Teaching Styles

The instructional approaches of North American schools are based on the characteristics of a male, white, middle-class norm. These include task orientation; focus on formal and non-personal attributes; attention to parts rather than the whole; emphasis on formal rules; linear thinking patterns; dispassionate but attentive behaviour; and use of "proper" English (Sleeter & Grant, 1988). In contrast, many females, ethnic minority cultures, and working-class students tend to be more person-oriented, focus on the whole rather than on parts, look for contextualized information, and show interest in human connections rather than rules (Sleeter & Grant, 1988; Gaskell, McLaren, & Novogrodsky, 1989). Moreover, there are striking differences within cultures depending on class, family structure, and home conditions (Nieto, 1992). What is clear is that students learn and perform better academically when instruction corresponds to their learning styles.

When learning styles are in conflict with the teaching style, students cannot respond effectively. Good teachers typically incorporate a range of pedagogical orientations rather than expect all students to fit into one mould of learning. In addition, various strategies may be employed to achieve certain objectives. For example, reduction in prejudice has been observed through techniques such as role-playing and co-operative learning. A meta-analysis of these two methods (McGregor, 1989) shows that both encourage a sense of control in students and maximize achievement in all children.

CONCLUSION

The bureaucratic problems of complex societal structures such as teacher education institutions and schools should not be underestimated. But the ethical imperatives of a multicultural democracy demand a pivotal role for teacher education (Ghosh, 1991). If education is slow to respond to social needs, teacher education institutions are perhaps the most conservative and unlikely to change. Pre-service teacher preparation is far behind developments in schools. Teachers do pick up multicultural and anti-racist perspectives and initiatives either to meet their needs or because of their own moral imperatives. This ad hoc method of response to a very important social need is less than satisfactory (Ghosh & Tarrow, 1993).

REVIEW QUESTIONS

1. What are some reasons why a multicultural education in schools requires multicultural teacher education?

2. Do present teacher education programs adequately prepare new teachers for giving all children in their classes an equal opportunity for education? Explain why or why not.

3. What does "educating the educators" mean? Use your own experiences to explain why this is important.

4. What are some reasons that explain why certain educators are reluctant to incorporate multiculturalism into their teaching? How might you convince them otherwise?

5. What kinds of messages are embedded in the hidden curriculum of teacher education? Do you think some students feel inadequate as a result of these messages?

6. Do cultural differences in values, attitudes, and behaviours among different ethnocultural groups affect the abilities of students? In what ways?

REFERENCES

Appiah, K.A. (1996). Race, culture, identity: Misunderstood connections. In K.A. Appiah and A. Gutman (Eds.), *Color conscious: The political morality of race*. Princeton, NJ: Princeton University.

Arshad-Ayaz, A. (2011). Making multicultural education work: A proposal for a transnational multicultural education. *Canadian Issues/Thèmes Canadiens*, Spring, 71–74.

Bagley, C., & Young, L. (1983). Class, socialization and cultural change: Antecedents of cognitive style in Jamaica and England. In C. Bagley & G. Verma (Eds.), *Multicultural childhood* (pp. 16–26). Hampshire, UK: Gower.

Banks, J. (1979). *Teaching strategies for ethnic studies* (2nd ed). Boston: Allyn & Bacon.

Banks, J.A. (Ed.). (1981). *Education in the 80s: Multiethnic education*. Washington, DC: National Education Association.

Berry, J. (1971). Ecological and cultural factors in spatial-perceptual development. *Canadian Journal of Behavioral Sciences, 3*, 324–336.

Bhabha, H. (1994). *The location of culture*. London: Routledge.

Bourdieu, P. (1973). Cultural reproduction and social reproduction. In R. Brown (Ed.), *Knowledge, education and cultural change* (pp. 71–112). London: Tavistock.

Bourdieu, R., & Passeron, J.C. (1977). *Reproduction in education, society, and culture*. Beverly Hills, CA: Sage.

Bowman, B.T. (1994). The challenge of diversity. *Phi Delta Kappan*, 218–224.

Bowman, B.T. (1989). Self-reflection as an element of professionalism. *Teachers College Record, 90*, 444–451.

Bowman, B.T., & Stott, E. (1993). Understanding development in a cultural context. In B. Mallory & R. New (Eds.), *Diversity and developmentally appropriate practices* (pp. 119–134). New York: Teachers College Press.

Brandt, R. (1987). On teaching thinking skills: A conversation with B. Othanel Smith. *Educational Leadership, 45*(2), 35–39.

Braun, C. (1976). Teacher expectation: Sociopsychological dynamics. *Review of Educational Research, 46*, 185–213.

Brittan, E. (1973). Teacher opinions on aspects of school life—Pupils and teachers. *Educational Research, 46*, 185–213.

Carter, R.T., & Goodwin, A.L. (1994). Racial identity and education. *Review of Research in Education, 20*, 291–336.

Cole, M., & Bruner, J.S. (1972). Preliminaries to a theory of cultural differences. In I.J. Gordon (Ed.), *Early childhood education, the seventy-first yearbook of the National Society for the Study of Education*. Chicago: University of Chicago Press.

Contreras, A.R. (1988). *Multicultural attitude and knowledge of education students at Indiana University*. Paper presented at the Annual Meeting of the American Educational Research Association. New Orleans, LA.

Cooper, H.M. (1979). Pygmalion grown up: A model for teacher expectation, communication and performance influence. *Review of Educational Research, 49*, 389–410.

Cornbleth, C. (1986). Ritual and rationality in teacher education reform. *Educational Researcher, 15*(4), 5–14.

Craft, M. (Ed.). (1981). *Teaching in a multicultural society: The task for teacher education*. Lewes, Sussex: Falmer Press.

Cremin, L.A. (1977). *The education of the educating professions*. Washington, DC: The American Association of Colleges for Teacher Education.

Delpit, L.D. (1988). The silenced dialogue: Power and pedagogy in educating other people's children. *Harvard Educational Review, 58*(3), 280–298.

De Vreede, E. (1986, September). *Teacher education and multicultural education: Baron von Monchhausen in the swamp*. Paper presented at the 11th Annual Conference of the Association of Teacher Educators in Europe, Toulouse, France.

Elder, D. (1981). Ability grouping as self-fulfilling prophecy: A micro-analysis of teacher-student interaction. *Sociology of Education, 54,* 151–162.

Freire, P. (1970). *Pedagogy of the oppressed.* New York: Seabury Press.

Friedrich, D. (2014). We brought it upon ourselves: University-based teacher education and the emergence of boot-camp-style routes to teacher certification. *Education Policy Analysis Archives, 22*(2), 1–12.

Gaskell, J., McLaren, A., & Novogrodsky, M. (1989). *Claiming an education: Feminism and Canadian schools.* Toronto: Our Schools/Our Selves Education Foundation.

Gay, G. (1986). Multicultural teacher education. In J.A. Banks & J. Lynch (Eds.), *Multicultural education in western societies* (pp. 154–178). London: Holt, Rinehart & Winston.

Geertz, C. (1973). *The interpretation of cultures.* New York: Basic Books.

Ghosh, R. (1991). L'éducation des maîtres pour une société multiculturelle. In F. Ouelett & M. Page (Eds.), *Pluralisme et éducation au Québec* (pp. 207–230). Montréal: Institut Québécois de Recherche sur la Culture.

Ghosh, R. (2011). The liberating potential of multiculturalism in Canada: Ideals and realities. *Canadian Issues/Thèmes Canadiens,* Spring, 3–7.

Ghosh, R., & Tarrow, N. (1993). Multiculturalism and teacher education: Views from Canada and USA. *Comparative Education, 29*(1), 81–92.

Giles, R. (1977). *West Indian experience in British schools.* London: Heinemann.

Gilligan, C. (1982). *In a different voice.* Cambridge, MA: Harvard University Press.

Giroux, H. (1981). *Ideology, culture and the process of schooling.* Philadelphia, PA: Temple University Press.

Giroux, H.A., & McLaren, P. (1986). Teacher education and the politics of engagement: The case for democratic schooling. *Harvard Educational Review, 56*(3), 213–238.

Goodenough, D. (1976). The role of individual differences in field dependence as a factor in learning and memory. *Psychological Bulletin, 83*(4), 675–694.

Grant, C.A. (1989). Urban teachers: Their new colleagues and curriculum. *Phi Delta Kappan, 70*(10), 764–770.

Grant, C.A., & Sleeter, C.E. (2011). *Doing multicultural education for achievement and equity* (2nd ed.). New York: Routledge.

Gundara, J.S. (2009). The future of intercultural studies in multicultural societies. In R. Cowen & A.M. Kazamias (Eds.), *International handbook of comparative education* (pp. 1009–1026). Amsterdam: Springer.

Hale, J.E. (1982). *Black children, their roots, culture and learning styles.* Provo, UT: Brigham Young University Press.

Harmingson, D. (1973). Towards judgment. *C.A.R.E. Occasional Publication.* No. 1.

Hayden-Benn, J. (2011). Teaching against the grain: An inner-city school in Montreal starts a social justice club. *Our Schools/Our Selves, 20*(2), 19–33.

Hofstede, G. (1980). Motivation, leadership and organization: Do American theories apply abroad? *Organizational Dynamics, 9,* 42–63.

Holt, J.C. (1982). *How children fail.* New York: Delta/Seymour Lawrence.

Huber, T., & Pewewardy, C. (1990). *Maximizing learning for all students: A review of literature on learning modalities, cognitive styles and approaches to meeting the needs of diverse learners.* (ERIC Document Reproduction Service No. ED324289).

Jackson, P.W. (1987). Facing our ignorance. *Teachers College Record, 88*(2), 384–389.

Kerekhoff, A., & Campbell, R. (1977). Black-white difference: In the educational attainment process. *Sociology of Education, 50,* 15–27.

Kluckhohn, F., & Strodtbect, F. (1961). *Variations in value orientations.* Evanston, IL: Row/Peterson.

Kozol, J. (1991). *Savage inequalities: Children in American schools.* New York: Crown Publications.

Larochelle-Audet, J., Borri-Anadon, C., McAndrew, M., & Potvin, M. (2013). *La formation initiale du personnel scolaire sur la diversité ethnoculturelle, religieuse et linguistique dans les universités québécoises: Portrait quantitatif et qualitative.* Montréal: CEETUM/ Chaire de recherche du Canada sur l'éducation et les rapports ethniques.

Liston, D.P., & Zeichner, K.M. (1987). Critical pedagogy and teacher education. *Journal of Education, 169*(3), 117–137.

Locke, D.C. (1988). Teaching culturally different students: Growing pine trees or bonsai trees. *Contemporary Education, 59*(3), 130–133.

Lusted, D. (1986). "Why pedagogy?" *Screen, 27*(5), 2–14.

Lynch, J. (1987, April). *Race, class, gender and the teacher education curriculum.* Paper presented at the American Educational Research Association, Washington, DC.

Macedo, D.P. (1993). Literacy for stupefaction: The pedagogy of big lies. *Harvard Educational Review, 63*(2), 183–206.

Marx, K. (1942). *Selected works* (Vol. 1). London: Lawrence & Wishart.

McDonald, J.R. (1988). The emergence of the teacher's voice: Implications for the new reform. *Teachers College Record, 89*(4), 471–486.

McGregor, J. (1989). *Teaching strategies for reducing prejudice.* Unpublished master's thesis, McGill University, Montreal, QC.

Milligan, C.S. (1993). *Multicultural content in teacher education.* Unpublished report, McGill University, Montreal, QC.

Mills, M. (1975). Public schools and the new segregation struggle. *Equal Opportunity Review,* 1–4. (ERIC Clearinghouse on Urban Education).

Moodley, K. (1981). Canadian ethnicity in comparative perspective. In T. Fernando & J. Dahlie (Eds.), *Ethnicity, power and the politics of culture* (pp. 6–21). Toronto: Methuen.

Mukherjee, T (1981). Views from teacher education: In-service training. In M. Craft (Ed.), *Teaching in a multicultural society: A task for teacher education* (pp. 118–124). Lewes, Sussex: Falmer Press.

National Council of Welfare. (1975). *Poor kids: A report by the National Council of Welfare on children in poverty in Canada.* Ottawa: National Council of Welfare.

National Crime Prevention Centre. (2012). *A statistical snapshot of youth at risk and youth offending in Canada.* Ottawa: Public Safety Canada. Retrieved from www.publicsafety.gc.ca/cnt/rsrcs/pblctns/ststclsnpsht-yth/ssyr-eng.pdf

Nieto, S. (1992). *Affirming diversity: The sociopolitical contexts of multicultural education.* New York: Longman.

Niyozov, S. (2008). Understanding pedagogy: Cross-cultural and comparative insights from Central Asia. In K. Mundy, K. Bickmore, R. Hayhoe, M. Madden, & K. Madjidi (Eds.), *Comparative and international education: Issues for teachers* (pp. 133–160). Toronto: Canadian Scholars' Press.

Noddings, N. (1986). Fidelity in teaching, teacher education, and research for teaching. *Harvard Educational Review, 56*(4), 496–510.

Parsonson, K. (1986). Review of the effects of learning styles on achievement. In R.J. Samuda & S.L. Kong (Eds.), *Multicultural education: Programmes and methods* (pp. 33–44). Kingston/Toronto: Intercultural Social Sciences Publication.

Perry, R., & Dickens, W. (1984). Perceived control in the college classroom: The effect of response-outcome contingency training and instructor expressiveness on student achievement and attributions. *Journal of Educational Psychology, 76*(6), 966–981.

Porter, J. (1965). *The vertical mosaic: An analysis of social class and poverty in Canada.* Toronto: University of Toronto Press.

Rich, S.J. (1985). Restoring power to teachers: The impact of "whole language." *Language Arts, 62*(7), 717–724.

Rist, R. (1970). Student social class and teacher expectations: The self-fulfilling prophecy in ghetto education. *Harvard Educational Review, 40*(3), 411–451.

Rosenthal, R., & Jacobson, L. (1968). *Pygmalion in the classroom: Teacher expectation and pupils' intellectual development.* New York: Holt, Rinehart & Winston.

Schulman, L.S. (1986). Paradigms and research programs in the study of teaching: A contemporary perspective. In M.C. Wittrock (Ed.), *Handbook of research on teaching* (3rd ed.) (pp. 3–36). New York: Macmillan.

Sleeter, C.E., & Grant, C.A. (1988). Mapping terrains of power: Student cultural knowledge versus classroom knowledge. In C.E. Sleeter (Ed.), *Empowerment through multicultural education* (pp. 49–68). Albany: State University of New York Press.

Stenhouse, L. (1975). Problems in research in teaching about race relations. In C. Bagley & G. Verma (Eds.), *Race and education across cultures* (pp. 305–321). London: Heineman.

Taylor, C. (1994). *Multiculturalism: Examining the politics of recognition.* Princeton, NJ: Princeton University Press.

Tomlinson, S. (1980). The educational performance of ethnic minority children. *New Community, 8*, 3.

ACTIVITY 5
"Repeated Exposure May Cause Empathy": Reflecting on How Our
Worldviews Are Shaped by Diversity

Purpose
- Impel students to reflect on the effect that their schoolteachers had on
  their early development, and to be aware of this in their own practice if
  they pursue the teaching profession
- Promote dialogue about the need for diversity in teacher recruitment
- Develop empathy in students by encouraging them to appreciate the
  unique contributions of teachers who represent diverse worldviews
- Emphasize how important it is for all teachers to represent commitment
  to multicultural education

Description
When students look back on their educational experiences, they often reflect
fondly on particular teachers who had a profound impact on their personal
development and growth. Particularly in early childhood, students look up
to their teachers as figures of authority and bearers of knowledge—not to
mention parental proxies. Acknowledging that teachers have significant
influence on their impressionable young students, we must also realize that
they rank among only a handful of adults with whom children develop
relationships in their early lives. Thus, it is worthwhile to consider what
kinds of individuals make up the labour force in education and what kinds
of worldviews they are able to share with their students.

In this activity, you will challenge your students to look back on their
schooling experiences and reflect on their own exposure to diversity from
an early age. Begin class discussion by informally asking students to think
back to their favourite teachers. Allow a few students to share stories or
anecdotes that describe what set these teachers apart in their memories.
After this preliminary discussion, ask students to think about all of the
teachers they have ever had, and to consider whether these teachers had
any characteristics in common. Students may recall that all their teachers
gave homework or that they were all caring, but perhaps certain students
will point out that their educational experiences are limited to teachers of
all or nearly all one gender or race. Follow up on such comments by asking
the students if they think this made any difference or if they feel like they
missed out on something.

In the next stage of discussion, prompt your students to think about what unique contributions they could make to their own classroom: What would set them apart from other teachers? What kinds of perspectives or insights would they share with their students? And what kinds of students could they relate to especially well? Relate back to the earlier discussion by asking what kinds of characteristics would have been appreciated in their past teachers.

At this point, ask your students to help you with a quick census of demographic information. You may choose to simply do a count of male and female students, or you might also survey the ratio of white students to those who represent visible minorities. (If you feel that another cultural component of identity is more relevant or less sensitive for discussion in your class, you can easily modify the activity to substitute that characteristic for either gender or ethnocultural background.) Now take the total number of students in the class and calculate the proportion of male students and visible minority students, as well as any male students who also represent visible minorities (assuming that these demographics are under-represented in your sample).

Finally, instruct your students to imagine that they all work in the same school and thus represent the demographics of the faculty. Remind the class that a child enrolled in elementary school will have six teachers in total from Grades 1 through 6. Now pose the following questions: What is the chance that a student will have only female teachers throughout elementary school? What is the chance that a student will have all white teachers? What is the chance of having a male teacher more than once? What is the chance of having a teacher that represents a visible minority more than once? You may choose to calculate the answer to these questions mathematically, or you can simply estimate odds on scale of very high to very low. Conclude the activity with a final discussion that asks students to consider the importance of children's exposure to diversity.

Curricular Connections

Mathematics: Introduce concepts of probability and chance, and ask students to correctly calculate the answers to the quantitative questions posed in the activity.

Science: Adapt the activity into a survival game that demonstrates the advantages of genetic diversity among animal populations; incorporate discussion of symbiotic relationships.

Language Arts: Encourage students to take demographic inventory of the authors represented in their textbook or required readings in the curriculum; afterwards, ask them to create recommended book lists to promote inclusion of more diverse voices and stories.

Physical Education: Break up a tennis or badminton match with same-gender teams in one round and mixed-gender teams in a second round; ask students to discuss if they thought they played the game differently based on who their teammates and competitors were.

Chapter 6

TEACHING STRATEGIES AND EVALUATION

Charlotte and Peesee are Grade 3 students in a Montreal English school. Charlotte belongs to an anglophone family, while Peesee is an Inuit girl from Canada's northernmost territory, Nunavut. Both are bright students, except when it comes to skills testing. Yesterday, Nancy, the class teacher, gave Charlotte and Peesee a test in which they were to make models using Lego and other building blocks. While Charlotte did the exercise quickly and easily, Peesee had a difficult time figuring out the materials and the exercise. This was not the case, however, when the arts and crafts teacher gave exercises that involved making things using traditional materials and techniques. The teachers are in a dilemma as to how to evaluate the two girls overall. Moreover, Charlotte's mother has recently expressed concern that her daughter may have a learning disability. The school principal, Ms. Cherif, communicated this to Nancy in hopes that she would begin filling out the appropriate paperwork. Ms. Cherif also suggested that Peesee might qualify for the special education program because of her linguistic difficulties. This way, both girls would be exempt from participating in the standardized assessment being piloted in the school at the end of the year.

- If you were the teacher in this situation, how would you respond?
- Do you think it is fair to evaluate certain students differently than their peers based on separate criteria or by using alternate methods?
- To what extent do children's mental and physical abilities affect their educational and life opportunities?

INTRODUCTION

Classroom teachers must be aware that there are many inequalities built into the school environment, structure, and curriculum, and they must alter their teaching strategies to make up for those inequalities. The goal of teaching is to get students thinking. Teaching methods can have diverse effects: they can make reality opaque or illuminated (Freire, in Shor & Freire, 1987). Illuminating reality is the process of knowing reality and how it is made. Freire stresses the importance of both content and the dynamism of the lecturer—the approach teachers take to initiate the learning process. Does a teacher's approach critically reorient students to society? Does it animate their critical thinking? Teaching can be an oral transfer of knowledge, or it can be a problem-posing illumination that challenges student thinking—"a *challenge* to be unveiled, and *never* a channel of transference of knowledge" (Shor & Freire, 1987, p. 40). Liberatory education should provoke students to challenge and rethink the way they see reality.

Various pedagogical approaches and strategies are particularly conducive to liberatory pedagogy while also serving the objectives of a redefined multicultural education. They are all multi-dimensional and consist of various methods. They focus on involving student experiences and developing positive identity, critical thinking, and empowerment. They provide a wide range of learning experiences that enhance a positive concept of self.

Do these strategies involve more work for teachers? This question is best answered if we focus on the potential to motivate and engage students in the dynamics of learning and becoming. Yes, "we must be careful here that teachers' involvement in matters beyond the boundaries of their own classrooms does not make excessive demands on their time, energy, and expertise, diverting their attention from their core mission with students" (Zeichner, 2009, p. 126). But if these methods can keep students from dropping out of school and life because of boredom and disciplinary problems, then teachers will not worry about too much work. But they must have patience with these approaches because they require skill and mastery. Gaining initial knowledge of the strategies and subsequent planning will undoubtedly be time-consuming; however, it is important to understand that once the pattern is established, these strategies can save time and energy for both teacher and students.

PEDAGOGICAL APPROACHES

Developing Skills

Learning to learn requires listening, language (reading), and thinking skills. Information processing through images and words is influenced by a person's intelligence, but the process of learning does not develop in isolation. Moreover, the process must be student-centred so that concepts are meaningful and relevant, and not just memorized data. An environment conducive to developing and fostering improved skills must be created through critical inquiry, that is, raising questions about historical and contemporary issues. Communication skills cannot be developed without concern for others. Listening is important and must be developed not only for learning, but also for considering and responding to others' points of view. Language is crucial not only because it describes the way we see the world, but also because it is a tool of power and therefore must be developed with care so as to make it inclusive (Gaskell, McLaren, & Novogrodsky, 1989).

Students need guidance from teachers to help them develop good thinking skills. Egocentric ways of reasoning are pervasive in society and school, and students are not generally taught to recognize such methods as bias. Examining other points of view, recognizing bias, and making decisions must be guided. Contextual thinking is a most basic cognitive skill, as it asks students to consider the "big picture." Students must be able to identify and define problems before they can proceed to problem solving. Knowledge should not be taken as information; rather, it is to be treated as a product that has been constructed by the mind. With practice, students learn how to discover for themselves strategies that lead to solutions, and this may help empower them. If they do not, teachers can provide them with subtle techniques through direct instruction. Over time, the use of these strategies will become spontaneous for students, at which point they become internalized. Transfer and application must be taught through questioning and example. Good thinking results from thinking "frames" (organized strategies) that foster better organization and support, and induce or motivate thought. "Thinking tools"—devices or ideas such as cognitive mapping, where students are prompted to construct a visual representation of concepts and to draw connections between them—help develop thinking skills. Higher-order thinking skills, including application, analysis, evaluation, and synthesis, should be integrated throughout the curriculum as essential cross-curricular competencies.

Developing Affective Aspects

Feminist theory focuses on the positive contributions that emotions make to knowledge and communication. It proposes taking emotions seriously and extending them from the private sphere of the family to the public sphere of the school. Emotional responses are normally not encouraged in the formal school system, which emphasizes logical thinking and reasoning. The argument here is that emotions are not opposed to reason, as is generally thought in education and society. Education means the development of the whole person, and this involves caring and attention to affective needs. Without attention to feelings of empathy, caring, and compassion for others, education is not complete. Hence, the development of feelings and emotions is an important aspect of multiculturalism and, like multiculturalism, cannot simply be appended to the content. It needs to be developed by example throughout the curriculum.

Deconstruction

Deconstruction is a method of decoding—for example, reversing binary opposites (good and bad), discussing them, and then generating new values. Cornell West (1993) calls this demystification. Deconstruction is an attempt to explain the function of specific social practices that sustain unequal power relations, such as patriarchy (a concept in which men have power over women). In recent education research related to classroom issues and school practices, the deconstruction approach has been applied to discussion of news media and current events with students (Galczynski, Tsagkaraki, & Ghosh, 2012), as well as more generally to unpacking concepts such as class (Gorski, 2012), privilege (Case, 2013), and deficit thinking (Fránquiz, Salazar, & Passos DeNicolo, 2011; Garcia & Guerra, 2004).

Anti-Racist Education

As an academic concept, anti-racist education is often seen as a successor to multicultural education. More often than not, however, anti-racist education and multicultural education are used synonymously. Those who find anti-racist education more useful as a concept primarily do so to distinguish it from the official view of multiculturalism and multicultural education. The official view, it is argued, "exoticizes" differences (colour, race, language, culture) rather than acknowledging how difference becomes a deficit or disadvantage. Multicultural education in this sense becomes monocultural education because one culture is exemplified. The official multiculturalism focuses on having classrooms of children from different cultural, ethnic, and racial backgrounds rather than considering different cultural perspectives and restructuring the decision-making setup to be more inclusive and representative.

According to Enid Lee, consultant on anti-racist education and organizational change, anti-racist/multicultural education must focus on "how the school is run in terms of who gets to be involved with decisions. It has to do with parents and how their voices are heard or not heard. It has to do with who gets hired in the school" (quoted in Au, 2009, p. 10). Similarly, decisions regarding syllabus structure and choice of instructional materials distinguish monocultural from truly multicultural (anti-racist) education. For instance, if the toys and games selected for a kindergarten class are reflective of the dominant culture, race, and language, then it will be essentially a monocultural classroom regardless of the presence of children from a number of different backgrounds (Au, 2009).

Anti-racist education emphasizes the political, historical, social, and economic aspects of all knowledge and subjects. It exposes the dominant ideology, provides alternative perspectives to the predominant Western worldview, and exposes the social construction of race and gender. For example, rather than blame the Third World alone for its problems, the anti-racist approach examines the relationship of developing countries to, and economic exploitation by, the West. It also challenges the assumption that European standards are universal (Gill, Singh, & Vance, 1987).

In contemporary society, few teachers are blatantly racist; however, to teach a subject like science uncritically inevitably maintains the dominance of one ideology. An anti-racist approach to science and health subjects offers the opportunity to debunk myths about the hierarchical classification of races. For instance, scientifically there is no such thing as race, but society has constructed racism. In terms of biological traits, 90 percent of *Homo sapiens* are thought to share the same genetic makeup. Anti-racist education methods, then, lead to a consideration of racial justice (Gill et al., 1987). Anti-racist education has three broad goals: (1) to attempt to integrate all minority groups into the education system; (2) to provide teachers and students with the knowledge and critical abilities to counter racism both within and outside of schools; and (3) to identify and change educational policies, procedures, and practices that foster racism (Canadian Race Relations Foundation, 1999). Anti-racist education has been implemented in Ontario and British Columbia; however, its implementation in British Columbia has been in the spirit of the official policy of multiculturalism, whereby racial difference is recognized but issues of power and privilege are by and large ignored.

In terms of strategy, it is unreasonable to expect a direct transformation from a monocultural to a multicultural/anti-racist education. A broad strategy to accomplish such a change can proceed along four phases. The first phase includes surface changes such as multicultural expressions (welcome signs in multiple languages, etc.) in schools; however, as Lee cautions, this should be a starting point, not a stopping point, as is often the case (in Au, 2009). From this point on, restructuring of the curriculum should begin. The second phase should include the creation of new teaching units and modules that are sensitive to the minorities hitherto excluded from the syllabus. During the third phase, the new units and modules that are sensitive to anti-racism are integrated into the main curriculum so that they do not remain peripheral but become embedded in the core curriculum. For instance, instead of starting with the Enlightenment, the civilization module in history class should also include Indian, Chinese, and other civilizations so that European civilization is not considered the norm and the beginning of the civilized world, and the latter are not labelled the "others." Finally, in the fourth phase, children can be expected to implement the new curriculum outside of the classroom/school. This can perhaps be termed as the social change stage leading to a non-racial education.

Questions about difference and differential treatment should be dealt with as a matter of routine throughout the curriculum, not only when they arise. Race-relations and prejudice-reduction strategies are not sufficient. Students need to internalize the idea that all human beings have rights. The race-relations approach is based on the concept of harmonious relations, but racism cannot be reduced by attempts to get along well together. As educators, we adhere to the belief that ability is distributed evenly across populations, even if we are aware that social and economic assets are not. Human beings are considered similar by virtue of their shared membership in the human race, but they are born unequal in multiple ways (Ghosh, 2012). Similarly, prejudice-reduction programs that deal with attitudes at the individual level rather than political, historical, and economic levels, where they interrelate, are less likely to be effective.

Our notion of redefined multicultural education is different from anti-racist education in two important ways. First, in conceptual terms, it moves beyond the critical perspective employed by anti-racist education by addressing a broader set of politicized differences that include not only race and class, but also gender, sexual orientation, and (dis)ability. Second, the redefined notion of multicultural education is more comprehensive and subsumes intercultural, anti-racial, and inter-ethnic perspectives.

Teaching about Cultures

The teaching of minority cultures and languages is important for minority children's identity and psychological survival. Self-concept is related to success in school, and teachers can be a positive force in this area by being knowledgeable about other cultures and showing sensitivity in cross-cultural interactions. In a multicultural society, the study of other cultures is absolutely essential, but isolating (and even trivializing) a child's culture is more likely to have detrimental effects, for several reasons. First, emphasis on the child's culture is likely to separate the child from the mainstream culture. A study of culture is valid when dealt with as a topic for intellectual discussion, but when it is relegated to folklore and festivals, culture is trivialized and minority children are subjected to a patronizing attitude. When taken in isolation, this "can be pressed in a patronizing, if not a racist way" (Rex, 1981, p. 39). Second, it is doubtful that emphasis on the child's culture alone will develop positive self-concept when the child faces discrimination *because* of membership in that culture. Teaching of cultures must be done within the larger framework of universal respect. Finally, what is often studied is a version of the culture the child does not live and is certainly not likely to face in her or his own life situations in *this* society. This confuses minority children and further marginalizes them. Indeed, "multicultural education is much more than learning facts and information about people's experiences, cultures, and histories. It includes a serious examination of Eurocentric cultural values, norms, and expectations that form the dominant perspectives through which many of us theorize about education and curriculum development" (Lee, Menkart, & Okazawa-Rey, 2006, p. xii). As such, multicultural education offers the opportunity to incorporate more diverse worldviews.

Teaching Controversial Issues

Teachers need to face controversial issues head on, even if it is painful to do so. Singh (1989) points out that teaching controversial issues related to racial and sexual discrimination involves moral issues and values. The teacher must be committed to the fundamental values of justice, fairness, and respect for others. To take a neutral approach, by avoiding discussion of racism and sexism, under the guise of avoiding indoctrination is harmful and evasive. Neither school nor society is neutral. A "neutral" approach is a stance that serves to perpetuate inequality. While the teacher must protect divergent views, teaching is designed to bring about certain outcomes. Racism and sexism are wrong, and to say so is not indoctrination. Rather, "to oppose [such] anti-democratic tendencies, we must take up the challenge of redefining and re-imagining teaching as a vital public service and schools as democratic public spheres. This means reminding teachers and everyone concerned about education of their responsibility to take ethical and risky positions and engage in practices currently at odds with both religious fundamentalism and the market-driven values that now dominate public schooling" (Giroux, 2012, p. 8). If the purpose of teaching is to bring about learning to act justly and fairly, the values held by students cannot be left to chance. Universal values such as fairness, respect, and equality are learned from concrete situations in the classroom, the school environment, and students' lives; it is "open-minded teaching … that succeeds in bringing about open-mindedness in pupils" (Singh, 1989, p. 232). Hidden

When teaching values, openness does not mean that every conviction is as good as the other or that conflicting values are resolved by lapsing into relativism. Relativism means that values are relative to the society that produced them. For example, child labour may be practiced in a particular society, but child labour undermines children's rights and therefore must be rejected as universally bad. There is nothing culturally justifiable in child labour. The important thing is that justification of a position should be built on analysis and should not be just a matter of personal preference. Values govern interpersonal relations, and both teachers and students must be aware of what they do and why they do it. This involves developing the mind as well as the heart. It is not enough to stop racism and sexism in the classroom—this may be superficial and temporary; instead, it is necessary to question the assumptions of school and societal organization that are based on barriers created around difference. Racist and sexist behaviours are not only unconstitutional, but they also violate human rights—they must be eradicated from society.

When students are encouraged to develop habits of questioning and thinking critically about their immediate environment, their beliefs, and their identities, the foundation is laid for them to become conscious and participating citizens. Critical questioning "involves asking not only 'Is this true?' but also 'Who says so?' 'Who benefits most when people believe it is true?' 'How are we taught to accept that it is true?' [and] 'What alternative ways of looking at the problem can we see?'" (Grant & Sleeter, 2009, p. 261). The teacher who is keen to discuss controversial issues and current events in his or her classroom can pique student interest by bringing up news that they may have already heard about on television, the Internet, and social media, or discussions with family and friends (Galczynski et al., 2012). Moreover, the teacher can engage his or her students by challenging the perceptions of youth in the media, as they "generally become visible in the media and in the public eye in [only] a negative manner; they are seen as dangerous, violent—a 'problem.' In some ways these images of youth are similar to the stereotypes and tensions that arise around cultural and ethnic difference and diversity" (Al-Shanti, 2011, p. 89).

At the same time, the professional expertise and experience of the teacher as a pedagogue is necessary to steer discussion of controversial issues in a productive direction, one that enables students to develop greater empathy for those whom society labels as "different" (Galczynski et al., 2012). The teacher needs to think about issues of difference, power, and privilege raised in the current events he or she decides to focus on, and then cultivate discussions with students in a manner appropriate for their level of maturity. In a multicultural framework, lessons that broach these issues cannot be taught as separate subjects; rather, they must be skilfully worked into everyday lesson plans. This is easy enough, however, as the multicultural teacher can use a current event as an introduction to the day's lesson or as a compelling supplement to regular curricular content. Creativity may be required on the part of the teacher, but with practice this pedagogical approach will become second nature.

INSTRUCTIONAL STRATEGIES

Using Student Experience

Teaching methods must give primacy to student culture, language, and experiences. School culture usually confirms white, male, middle-class voices and excludes or disparages others. Teachers must learn how to understand, validate, and analyze the experiences of students from all backgrounds. They must apply and develop conditions for learning that incorporate student experiences and enable students to assert their voices. The notion of voice must be part of the reconstruction of identity in a curriculum built on difference. Dignifying minority cultures and experiences in a meaningful way leads to the empowerment of minority students.

This does not mean endorsing all student experiences uncritically, but rather examining all experiences. The emphasis must be on interpersonal, affective, and cognitive experiences. How quickly teachers can learn about their students—their experiences, intellectual abilities, feelings of joy or alienation, and living conditions—will influence their teaching. In this sense, teachers are researchers and must learn to listen to students. In combining research with teaching, they involve their students and genuinely motivate them while narrowing the distance between them. Moreover, it is imperative to know about the lives of their students. For example, why do some students not do their work? The answer may have nothing to do with what actually happens at school and can be difficult to discern on the part of the teacher. For instance, as is common among students from lower socio-economic backgrounds, one reason the student may not be learning could be undernourishment or ill health. As Freire said, "[when] I began to eat better, I began to understand better what I was reading" (Shor & Freire, 1987, p. 29). Teachers need to be cognizant that their students' lives inside and outside of the classroom are sometimes incompatible, and that this can have a significant effect on their motivation and achievement in school. It is important for teachers to recognize the reality of their students' experiences in order to set more reasonable expectations, design more meaningful lessons and activities, and develop more equitable methods of evaluation.

Freire (Shor & Freire, 1987) suggests one way of using student experiences in teaching: Starting from students' descriptions of their daily experiences, teachers can take a topic of student interest, such as music, human psychology, physics of motion, or sports, and then move out to explore the topics together. This allows critical participation of students in their own education. For example, teachers can begin with popular thinking from a non-expert's point of view: What is gravity? What are emotions? How many kinds of music are there? Students can work in groups, report to class, and compare their points of view with others. The teacher can then think scientifically with them about this material. Situated research moves students beyond the limits that restrict them in traditional methods and curricula, and makes them active researchers. It gives "texture" to teaching and moves away from purely abstract concepts. Labinowicz (1985) points out that in math "we see what we understand rather than understand what we see" (p. 7). Even the basic operations in mathematics problem solving can be illustrated through daily activities. The central issue of math teaching is finding meaning rather than precision. Involving student experiences, as Dewey often suggested, is to engage feelings and emotions in the learning process. This is an essential aspect of multicultural education; in this way, multicultural education moves beyond human rights education.

Issue-Based Global Perspective

Multiple and global perspectives provide new and interesting ways of teaching that give students alternatives in order to show that there is no single answer. Such perspectives reveal several myths regarding the notion of European superiority. For example, did you know that the first successful heart surgeon, Daniel Hale Williams, was a black man? That geometry and other mathematical sciences originated in Egypt (Duncan, 1986)? That the concept of zero, developed in India, spread to the Arab world, was brought to Italy, and eventually to Britain (Williams, 1965)? Studying such issues as environmental problems helps students connect with other parts of the world through experiences that are not contained by national borders.

Issue-based study involves activities such as designing experiments, postulating and testing hypotheses, measuring, observing, recording, communicating, and working together. Basic math and science facts can be applied to global problems. A global approach cannot be divorced from history. For example, many ethnic conflicts in the world today have their roots in colonialism. Teaching students this will allow them to see that wealth does not exist without poverty, and that the Industrial Revolution in England was made possible because of the supply of raw materials from British colonies. Similarly, domination by men would not be possible without the subjugation of women.

Teaching Values

According to Rokeach (1973), values refer to either (1) means (modes of conduct), or instrumental values, such as honesty, love, responsibility, and courage; or (2) ends, or terminal values, such as freedom, equality, world peace, and inner harmony. As such, critical thinking needs to be applied to moral problems in the appropriate context. Moral values have "good" or "right" associated with them. Teachers and students need to consider alternatives, and discuss outcomes. Teachers must ask themselves what their values are and how they are produced and sustained. Students need not only moral leadership, but also guidance to sort out values. There is much more to teaching values than rationality because values involve the affective aspect—the inner self. Students acquire moral values by constructing them for themselves and by interacting with other pe/ must help students work out mutually acceptable solutions throug. tion of human rights principles, discussion, and problem solving.

Banks (1992) has developed a value inquiry model for teachers to use to help students acquire moral values. After choosing a story or scenario, teachers can ask students to do the following:

1. Define the value problem: What is the value problem being faced?
2. Describe the behaviour, and the values exemplified by the behaviour, and its conflict with other values: What does each person think is important? What do they think is right? What do they value? Do their ideas/beliefs conflict?
3. Think about the sources of the values being discussed: How did each person develop these values? What are some other related values?
4. Make a choice: what decision would you make in the situation depicted in the story? What are the possible consequences of the decision made in the story? How different could your decision be?

Multicultural education demands a democratic and morally responsible attitude to students' values if students are to become sensitive to differential treatment based on sex, race/ethnicity, and class. Developing and clarifying a set of values involves seeing how they conflict and considering the consequences of choices within the context of human dignity. Teachers need to create an environment in which democratic principles of equity, fairness, and justice are present. It is essential to discuss the purpose of education and the values exemplified by schools: Who is served by education? Who is disadvantaged? Why are cooperation and caring not seen as being as valuable as rationality and analytic thought? Students must question the Western, male, middle-class values that restrict the emotional development of dominant-group children, as well as minority children, whose own values are at variance. According to Martin (1985), when the "hierarchy of values is rejected, teaching methods, learning activities, classroom atmospheres, teacher-pupil relationships, school structures, [and] attitudes towards education may all be affected" (p. 198). In addition to the three R's (reading, writing, and arithmetic), Martin suggests that schools add the three C's: caring, concern, and connection.

Developing Learning Experiences

Crawford (1993) suggests several phases in the development of multicultural learning experiences. The first phase, the introduction, should consist of orientation, focus, and purpose-setting activities. Students and teacher together determine what students know and are interested in. The second phase, the theme/topic phase, develops the content through planned learning experiences, involving several subject areas and taking into account instructional groupings (co-operative learning); classroom organization and management to locate appropriate material (library work); and consultation with the teacher and the exchange of ideas among students. Students must have opportunities to share activities through various media and displays. The third phase is generalization, in which integration takes place and leads to higher-level thinking. The last phase allows for reflection on what has been learned and its implications.

Dialogic/Discussion Method

The dialogic method is a means of communicating. Discussion is not chatting. It begins with teacher and student reflecting together on familiar topics, starting from the concrete and gradually guiding students to detach themselves and consider the abstract. The choice of theme is critical: while a theme can be chosen from the formal curriculum, it must be related to students' lives. The themes generate ideas because they are important to the students. Teachers can start with what students want to know and lead the discussion to incorporate curricular objectives. This method can involve individual or group work, library research, writing, student presentations, or fieldwork. Students are able to construct peer relations instead of authority-dependent relations. When students are working on their own, teachers are able to do research on students. With skill, teachers can engage shy students (often from minority groups) in asking questions and participating in discussions. Teacher lectures can help students if the need arises. While students present their own analyses, teachers must bring all of the perspectives together and provide a historical and global view.

Socratic Questioning

Teacher questioning is an important aspect of learning as well as a significant means of student validation. Teachers must be skilled in asking questions about a text the class has read to improve student understanding of basic ideas and values. The Greek philosopher Socrates (470–399 BC) used questioning for self-examination and to encourage critical thinking about one's own life. Students must likewise learn to ask critical questions about texts and about power: who has it, why, what kind of power, and how it is used.

A simple method of applying this to classroom practice asks students to take sides on a particular issue—literally. In an appeal to kinesthetic learners, the teacher can designate opposite sides of the classroom as representative of the positions "for" or "against" the issue being debated. Students are asked to sit on the side that aligns with their own opinion. As class discussion proceeds, students may decide to relocate in response to the ideas presented and questions posed by their peers. The teacher may also designate an "undecided" section, which can temporarily placate students who have not made up their minds on the issue and would like to hear more from their classmates before advocating for a particular side.

Role-Play

This method puts the student in another person's shoes. Role-play does not necessarily involve acting but does require the student to put him or herself in the place of an individual in a film, story, or real-life situation (for example, one that involves racism or sexism) and live through the experience. A series of questions (posed by the teacher or other students, or self-generated) guides students to experience how others feel. The feeling should be made explicit and discussed. Role-play activities often involve considerable preparation; however, the teacher may ask his or her students to research their particular roles on their own to simplify the planning process. Research on role-play as a tool for the promotion of multiculturalism (Ogawa, 2010; Gordon, 2012) suggests that this strategy helps students develop understanding and empathy.

Co-operative Learning

To be effective and truly engaging for all students, co-operative learning often requires extensive preparation. Nevertheless, it has been shown to have a positive effect on students, helping to raise achievement, develop positive attitudes and respect for difference, increase the ability to work together to solve problems, and improve race relations (Slavin, 1987). This technique suits students from many non-Western cultures, as well as females. The fear that some students may tend to dominate the process can be avoided by keeping groups small, pairing students of different backgrounds but changing groupings often, and giving students responsibility for their own learning. Co-operative learning is a valuable and useful tool in multicultural education, and teachers are encouraged to consult the literature on the various strategies used (Aronson, 1978; Cartwright & Zander, 1968; Dishon & O'Leary, 1984; Johnson, 1981). This pedagogical strategy can be implemented directly in the classroom or virtually, through technology and social media (Hossain & Aydin, 2011; Nicolson & Uematsu, 2013).

One specific strategy that can be used to facilitate co-operative learning is the jigsaw method. In jigsaw activities, heterogeneous groups are formed (by the teacher or the students themselves), topics are discussed, and material distributed. Each small group of four to six students assigns an important but different role or task to each individual group member. Students first study individually, then join with other classmates who have the same information to discuss and critique the topic, and finally return to their original groups to tutor the rest of their group on their area of specialization. Because each task is important, all students must contribute in an interdependent way. Although considerable planning is required, in the long run the workload becomes minimal, as the teacher becomes more efficient at designing tasks and students become more comfortable with the activity format.

EVALUATION

Evaluation is an important part of education. It provides feedback regarding how students relate to what is taught. It also provides feedback on a teacher's ability to impart knowledge. However, evaluation can also be highly political and used as a power tool rather than a diagnostic tool. Used judiciously, it can point to the reasons why some students might not be able to assimilate the imparted knowledge.

It is as important to rethink and redefine evaluation as it is to redefine multicultural education. Without one, the other might not be able to achieve the results it seeks. It is important to question the basic purpose of evaluation: Is it a means to an end or an end in itself? Seen as an end, evaluation can be political and may discriminate against certain students. As an end in itself, evaluation is linked to our value judgments about what knowledge is important. It thus loses objectivity and the purpose for which it is used in the first place. Evaluation should be understood as a means to an end: the production and reproduction of knowledge. It should aim to measure the quality rather than just the quantity of knowledge a student acquires.

It is also important to determine the target of evaluation; that is, who should be assessed? Should the instruments assess only the students or should the ability of/method used by the teacher to impart knowledge also be assessed? Similarly, it is important to ask what should be assessed. Should it be competency in basic skills, such as language, writing, and math, or overarching achievements, such as good citizenship and critical thinking? Are the standardized instruments of evaluation adequate to assess all students in a classroom or the educational system? Raising these questions is important not only for the transparency and objectivity of the evaluation system, but also for the effective functioning of a multicultural education system.

There are fundamental problems with the traditional system of evaluation in terms of its multicultural soundness. The traditional instruments of evaluation are based on particular definitions of excellence and achievement. These definitions favour a male, middle-class, European/North American student and are culturally biased against females and students belonging to minority ethnocultural groups. Monocultural evaluation tends to label students and focus attention on their lack of ability as determined by the values and codes of a particular culture, rather than on the discriminatory nature of the examination and assessment process itself. Such arguments have been raised, for instance, against the monocultural character of IQ tests, which are more suitable for the white, middle-class, male students than for any other segment of society. Similar objections have been raised against entrance exams for professional colleges. Sedlacek and Sue (1995), for instance, have argued that evaluation measures and techniques that have established reliability and validity in white, male, middle-class academic milieux are not suitable for assessing female or working-class students or those from other cultural and racial groups.

Evaluative instruments, especially qualitative instruments, tend to hide the biases of the dominant culture while highlighting the differences in students from minority cultures. Qualitative evaluations are usually based on questions and values important to the dominant culture. They tend to focus on attributes possessed and valued by the dominant group, and perpetuate difference and inequality as a result.

Quantitative exam grades may appear to be objective but they are based on a value system that is not shared by all who are tested and evaluated. This is because traditional quantitative evaluation techniques are based on the assumption that knowledge can be measured in quantitative terms. They are aimed at testing only that part of knowledge that is deemed important to the dominant culture. These kinds of approaches have repercussions on a global scale, as countries strive to come out on top of international rankings of student achievement through large, cross-national assessments such as the Organisation for Economic Co-operation and Development's Programme for International Student Assessment (PISA) and the International Association for the Evaluation of Educational Achievement's (IEA) Trends in International Mathematics and Science Study (TIMSS). Such assessments have far-reaching effects, because "the power that emanates from global education rankings is the power to precisely define what knowledge is. And if this most valuable form of knowledge is seen as cascading down from those nations at the top of the rankings, then those nations … are validated in their practices of knowledge-production, and so lower-ranking nations will try to emulate those practices" (Galczynski, 2014). The problem is that large-scale international assessments have been limited to just a handful of subject areas (science, mathematics, reading) and thus interpret knowledge in a very limited scope. The notion of multiple intelligences (Gardner, 1983), on the other hand, suggests that other intelligences, such as musical, physical, social, and emotional, should also be evaluated.

Quantification of evaluation procedures can also lead to unhealthy competition among students. Too much competition for grades has the potential to restrict students' learning space. Students might develop strategies that are more conducive to getting numerical grades than to reflecting, contemplating, and internalizing what is taught. Most importantly, this deflects attention from creativity and innovation, which are so important in today's world.

Considerations for Multiculturally Relevant Evaluation

The aims of evaluation are related to the aims of education. Do we want to assess what students do or do not know, or do we want to evaluate how they think and what kinds of moral judgments they can make? Who is the evaluation for? Will it improve teaching and learning? What, how, and why we assess are linked with our ideas of what knowledge is important, how it is acquired, and why we need to acquire that knowledge—is it because of exams?

A multiculturally relevant evaluation system must be based on a different set of educational goals. Evaluation instruments that are sensitive to the many cultures that populate our schools and society should be developed. Those who develop these instruments must recognize that the goal of evaluation and assessment is not to establish singular, universal standards. A co-operative rather than competitive assessment system, for instance, has the potential to create learning spaces. By lifting the pressure from students to "excel," such a system will create the space for reasoning and reflection.

Whereas all assessments are conducted and interpreted within a specific cultural context, the cultural assumptions that underlie assessments have often been ignored. Indeed, there are fundamental problems with evaluation in terms of its multicultural soundness. These problems include the following:

- The knowledge for which students are tested excludes many students and represents the experiences of the dominant class. In this way, the assessment procedures discriminate against culturally different students because some students cannot relate to the knowledge that is taught.
- Evaluations are based on a particular definition of excellence and achievement that tends to favour a male, European, middle-class norm while ignoring female and culturally different students. Therefore, the tests (especially standardized tests) are culturally biased toward some.
- The concept of multiple intelligences (Gardner, 1983) requires that we test all kinds of intelligence and attributes, such as caring and feeling as well as reasoning and thinking; however, existing evaluations tend not to do so.

- One assumption in evaluation procedures is that knowledge is a quantifiable and measurable commodity. But, as Freire points out, it is impossible to measure knowledge with rulers, as if 20 feet of knowledge were made in class today (Shor & Freire, 1987).
- The quantification of inequalities perpetuates the hierarchy through supposed equal opportunity. Test scores that appear in the form of numbers look objective but, in reality, hide many biases.
- Exam grades label students and focus attention on their "disabilities" rather than on the discrimination of the system.
- Schools traditionally track students toward non-professional subjects when they do not identify with prescribed curriculum or fit into given teaching styles. For example, lack of proficiency in language of instruction is often given as a reason for placing bright students in academically unchallenging classes. Such students may need some specialized instruction in language to continue. When students are grouped along class, race, and gender lines, streaming or tracking constitutes discrimination.

A multiculturally relevant evaluation system must be based on a different set of educational goals. New measures must have a broader framework of values, ways of knowing, and modes of learning. Such a framework requires a redefinition of excellence and of the purpose of testing. Standardized tests should be avoided as much as possible. Teacher-made tests should search for the best ways to determine competence, rather than failure. Tests should be based on considerations such as how they will improve learning and how they relate to students. If testing is to improve learning, it should be continuous (as a data-gathering system throughout the year), involve a variety of data, be co-operative rather than competitive, and be used to improve teaching. Teachers must challenge the real cause of underachievement. They must use evaluation as a diagnostic tool rather than a power tool. Evaluation presupposes a power relation: "Measuring levels of achievement is not a technical issue, but a political one" (Gaskell et al., 1989, p. 18).

While an increasing number of teachers are "doing" multicultural education, few have adequate training in both instrument development and the multicultural issues involved in testing and evaluation. One proposed solution to this problem is to increase interaction between those teachers with a quantitative orientation and those with interest and expertise in multicultural issues so that there is a free flow of ideas and information that can be used to cooperatively develop multicultural evaluation techniques. Formal training in evaluation methods that are sensitive to multicultural education should also be provided to teachers at both the in-service and pre-service stages.

In order to make present evaluation systems more sensitive to the needs of a redefined multicultural education, they should be based on an objective understanding of different cultural contexts rather than just labels, such as "pass," "fail," and letter grades. Testing should be made more conducive to the learning process. Ongoing evaluation (spread over a certain learning period), for instance, can result in a better understanding of students' learning abilities. Furthermore, students should be evaluated not only for their problem-solving skills; according to Gardner's (1983) concept of multiple intelligences, students should be tested for all kinds of intelligence and attributes, such as caring and feeling as well as reasoning and thinking. Standardized testing procedures based on the values of the dominant culture can only strengthen hierarchies and biases. Testing should be more inclusive of the value systems of the body of students it aims to evaluate.

Moreover, different cultural contexts must be taken into account when exams are being conceptualized. What Helms (1992) and Sedlacek and Sue (1995) note for psychological education is equally relevant to other branches of education. They observe that at the conceptualization stage there is a lack of developmental multicultural thinking. Cultural groups other than the dominant one are "thrown in" to "see how their test results compare with those of the population on which the test was normed" (Sedlacek & Sue, 1995, p. 2). A truly multicultural evaluation should be geared towards "understanding" the causes of underachievement rather than simply being the marker of failure (or success). Instruments that have the capacity to label students in terms of achiever/underachiever or good/bad should be modified.

CONCLUSION

This chapter has discussed some teaching strategies that take into account students who are "different." Both teaching strategies and evaluation methods are based on the goals of education. The present goals and evaluations do not emphasize the integration and inclusion of minority-group children. An essential part of a redefined multicultural education is redefining what schools should strive for, broadening the framework of values and how things should be done, and recasting the concept of excellence and achievement and, therefore, of evaluation.

REVIEW QUESTIONS

1. From the perspective of a teacher, which of the approaches and strategies described in this chapter would you feel most comfortable implementing in the classroom? Explain why.

2. From the perspective of a student, which of the approaches and strategies described in this chapter would interest you most in the classroom? Explain why.

3. How do the approaches and strategies discussed in this chapter address the needs of all different kinds of students?

4. Do you think that taking a multicultural approach to teaching requires a lot of work? Is this an extra demand placed on teachers, or is it the responsibility of all good educators?

5. How can particular methods of testing discriminate against students who are perceived as different?

6. What should be the purpose of evaluation in a redefined multicultural education? Can it be compatible with the realities of the teaching profession?

7. From the perspective of a teacher, what kinds of evaluation methods do you consider to be most fair: letter grades (A–F), numerical percentages (0–100 percent), rank-based grades (percentiles, bell curves), categorical grades, pass or fail marks, or peer evaluation methods?

8. From the perspective of a student, what kinds of evaluation methods do you consider to be most fair: letter grades (A–F), numerical percentages (0–100 percent), rank-based grades (percentiles, bell curves), categorical grades, pass or fail marks, or peer evaluation methods?

9. Is it fair to eliminate awarding grades from the evaluation process altogether? Is this compatible with the realities of the teaching profession?

REFERENCES

Al-Shanti, N. (2011). Perceptions of difference and change: Seeing value in diversity. *Our Schools/Our Selves, 20*(2), 83–99.

Aronson, E. (1978). *The jigsaw classroom.* Beverly Hills, CA: Sage.

Au, W. (Ed.). (2009). *Rethinking multicultural education: Teaching for racial and cultural justice.* Milwaukee, WI: Rethinking Schools.

Banks, J.A. (1992). A curriculum for empowerment, action and change. In K. Moodley (Ed.), *Beyond multicultural education: International perspectives* (pp. 154–170). Calgary: Detselig.

Canadian Race Relations Foundation. (1999). *Race Relations Bulletin, 2*(2), 1–8.

Cartwright, D., & Zander, A. (Eds.). (1968). *Group dynamics.* New York: Harper & Row.

Case, K.A. (Ed.). (2013). *Deconstructing privilege: Teaching and learning as allies in the classroom.* New York: Routledge.

Crawford, L.W. (1993). *Language and literacy learning in multicultural classrooms.* Boston: Allyn and Bacon.

Dishon, D., & O'Leary, P. (1984). *A guidebook for cooperative learning*. Holmes Beach, FL: Learning Publications.

Duncan, C.G. (1986). Towards a multicultural curriculum—Secondary. In R.K. Arora & C.G. Duncan (Eds.), *Multicultural education: Towards good practice* (pp. 62–73). London: Routledge.

Fránquiz, M.E., Salazar, M.C., & Passos DeNicolo, C. (2011). Challenging majoritarian tales: Portraits of bilingual teachers deconstructing deficit views of bilingual learners. *Bilingual Research Journal, 34*(3), 279–300.

Galczynski, M. (2014, in press). Developing a clearer snapshot of educational quality through the lens of international large-scale assessments: A meta-interpretation of PISA, TIMSS, PIRLS, and ICCS. In D.B. Napier (Ed.), *Qualities of Education in a Globalised World*. Rotterdam: Sense Publishers.

Galczynski, M., Tsagkaraki, V., & Ghosh, R. (2012). Unpacking multiculturalism in the classroom: Using current events to explore the politics of difference. *Canadian Ethnic Studies, 43*(3), 145–164.

Garcia, S.B., & Guerra, P.L. (2004). Deconstructing deficit thinking: Working with educators to create more equitable learning environments. *Education and Urban Society, 36*(2), 150–168.

Gardner, H. (1983). *Frames of mind: The theory of multiple intelligences*. New York: Basic Books.

Gaskell, J., McLaren, A., & Novogrodsky, M. (1989). *Claiming an education: Feminism and Canadian schools*. Toronto: Our Schools/Our Selves Education Foundation.

Gill, D., Singh, E., & Vance, M. (1987). Multicultural versus anti-racist science: Biology. In D. Gill & L. Levidow (Eds.), *Anti-racist science teaching* (pp. 124–135). London: Free Association Books.

Ghosh, R. (2012). Diversity and excellence in higher education: Is there a conflict? *Comparative Education Review, 56*(2), 349–365

Giroux, H. (2012). *Education and the crisis of public values: Challenging the assault on teachers, students, and public education*. New York: Peter Lang.

Gordon, T. (2012). Using role-play to foster transformational and social action multiculturalism in the ESL classroom. *TESOL Journal, 3*(4), 698–721.

Gorski, P.C. (2012). Perceiving the problem of poverty and schooling: Deconstructing the class stereotypes that mis-shape education practice and policy. *Equity and Excellence in Education, 45*(2), 302–319.

Grant, C.A., & Sleeter, C.E. (2009). *Turning on learning: Five approaches for multicultural teaching plans for race, class, gender and disability* (5th ed.). Hoboken, NJ: Wiley.

Helms, J.E. (1992). Why is there no study of cultural equivalence in standardized cognitive ability testing? *American Psychologist, 47*(9), 1083–1101.

Hossain, M.M., & Aydin, H. (2011). A Web 2.0–based collaborative model for multicultural education. *Multicultural Education & Technology Journal, 5*(2), 116–128.

Johnson, D.W. (1981). Student-student interaction: The neglected variable in education. *Educational Researcher, 10*, 5–10.

Labinowicz, E. (1985). *Learning from children: New beginnings for teaching numerical thinking.* Reading, MA: Addison-Wesley.

Lee, E., Menkart, D., & Okazawa-Rey, M. (2006). *Beyond heroes and holidays: A practical guide to K–12 anti-racist, multicultural education and staff development* (3rd ed.). Washington, DC: Teaching for Change.

Martin, J.R. (1985). *Reclaiming a conversation: The ideal of the educated woman.* New Haven, CT: Yale University Press.

Nicolson, M., & Uematsu, K. (2013). Collaborative learning, face-to-face or virtual: The advantages of a blended learning approach in an intercultural research group. *International Journal of Research & Method in Education, 36*(3), 268–278.

Ogawa, N. (2010). Intercultural collaborative learning: Using role-play as a tool. *International Journal of Human Activity Theory, 3*(3), 61–72.

Rex, J. (1981). Aims and objectives. In M. Craft (Ed.), *Teaching in a multicultural society: A task for teacher education* (pp. 36–52). Lewes, Sussex: Falmer Press.

Rokeach, M. (1973). *The nature of human values.* New York: The Free Press.

Sedlacek, W.E., & Sue, H.K. (1995). Multicultural assessment. *ERIC Digest.* Retrieved from ericae.net/db/edo/ED391112.htm

Shor, I., & Freire, P. (1987). *A pedagogy for liberation: Dialogues on transforming education.* South Hadley, MA: Bergin & Garvey.

Singh, B.R. (1989). Neutrality and commitment in teaching moral and social issues in a multicultural society. *Educational Review, 41*(3), 227–242.

Slavin, R.E. (1987). Cooperative learning and the cooperative school. *Educational Leadership, 45*(3), 7–13.

West, C. (1993). The new cultural politics of difference. In M. Carthy & W. Crichlow (Eds.), *Race, identity and reproduction in education* (pp. 11–23). New York: Routledge.

Williams, S.E. (1965). *Stories of mathematics.* London: Evans.

Zeichner, K.M. (2009). *Teachers and the struggle for social justice.* New York: Routledge.

ACTIVITY 6

"Your Feedback Is Important to Us": Generating Discussion of Multicultural Topics through User Comments

Purpose

- Spark dialogue on culturally sensitive topics through technological platforms
- Create a safe discussion space for students within the classroom
- Help students recognize the need for critical thinking and the danger of inaction
- Promote participatory citizenship among students by encouraging them to engage with events taking place in their communities, country, and the world

Description

It is well documented that some teachers are reluctant to discuss current events, let alone controversial ones, in their classrooms. While a teacher may strive to remain neutral on political or global developments, the pedagogical decision to prevent students from having a space to voice their opinions on important issues is not neutral at all. Such censorship does a great disservice to students because it promotes the status quo, allows ignorant ideas to go unchallenged, and fails to recognize current events as a source of legitimate knowledge production—opting instead for the packaged material found in standardized curriculum and textbooks.

Students need to be encouraged to engage in dialogue with one another in order to prepare themselves for democratic participation in society. Current events reported in news media offer the opportunity for a teacher to capitalize on teachable moments, especially because students are exposed to and already may be talking about controversial topics outside of school. It is important for the teacher to be a skilful facilitator, however, if class discussion it to be productive and meaningful for students.

In this activity, class discussion of current events is sparked through analysis of user comments posted on websites or through social media platforms. When there is a particular topic you would like to broach with your students, find a concise news report on the topic from a media source that allows readers to post comments in response to it. Ask your students to read the article prior to class. When each student comes into the classroom the following day, hand him or her a printout of one discussion thread in response to the article;

this should include just a few comments conveying users' conversation back and forth on a particular point in relation to the news story. Many websites even allow readers to "like" or "dislike" other users' comments, so this can be included on the printout as well. Alternatively, you might draw on comments generated through a social media feed such as Twitter, which would construct a discussion thread through the use of a relevant keyword hashtag.

To begin discussion, ask your students to pair up with the person next to them and briefly look over their discussion thread printouts. A few minutes later, open discussion to the entire class and ask if anyone would like to respond to something contained in their discussion thread. Because the discussion threads consist of anonymous and unfiltered responses, certain comments may include inappropriate remarks. Others may be completely off topic. It is important to include some of these remarks in this activity because your students will be able to see whether other users responded positively or negatively to them.

With articles related to culturally sensitive topics—for example, terrorism—your students will likely read remarks that are racist, Islamophobic, anti-Semitic, or otherwise hateful in nature. Yet such comments will be introduced to your class more constructively, as you can include examples of extremist behaviour among individuals from mainstream groups. As the teacher, you will be able to point out how unacceptable such attitudes are, but your students will also likely criticize the authors of such inflammatory comments for "trolling," or posting with the malignant intent of offending others. When you are ready to conclude class discussion, be sure to remind students that ignorant attitudes are a real phenomenon and that it is the responsibility of democratic citizens to speak out against them.

Curricular Connections

Mathematics: Utilize the "likes" and "dislikes" on user comments (often represented with icons of thumbs pointing up or down) to supplement lessons on proportions, fractions, or creating graphic charts.

Fine Arts: Introduce students to important works of protest art and ask them to design their own posters in response to provocative user comments.

Music: Have students watch YouTube videos of diverse musical performers and draw on user comments to discuss terminology appropriate for music appreciation and critique.

Social Studies: Design an activity in which students role-play as individuals with different perspectives on historical events and create their own discussion threads in response to the representation of key issues on encyclopedic websites.

USEFUL WEBSITES ON MULTICULTURAL EDUCATION

PRIMARY SOURCE DOCUMENTS

Canadian Charter of Rights and Freedoms
Part 1 of the Government of Canada's Constitution Act (1982).
www.laws-lois.justice.gc.ca/eng/Const/page-15.html#h-38

Canadian Human Rights Act
The Government of Canada's act (R.S.C., 1985, c. H-6) to extend the laws in Canada that proscribe discrimination.
www.laws-lois.justice.gc.ca/eng/acts/h-6/index.html

Canadian Multiculturalism
Citizenship and Immigration Canada's mandate for promotion of inclusive citizenship.
www.cic.gc.ca/english/multiculturalism/multi.asp

Canadian Multiculturalism Act
The Government of Canada's act (R.S.C., 1985, c. 24 (4th Supp.)) for the preservation and enhancement of multiculturalism in Canada.
www.laws.justice.gc.ca/eng/acts/C-18.7/index.html

Declaration on the Rights of Indigenous Peoples
The United Nations proclamation (2007) of the rights of indigenous peoples as a standard of achievement to be pursued in a spirit of partnership and mutual respect.
www.undesadspd.org/IndigenousPeoples/DeclarationontheRightsofIndigenousPeoples.aspx

Universal Declaration of Human Rights
The United Nations proclamation (1948) of universal human rights as a common standard of achievement for all peoples and all nations.
www.un.org/en/documents/udhr

EDUCATIONAL ORGANIZATIONS

Aboriginal Affairs and Northern Development Canada (AANDC)
Federal department that supports Aboriginal people (First Nations, Inuit, and Métis) and Northerners in their efforts to improve social well-being and economic prosperity; develop healthier, more sustainable communities; and participate more fully in Canada's political, social, and economic development.
www.aadnc-aandc.gc.ca

American Association of Colleges for Teacher Education (AACTE)
National alliance of 800 American educator preparation programs dedicated to the professional development of teachers and school leaders; emphasizes a commitment to cultural pluralism and provides a national forum for educator development in the areas of human rights, social justice, educational quality, and multicultural and global education.
www.aacte.org/programs/multicultural-diversity

Association of Universities and Colleges of Canada (AUCC)
National voice for Canadian universities promotes policy initiatives focused on social science research, global connections, and increased access to university education for Aboriginal Canadians; runs award-winning *University Affairs* magazine and website.
www.aucc.ca

Canadian School Boards Association (CSBA)
Association of provincial school boards that represent elementary and secondary school students across Canada; website features CSBA's blog and resources on initiatives related to Aboriginal education, student health and wellness, and professional development.
www.cdnsba.org

Council of Ministers of Education, Canada (CMEC)
Intergovernmental body that contributes to the exercise of the exclusive jurisdiction of provinces and territories over education.
www.cmec.ca

INFORMATION RESOURCES

Association for Canadian Studies (ACS)
Organization that initiates and supports activities in the areas of research, teaching, communications, and training students in the field of Canadian studies, especially in interdisciplinary and multidisciplinary perspectives on topics such as multiculturalism and diversity, identity and values, and political participation; publishes *Canadian Issues, Canadian Diversity*, and the *Canadian Journal for Social Research*.
www.acs-aec.ca

Education Resources Information Center (ERIC)
Digital library of education research and information sponsored by the Institute of Education Sciences (IES) of the US Department of Education; provides a comprehensive, easy-to-use, searchable bibliographic and full-text database of education research and information for educators, researchers, and the general public.
www.eric.ed.gov

Geo Gratis
Natural Resources Canada's search tool that allows users to discover and download free maps, data, and publications.
www.geogratis.gc.ca

How Canada Performs
A multi-year research program conducted by the Conference Board of Canada, a non-profit policy think tank; includes analysis of societal factors such as income inequality, poverty, literacy, graduation rates, and acceptance of diversity.
www.conferenceboard.ca/hcp/details.aspx

Library and Archives Canada
National collection of Library and Archives Canada, the shared documentary heritage of all Canadians; allows users to browse databases, digitized microforms, virtual collections, and educational resources on topics including Aboriginal heritage, ethnocultural groups, censuses, immigration, and national identity in English or French.
www.collectionscanada.gc.ca

Multicultural Canada
Digitization project of newspapers, interviews, photographs, and print and material culture aimed at sharing the stories of cultural groups that make up Canadian history; includes learning modules for educators and students, as well as the extensively researched Encyclopedia of Canada's Peoples.
www.multiculturalcanada.ca

Statistics Canada
The Government of Canada's reference database on topics including education, population and demography, Aboriginal peoples, languages, children and youth, and culture and leisure.
www.statcan.gc.ca

Status and Trends in the Education of Racial and Ethnic Minorities
National Center for Education Statistics' report that examines the educational progress and challenges of students in the United States by race/ethnicity.
www.nces.ed.gov/pubs2010/2010015/index.asp

ADVOCACY GROUPS WITH RESOURCES FOR EDUCATORS

Canadian Multicultural Education Foundation (CMEF)
Non-profit volunteer society founded by veteran educators to promote public awareness of the opportunities and benefits of an evolving multicultural society in Canada; offers a series of resources useful for teachers as they work with students and parents from immigrant backgrounds, including Somali-Canadian and South Sudanese–Canadian families.
www.cmef.ca/Programs/TeacherResources.aspx

Center for Teaching Quality (CTQ)
North Carolina–based non-profit aims to connect, prepare, and mobilize teacher-leaders to transform schools; resources for "teacherpreneurs," innovative teachers who lead but don't leave, are browsable in categories such as classroom practice, leadership, school redesign, and teacher evaluation.
www.teachingquality.org/resources

Classroom Connections
Organization dedicated to improving learning opportunities, experiences, and outcomes for Canadian youth, in addition to building self-sufficiency in First Nations communities across Canada; offers innovative award-winning educational materi-

als, including the Cultivating Peace and Cultivate Your Commitment to Canada resource series, designed to engage and motivate youth by providing non-traditional learning opportunities that are authentic and meaningful.
www.classroomconnections.ca/en/othresources.html

Educators Against Hate
Subsection of the Partners Against Hate project, which shares education and counteraction strategies for young people and the wide range of community-based professionals who work and interact with youth, including educators, parents, law enforcement officials, and community/business leaders.
www.partnersagainsthate.org/educators/index.html

Fighting Antisemitism Together (FAST)
Coalition of non-Jewish Canadian business and community leaders funding education and other projects to encourage other non-Jews to speak out against anti-Semitism; includes the free downloadable *Choose Your Voice* kit, supported by connections to provincial curriculum standards.
www.fightingantisemitism.ca/cyv_curriculum.html

First Nations Education Steering Committee (FNESC)
British Columbia–based independent society of First Nations community representatives that works to support First Nations communities in working together to advance education issues, develop new First Peoples curriculum and classroom resources to create more inclusive schools and classrooms, and better inform all students about First Nations issues and realities.
www.fnesc.ca/curriculum

Gay, Lesbian, and Straight Education Network (GLSEN)
US-based education organization focused on ensuring safe schools through the prevention of student bullying, discrimination, and/or falling through the cracks; offers educator resources for LGBT-inclusive curriculum and lesson plans on bullying, bias, and diversity.
www.glsen.org/educate/resources

Harmony Movement: Be the Change
Ontario-based provider of education programs promoting diversity, equity, and inclusion; offers downloadable versions of the *Change through Equity Resource Guide* and *Educator's Equity Workbook* (also available in French).
www.harmony.ca/resources

Institute for Humane Education (IHE)

Maine-based organization that offers programs and resources designed to train, educate, and inspire people to become humane educators and change-makers; website includes an award-winning resource centre that features suggested lesson plans, activities, books, and links.
www.humaneeducation.org/blog/category/resources

Lesbian, Gay, Bisexual and Trans-identified (LGBT) Family Coalition (Coalition des familles homoparentales)

Advocacy for the legal and social recognition of LGBT families, including workshops and resources for professionals working with youth.
www.familleshomoparentales.org

MediaSmarts: Canada's Centre for Digital and Media Literacy

Non-profit charitable organization for digital and media literacy, whose efforts help children and youth develop the critical thinking skills to engage with media as active and informed digital citizens; offers database of teacher resources that can be browsed by topic, grade, subject area, and province/territory.
www.mediasmarts.ca/teacher-resources

Oyate

Organization working to see Native peoples' lives and histories portrayed with honesty and integrity through critical evaluation of books and curricula with Native themes; website offers resources to help parents and educators provide their children with historically accurate, culturally appropriate information about Native peoples—including *How to Tell the Difference: A Guide for Evaluating Children's Books for Anti-Indian Bias.*
www.oyate.org/index.php/resources

The Representation Project

Organization formerly known as MissRepresentation.org uses film and media content to expose injustices created by gender stereotypes and to shift people's consciousness towards change; distributes educational tools and resources such as conversation starter tool kits for young people and families, as well as a multimedia curriculum that can be purchased by school districts or universities.
www.therepresentationproject.org

Safe@School

Collaborative project between the Ontario Teachers' Federation (OTF) and the Centre ontarien de prévention des agressions (COPA) offers teachers and the educational community a selection of relevant resources, including professional learning modules on equity and inclusive education (with lesson plans and tool kits focused on homophobia, racism, and sexism) and bullying prevention. www.safeatschool.ca

See Jane: Gender Equality Lessons for Schools

The Geena Davis Institute on Gender in Media's programming arm presents a series of lessons focused on gender, self-image, and equality, introducing topics such as media and bullying in the context of gender equality. www.seejane.org/education

Southern Institute for Education and Research

Tulane University–based non-profit race relations centre dedicated to improving ethnic relations in the Deep South through tolerance education and communications training; offers teaching guides on topics related to civil rights education, Holocaust education, oral history, and cross-cultural communication. www.southerninstitute.info

Teaching for Change: Building Social Justice Starting in the Classroom

Washington, DC–based organization provides parents and teachers with social justice–focused professional development and resources, including participatory lessons that go beyond a hero's version of history and a curriculum that helps students become active citizens rather than passive consumers; its publications include *Beyond Heroes and Holidays* and *Putting the Movement Back into Civil Rights Teaching* classroom resource guides. www.teachingforchange.org/free-classroom-resources-from-teaching-for-change

Teaching Tolerance

The Southern Poverty Law Center's award-winning project dedicated to reducing prejudice, improving inter-group relations, and supporting equitable school experiences for children; provides free curricular materials—including lesson plans, activity ideas, film kits, and a biannual magazine—to Canadian and American teachers. www.tolerance.org

ADDITIONAL ADVOCACY GROUPS

American Indian Movement (AIM)

US-based community organization with a mandate to turn the attention of Indian people toward a renewal of spirituality that would impart the strength of resolve needed to reverse the policies of the United States, Canada, and colonialist governments of Central and South America; website includes a role-play classroom activity on the misappropriation of Native Americans as sports mascots. www.aimovement.org

Anti-Defamation League (ADL)

American civil rights/human relations agency fights anti-Semitism and all forms of bigotry, defending democratic ideals and protecting civil rights on issues ranging from disability rights to immigration reform to ending workplace discrimination against LGBT employees; education and outreach programs cover topics such as anti-bias education, interfaith affairs, Hispanic/Latino affairs, and Holocaust education. www.adl.org/education-outreach

Canada Without Poverty (CWP)

Non-profit national anti-poverty organization, which leads the Dignity for All outreach initiative and the Ethno-Cultural Project, aimed at low-income individuals and families from under-represented ethno-cultural-racial-faith based groups. www.cwp-csp.ca

Canadian Anti-racism Education and Research Society (CAERS)

National volunteer organization that leads lobbying, community, and educational initiatives; operates the Stop Racism and Hate Collective, which features digital news reports, articles, anti-racism videos, legal remedies, and relevant links. www.stopracism.ca

Canadian Centre for Diversity: See Different

Ontario-based organization with mission to inform and educate Canadian society about the value of diversity, difference, and inclusion; leads interactive in-school workshops that focus on leadership and facilitation training, discussions around school-specific diversity issues, and collaboration on school-wide initiatives. www.centrefordiversity.ca

Canadian Centre for Policy Alternatives (CCPA)

Independent, non-partisan research institute concerned with offering balanced debate, myth-busting, and solutions regarding issues of social, economic, and environmental justice; leads initiatives such as Making Women Count and the Climate Justice Project. www.policyalternatives.ca

Canadian Disability Policy Alliance (CDPA)

Government-funded national collaboration of disability researchers, students, community disability organizations, and federal and provincial policy-makers aimed at creating and mobilizing knowledge to enhance disability policy in Canada, and to promote equity and opportunity for disabled Canadians.

www.disabilitypolicyalliance.ca

Canadian Immigrant: Arrive. Succeed. Inspire.

Online and print resource that highlights immigrants' success stories and offers columns from experts in fields such as immigration law, banking, careers, and real estate; includes a multicultural calendar, as well as subsections on education, culture clash, and being "Canadian."

www.canadianimmigrant.ca

Canadian Race Relations Foundation (CRRF)

National foundation that advances understanding of past and current causes and manifestations of racism, and recommends approaches to eliminating racism and strengthening Canadian identity as it refers to the principles of equality, fairness, justice, and human dignity; offers free publications covering topics such as hate crimes, Islamophobia, and anti-Semitism.

www.crr.ca

Canadian Teachers' Federation (CTF)

National alliance of provincial and territorial teacher organizations that represent nearly 200,000 elementary and secondary school teachers across Canada; focuses on issues including diversity and human rights, status of women, Aboriginal education, poverty, and cyberbullying.

www.ctf-fce.ca

Canadian Women's Foundation

National foundation that specializes in helping women and girls move out of violence and poverty and into confidence; shares inspirational stories of women in its publication, *SHE Magazine*.

www.canadianwomen.org

Centre for Social Justice (CSJ)

Ontario-based advocacy organization that seeks to strengthen the struggle for social justice by focusing on key factors such as economic, racial, gender, and

health inequality, and Aboriginal issues.
www.socialjustice.org

Council of Canadians with Disabilities (CCD)

National human rights organization of people with disabilities working for an inclusive and accessible Canada.
www.ccdonline.ca

GLAAD

American lesbian, gay, bisexual, and transgender media advocacy organization specializing in analysis of news and entertainment media, including Latino/ Spanish-language media and digital communications strategies; publishes annual reports such as *Where We Are on TV*, which scrutinizes representations of diversity among television characters.
www.glaad.org/publications

Learning Disabilities Association of Canada (LDAC)

Non-profit voluntary organization dedicated to serving as the national voice for persons with learning disabilities and those who support them; includes the youth2youth program aimed at helping students transition from secondary education to university and beyond.
www.ldac-acta.ca

Multicultural Education Alliance (MEA): Promoting Equal Educational Opportunities for Our Students, Schools, and Communities

Florida-based active outreach non-profit organization that encourages partnerships with businesses to create programs that will prepare children for workforce participation.
www.multiculturaleducationalliance.org

Muslim Educational Network, Training and Outreach Service (MENTORS)

Non-profit Muslim organization that provides professional support to Muslim schools, teachers, and students, as well as accommodation for Muslim students within the public school system.
www.mentorscanada.com

National Association for Multicultural Education (NAME): Advancing and Advocating for Social Justice and Equity

American non-profit, volunteer-driven organization that advances and advocates for equity and social justice through multicultural education; distributes annual awards for excellence and innovation in multicultural education. www.nameorg.org

National Education Policy Center (NEPC)

University of Colorado, Boulder–based group disseminates high-quality, peer-reviewed research to inform policy discussions and combat "truthiness" in education; produces Best of the Ed Blogs feature on insightful policy blog discussions and distributes the Bunkum Awards to highlight nonsensical, confusing, and disingenuous education reports produced by think tanks. www.nepc.colorado.edu

National Educational Association of Disabled Students (NEADS)

Consumer organization with a mandate to encourage the self-empowerment of postsecondary students with disabilities; offers free publications on topics such as success in STEM (science, technology, engineering, and mathematics) fields, making extracurricular activities inclusive, and helping students make the transition to university. www.neads.ca

MULTICULTURAL RESOURCES FOR EDUCATORS

Asia Society: Resources for Schools

Educational organization dedicated to promoting mutual understanding and strengthening partnerships among peoples, leaders, and institutions of Asia and North America in a global context; offers culturally sensitive lesson plans for elementary and secondary students, as well as professional learning and community partnership ideas. www.asiasociety.org/education/resources-schools/term

Association for Library Service to Children (ALSC)

American organization dedicated to the support and enhancement of library services for children, from creative programming and best practices to continuing education and professional connections; website includes an "Educators" page with links to recommended multicultural booklists and professional tools. www.ala.org/alsc/audiencemenus/educators

CanTeach

Database of elementary-level resources that consists of lesson plans and strategies, and offers links to other sites related to various educational topics; includes

a subsection with materials focused on First Nations content.
www.canteach.ca

Celebrating Cultural Diversity Through Children's Literature
Annotated bibliographies of children's multicultural books appropriate for elementary grades and categorized by literary genre; cultural groups represented include African Americans, Chinese Americans, Latino/Hispanic Americans, Japanese Americans, Jewish Americans, Native Americans, and Korean Americans.
www.multiculturalchildrenslit.com

Critical Multicultural Pavilion
EdChange-sponsored resource collection that gathers together printable handouts, awareness activities, equity and diversity quizzes, multicultural links, and other relevant teacher resources.
www.edchange.org/multicultural/index.html

Education.com
Large database of printable classroom activities and lessons for students of all grade levels and for most curricular areas; includes a subsection on classroom diversity with interesting articles highlighting the needs of ethnically diverse students, rural students, gay or questioning students, and second-language learners.
www.education.com/topic/diversity-in-education

Environmental Health Science Education
US Department of Health and Human Services' National Institute of Environmental Health Sciences (NIEHS) website provides educators, students, and scientists with easy access to reliable tools, resources, and classroom materials aimed at increasing awareness of the link between the environment and human health.
www.niehs.nih.gov/health/scied/index.cfm

HotChalk Lesson Plans
Large database of teacher-designed lesson plans that includes curricular subsections focused on cultural heritage and diversity.
www.lessonplanspage.com/cultural-heritage-diversity/

In The Mix: Reality Television for Teens
American Public Broadcasting Service (PBS) television network's award-winning TV series by teens, for teens includes printable resources for educators; les-

son plans and discussion guides cover topics such as diversity, ethics, school violence and conflict resolution, teen immigrants, and media and financial literacy.
www.pbs.org/inthemix/educators/lessons

Incorporating Multicultural Content into Your Teaching

Michigan State University–hosted resource page that offers strategies for multicultural curriculum transformation—or how to design curricula, programs, and courses that incorporate multicultural content and acknowledge diverse student populations.
www.fod.msu.edu/oir/incorporating-multicultural-content-your-teaching

Multicultural Literacy

Reading is Fundamental (RIF) campaign to encourage children to explore and learn about their own and others' culture, as well as to promote and support early childhood literacy specifically among African American, Hispanic, and American Indian communities; links include interactive literacy websites for children and multicultural booklists for targeted grade levels.
www.rif.org/us/literacy-resources/multicultural.htm

National Geographic Education

National Geographic Society affiliate's educational programs strive to promote geo-literacy as an essential skill for understanding how the world works and how people and places are connected; free downloadable resources include activities, lessons, and units for teachers and students, as well as for families and informal educators.
www.education.nationalgeographic.com/education/teaching-resources

PaperTigers: Books + Water

Website, blog, and outreach program centred on multicultural children's and young adult books and reading as ways of fostering empathy, understanding, and peace; embraces multicultural books in English from all over the world, with a particular focus on the Pacific Rim and South Asia.
www.papertigers.org/indexOld.html

Rock and Roll Hall of Fame and Museum

Cleveland-based museum's award-winning education programs focus on how music is changing our world as well as reflecting it; resources include downloadable interdisciplinary lesson plans.
www.rockhall.com/education/resources/lesson-plans

Scholastic

Corporate book publisher and distributor encourages the intellectual and personal growth of children, beginning with literacy as the cornerstone of all learning; offers searchable database with free lesson plans, unit plans, discussion guides, and extension activities—including a subsection with culturally informed curriculum to help meet the challenges of the diverse classroom.
www.teacher.scholastic.com/professional/teachdive

Symmetry and Pattern: The Art of Oriental Carpets

Collaborative project of Washington, DC's Textile Museum and Drexel University's Math Forum focuses on the study of pattern as the intersection of art and mathematics; educational resources include student activities.
www.mathforum.org/geometry/rugs/resources

Teaching Diverse Learners

Resource dedicated to enhancing the capacity of teachers to work effectively and equitably with English language learners created by the Education Alliance at Brown University; includes subsections on policy, families and communities, teaching and learning strategies, and assessment.
www.brown.edu/academics/education-alliance/teaching-diverse-learners

A World of Difference Institute: Recommended Multicultural and Anti-Bias Books for Children

Anti-Defamation League's bibliographic collection of children's books intended for educators, parents, and other caregivers of early childhood and elementary aged children; categories include biography, cultural and religious groups; customs and traditions; folktales, legends, and poems; and prejudice and discrimination.
archive.adl.org/bibliography

ADDITIONAL RESOURCES FOR EDUCATORS

Annenberg Learner: Teacher Resources and Professional Development across the Curriculum

The Annenberg Foundation's multimedia resource page to help teachers increase their expertise in their fields and assist them in improving their teaching methods; includes database of browsable lesson plans.
www.learner.org/resources/lessonplanbrowse.html

Artsedge

The Kennedy Center's free digital resource for teaching and learning in, through, and about the arts; includes a lesson database and "How To" finder for tips, guides, and articles to support teaching in and with the arts.

www.artsedge.kennedy-center.org/educators.aspx

Discovery Education

Discovery Channel affiliate offers a broad range of free classroom resources (including interactive games, puzzles, lesson plans, and videos) aimed at fostering deeper student engagement in learning.

www.discoveryeducation.com/teachers

EDSITEment! The Best of Humanities on the Web

Partnership between the National Endowment for the Humanities, the National Trust for the Humanities, and the Verizon Foundation offers a treasure trove for teachers, students, and parents searching for high-quality lesson plans in the subject areas of literature and language arts, foreign languages, art and culture, and history and social studies.

www.edsitement.neh.gov/lesson-plans

Education Week Teacher

Independent, non-profit publisher Editorial Projects in Education's blog is targeted towards teacher-leaders and aimed at raising awareness and understanding of critical issues facing American schools; offers a wealth of news and information, webinars, and the Education Week Teacher Book Club.

www.edweek.org/tm

EducationWorld: The Educator's Best Friend

Large resource database, updated daily, that offers lesson plans and classroom materials for educators.

www.educationworld.com/a_lesson

Edutopia

George Lucas Educational Foundation's comprehensive blog designed to inspire, inform, and accelerate positive change in schools by shining a spotlight on evidence-based strategies and best practices that improve learning and engagement for students.

www.edutopia.org

Great Websites for Kids
Compilation of exemplary websites geared to children from birth to age 14, as evaluated by a committee of Association for Library Service to Children members.
gws.ala.org

Leading English Education and Resource Network (LEARN)
Quebec-based non-profit educational foundation offers online learning services to students, educators, administrators, and parents in all curricular areas at various educational levels (elementary, secondary, adult, and vocational).
www.learnquebec.ca

The National Archives Experience: DocsTeach
Immersive website featuring find-and-use activities crafted by educators using documents from the US National Archives, intended to help students think through primary source documents for contextual understanding and glean information to make informed judgments; features a creation tool for teachers to make personalized interactive activities.
www.docsteach.org

National Education Association (NEA): Great Public Schools for Every Student
Largest American professional employee organization committed to advancing the cause of public education; hosts database of lesson plans browsable by monthly relevance.
www.nea.org/tools/LessonPlans.html

Teach Primary
UK-based magazine for primary educators includes searchable database of elementary-level learning resources, including lesson plans and professional development strategies.
www.teachprimary.com/learning_resources

Teachers Network
Large database that includes curricular materials for students at all grade levels; includes lesson plans submitted by veteran teachers, as well as lessons designed by new teachers for new teachers.
www.teachersnetwork.org/lessonplans

USA TODAY Education

Lesson library, which includes 12 subject areas, supports educational initiatives of American educators; many lessons are paired with articles from *USA TODAY* to give students a relevant reading source.

www.usatodayeducation.com/k12/lesson-library

MULTICULTURAL OPEN-ACCESS PUBLICATIONS FOR EDUCATORS

Canadian Ethnic Studies

Canadian Ethnic Studies Association's fully refereed, interdisciplinary journal devoted to the study of ethnicity, immigration, inter-group relations, and the history and cultural life of ethnic groups in Canada.

muse.jhu.edu/journals/canadian_ethnic_studies

Canadian Journal for Social Research

Association for Canadian Studies' bilingual (French/English) publication geared towards the dissemination of social research on Canadian themes; select issues of partner publications *Canadian Issues* and *Canadian Diversity* are also available through the website.

www.acs-aec.ca/en/publications/canadian-journal-social-research

Canadian Journal of Native Studies (CJNS)

Manitoba-based, internationally-refereed periodical that biannually publishes articles and reviews concerning Aboriginal people and Aboriginal affairs in Canada, the United States, and other countries.

www3.brandonu.ca/library/CJNS

Democracy and Education

Open-access since 2011, this journal aims to provoke rigorous, open, and inclusive engagement with the challenges of educating youth for active participation in a democratic society.

www.democracyeducationjournal.org

Diversities

Scholarly and professional journal, published by UNESCO, provides a platform for international interdisciplinary and policy-related social science research in the fields of migration, multicultural policies, and human rights; formerly the *International Journal on Multicultural Societies*.

www.unesco.org/new/en/social-and-human-sciences/resources/periodicals/diversities

Feminist Teacher

University of Illinois Press publication provides discussions of such topics as multiculturalism, interdisciplinarity, and distance education in a feminist context; serves as a medium in which educators can describe strategies that have worked in their classrooms, theorize about successes or failures, and reveal the rich variety of feminist pedagogical approaches.

muse.jhu.edu/journals/feminist_teacher

Fourth World Journal

Biannual publication from the Center for World Indigenous Studies (CWIS), an independent, US-based, non-profit research and education organization dedicated to wider understanding and appreciation of the ideas and knowledge of indigenous peoples and the social, economic, and political realities of indigenous nations—or "Fourth World Nations," a term used to define the relationships between ancient, tribal, and non-industrial nations and modern industrialized nation-states.

www.cwis.org/FWJ/issues

International Journal of Multicultural Education (IJME)

Peer-reviewed journal for scholars, practitioners, and students of multicultural education committed to promoting educational equity for all, cross-cultural understanding, and global awareness at all levels of education including leadership and policies.

www.ijme-journal.org

Intersections and Inequalities

Annual publication of the University of Maryland's Consortium on Race, Gender and Ethnicity; explores the intersections of race, gender, ethnicity, and other dimensions of inequality as they shape the construction and representation of identities, behaviour, and complex social relations.

www.crge.umd.edu/publications.html

Journal of Multiculturalism in Education

West Texas A&M University–based peer-reviewed professional research journal whose primary purpose is the collection and dissemination of multiculturalism in education research, theory, and practice on all multiculturally related aspects of primary, secondary, and post-secondary education around the world.

www.wtamu.edu/journal/multiculturalism-in-education.aspx

Journal of Praxis in Multicultural Education
Peer-reviewed journal committed to publishing manuscripts written by teachers and higher education researchers that embody the true definition of praxis; demonstrates teacher learning through a dialectical union of reflection and action.
digitalscholarship.unlv.edu/jpme

Language Magazine: The Journal of Communication and Education
Engaging monthly publication featuring articles that offer a global perspective on language learning and language learners.
www.languagemagazine.com

Multicultural Education Review (MER)
Korean Association for Multicultural Education's biannual peer-reviewed international journal for research in multicultural education; aims to provide an international, multidisciplinary forum for the discussion of educational issues, to explore various aspects of policy and practice in multicultural education around the world.
journals.sfu.ca/mer

Our Schools/Our Selves
Canadian Centre for Policy Alternatives' quarterly journal on education, which includes debates and discussion on topics such as Aboriginal education, anti-racism classroom programs, sex education, peace studies, commercialism, environmental education, child care, and authentic classroom assessment; access to select articles requires subscription.
www.policyalternatives.ca/publications/ourschools-ourselves

Radical Teacher
Biannual magazine examines the root causes of inequality and promotes progressive social change; includes articles on classroom practices and curriculum, as well as educational issues related to gender and sexuality, disability, culture, globalization, privatization, race, class, and other similar topics.
muse.jhu.edu/journals/radical_teacher

Rethinking Schools
American activist publication committed to equity and the vision that public education is central to the creation of a humane, caring, multiracial democracy; emphasizes problems facing urban schools, particularly issues of race, with articles written by and for teachers, parents, and students.
www.rethinkingschools.org

Understanding and Dismantling Privilege (UDP)

Interdisciplinary journal focusing on the intersectional aspects of privilege, bridging academia and practice, highlighting activism, and offering a forum for creative introspection on issues of inequity, power, and privilege.
www.wpcjournal.com/issue/archive

Yes! Magazine

Non-profit, ad-free publication empowers people with the vision and tools to create a healthy planet and vibrant communities through powerful ideas and practical actions; offers curriculum and resources for visual learning, and teaching sustainability, peace and justice, innovation, and happiness.
www.yesmagazine.org/for-teachers/curriculum-resources

ADDITIONAL OPEN-ACCESS PUBLICATIONS FOR EDUCATORS

American Teacher

American Federation of Teachers (AFT) union publication covers a wide range of activities of interest to pre-K–12 educators, including classroom resources and reports on education reform efforts, teachers' rights, union organizing, effective teaching techniques, and other education and labour issues; partner journal *American Educator* is available through the same website.
www.aft.org/newspubs/periodicals

Canadian Teacher Magazine

Independent national magazine designed to keep Canadian teachers abreast of current trends in their field by offering informative articles on instructional strategies and methodology, classroom management, professional and personal development, and national and international issues.
www.canadianteachermagazine.com

Education and Treatment of Children

Quarterly journal devoted to the dissemination of information concerning the development of services for children and youth; designed to be valuable to educators and other child-care professionals in enhancing their teaching/training effectiveness.
muse.jhu.edu/journals/education_and_treatment_of_children

Education Canada

Canadian Education Association (CEA) magazine encourages thoughtful consideration of educational issues and ideas from a Canadian perspective, informs readers about current educational research, and promotes dialogue and discussion about teaching and learning wherever they occur.
www.cea-ace.ca/education-canada

International Journal of Adolescence and Youth (IJAY)

Aims to identify, examine, and compare particular issues, problems, and policies related to adolescents and youth throughout the world; subject areas covered include education, family relationships, sex education, delinquency, homelessness, and social policy.
www.tandfonline.com/loi/rady20

LEARNing Landscapes

Peer-reviewed, biannual journal that works to bridge theory and practice by publishing submissions from individuals who represent the wider educational community; includes a media library with interviews, poetry readings, and other engaging content from published authors.
www.learninglandscapes.ca

McGill Journal of Education (MJE)

Peer-reviewed, interdisciplinary, bilingual (English/French) scholarly journal embraces a broad concept of education and is dedicated to connecting educational research, theory, policy, and practice by inviting thoughtful and critical submissions from scholars and practitioners working in diverse areas of education and learning in Quebec, Canada, and internationally.
www.mje.mcgill.ca

TEACH Magazine

Canada's largest national education publication covers issues and topics of interest to any K–12 educator, from fundraising to curriculum development to the integration of technology; each issue contains pragmatic and hands-on content.
www.teachmag.com

Teacher

Newsmagazine of the British Columbia Teachers' Federation; archived issues are fully digitized and available for smartphone and tablet viewing.

www.bctf.ca/publications/TeacherNewsmag.aspx

Voices of Practitioners: Teacher Research in Early Childhood Education

Peer-reviewed, professional journal publishes informative articles, resources, and tools to promote the participation of early childhood teachers in teacher research; partner publications *Young Children* and *Teaching Young Children* are available through the same website.

www.naeyc.org/publications/vop

CANADIAN UNIVERSITY-BASED RESEARCH CENTRES

Aboriginal Education Research Centre (AERC)

University of Saskatchewan

www.aerc.usask.ca

Acadia Centre for the Study of Ethnocultural Diversity (ACSED)

Acadia University

www.acadiau.ca/ACSED

Canadian Research Centre on Inclusive Education

Western University

www.edu.uwo.ca/inclusive_education

Centre d'études ethniques des universités montréalaises (CEETUM)

Université de Montréal

www.ceetum.umontreal.ca

Centre for Global Citizenship Education and Research (CGCER)

University of Alberta

www.cgcer.ualberta.ca

Centre for Intercultural Education
NorQuest College
www.norquest.ca/norquest-centres/centre-for-intercultural-education.aspx

Centre for Leadership and Diversity (CLD)
Ontario Institute of Studies in Education at the University of Toronto
www.oise.utoronto.ca/cld

Centre for Studies in Religion and Society (CSRS)
University of Victoria
www.csrs.uvic.ca

Centre for Urban Schooling (CUS)
Ontario Institute of Studies in Education at the University of Toronto
www.cus.oise.utoronto.ca

York Centre for Education and Community (YCEC)
York University
www.ycec.edu.yorku.ca

AMERICAN UNIVERSITY-BASED RESEARCH CENTRES

Center for Intercultural and Multilingual Advocacy (CIMA)
Kansas State University
www.coe.ksu.edu/departments/cima

Center for Intercultural Education and Development (CIED)
Georgetown University
www.cied.georgetown.edu

Center for Multicultural Education
University of Nevada, Las Vegas
faculty.unlv.edu/troutman/multicultural

Center for Multicultural Education (CME)
University of Washington
www.education.uw.edu/cme

Center for Research on Education, Diversity, and Excellence (CREDE)
University of Hawai'i at Mānoa
www.manoa.hawaii.edu/coe/crede

Center for the Study of Race, Politics, and Culture (CSRPC)
University of Chicago
www.csrpc.uchicago.edu

Center for Urban and Multicultural Education (CUME)
Indiana University School of Education
www.education.iupui.edu/CUME

Center for Urban Education (CUE)
University of Southern California Rossier School of Education
www.cue.usc.edu

Center of Diversity and Community (CoDaC)
University of Oregon
codac.uoregon.edu

Consortium on Race, Gender and Ethnicity (CRGE)
University of Maryland
www.crge.umd.edu

Haas Institute for a Fair and Inclusive Society
University of California, Berkeley
www.diversity.berkeley.edu/haas-institute

Inclusion Institutes
School of Education of Syracuse University
soeweb.syr.edu/centers_institutes/inclusion_institute

Kirwan Institute for the Study of Race and Ethnicity
Ohio State University
www.kirwaninstitute.osu.edu

Matrix Center for the Advancement of Social Equity and Inclusion
University of Colorado, Colorado Springs
www.uccs.edu/~matrix

National Center for Institutional Diversity (NCID)
University of Michigan
www.ncid.umich.edu

Paulo Freire Institute
University of California, Los Angeles
www.paulofreireinstitute.org

School of Education, Teaching, and Health (SETH) Institute for Innovation in Education
American University
www.american.edu/cas/seth/iie/index.cfm

Urban Education Institute (UEI)
University of Chicago
www.uei.uchicago.edu

MULTICULTURAL LINKS PAGES

Center for Multilingual, Multicultural Research
Organized research and information dissemination unit at the University of Southern California offers an index of links to multicultural education, teacher education, language policy, ethnocultural studies, and professional organization resources.
www.usc.edu/dept/education/CMMR

Diversity Resources
Directory of links compiled by public-education advocacy group, the National Education Association (NEA).
www.nea.org/home/12969.htm

The Diversity Toolkit
University of Calgary–hosted compilation of Web-based diversity resources, organized in provincial, national, and international source indexes.
www.ucalgary.ca/dtoolkit/resources

DiversityWatch
Ryerson University School of Journalism–run directory of grassroots, affiliate, advocacy, and political groups promoting cultural or diversity issues.
www.diversitywatch.ryerson.ca/links

Kids Becoming Global Citizens: Resources for Parents and Educators
The Global Fund for Children's directory of high-quality resources for teaching children about diversity, tolerance, and global citizenship; subsections include tolerance, anti-bias, and diversity education; activism and service learning; and global citizenship and stewardship.
www.globalfundforchildren.org/store/resources

Multicultural Education and Ethnic Groups
Compilation of Web resources concerning multicultural education and diversity hosted by California State University, Stanislaus; provides links to lesson plans, cultural calendars, articles, and other documents.
ivy.csustan.edu/lboyer/multicultural

Multicultural Education Internet Resource Guide
Northern Arizona University–hosted directory created to help multicultural educators locate online educational resources, including lesson plans, photo galleries, stories, maps, and virtual field trips, as well as a listing of professional organizations.
www.jan.ucc.nau.edu/~jar/Multi.html

Teaching to Diversity: ESL, Learning Assistance, Special Education
Subsite of the British Columbia Teachers' Federation (BCTF) designed to support educators of school-aged students of all abilities with information, strategies, and resources related to special education, learning assistance, and ESL; includes link to BCTF's social justice page with additional links for diversity issues such as anti-racism, homophobia and heterosexism, poverty, and status of women.
www.bctf.ca/TeachingToDiversity

WISE: Working to Improve Schools and Education

Ithaca College–based comprehensive resource site for articles and links related to multicultural topics; directory index includes multicultural education and culturally responsive teaching; ability grouping, tracking, and alternatives; linguistic diversity; gender issues; sexual orientation; and separate subsections on the experiences and issues facing African Americans, American Indians, Arab Americans/Muslims, Asian Americans, and Latinos, in addition to whiteness studies.

www.ithaca.edu/wise

ABOUT THE AUTHORS

Ratna Ghosh, C.M., O.C., Ph.D., F.R.S.C., is James McGill Professor and William C. Macdonald Professor of Education at McGill University. A member of the Orders of Canada and Quebec, as well as a Fellow of the Royal Society of Canada, she has previously served as Dean of Education at McGill, President of the Shastri Indo-Canadian Institute, and President of the American Comparative and International Education Society. Her publications, grants, and teaching reflect her varied research interests in multiculturalism, international education, and women and development. She is the recipient of several awards from national and international organizations, and was featured in *Time* magazine as one of "Canada's Best in Education." The second edition of her book *Education and the Politics of Difference* (co-authored with Ali Abdi) was published in 2013.

Mariusz Galczynski, Ph.D., is a lecturer at McGill University and administrator of the Quebec Ministry of Education's English Exam for Teacher Certification. A former secondary school teacher in Texas and Illinois, his research interests include multicultural education, comparative education, teacher policy and professionalization, and assessment literacy.

INDEX